D1559162

COLUMBIA UNIVERSITY STUDIES
IN ENGLISH AND COMPARATIVE LITERATURE
NUMBER 124

RUSSIA IN THE INTELLECTUAL LIFE
OF EIGHTEENTH-CENTURY FRANCE

RUSSIA
IN THE INTELLECTUAL LIFE
OF EIGHTEENTH-CENTURY
FRANCE

BY

DIMITRI S. von MOHRENSCHILDT

OCTAGON BOOKS

A DIVISION OF FARRAR, STRAUS AND GIROUX

New York   1972

Reprinted 1972

by special arrangement with Columbia University Press

OCTAGON BOOKS

A DIVISION OF FARRAR, STRAUS & GIROUX, INC.

19 Union Square West

New York, N. Y. 10003

Library of Congress Cataloging in Publication Data

Von Mohrenschildt, Dimitri Sergius, 1902-
    Russia in the intellectual life of eighteenth-century France.

    (Columbia University studies in English and comparative literature, no. 124)
    Original ed. issued also as thesis, Columbia University, 1936.

    Bibliography: p.

        1. France—Relations (general) with Russia.
        2. Russia—Relations (general) with France.
        3. Literature, Comparative—French and Russian.
        4. Literature, Comparative—Russian and French.
        5. France—Intellectual life.
        6. French literature—18th century—History and criticism.
        7. Russians in France.
        8. French in Russia. I. Title. II. Series.

DC59.8.R8V6   1972   301.29′44′047   71-159255
ISBN 0-374-98088-8

Manufactured by Braun-Brumfield, Inc.
Ann Arbor, Michigan

Printed in the United States of America

To

BABET

PREFACE

THE aim of this work is to determine the nature and extent of Russian influence in France during the eighteenth century. The first part deals with the direct relations between eighteenth-century French and Russian society; the second, with the rôle of Russia in the historical, political and imaginative literature of France.

The cultural inheritance which Russia received from France has already been studied extensively, and since the publication in 1910 of Emile Haumant's *La Culture française en Russie,* there is little to be added on this subject. On the other hand, studies of cosmopolitan tendencies in France, especially in the second half of the century, have usually been confined to England and Germany. Russia's influence, however, has not as yet received sufficient attention. *Le XVIIIe siècle français,* observed Mansuy, *sera presque aussi russe qu'anglais: tout le monde y aura quelque chose à dire sur le grand pays slave* . . . It is largely in an endeavor to substantiate this statement that the present work has been undertaken.

The first part of this study is partially based on the works of well-known students of Franco-Russian relations: Pingaud, Rambaud, Larivière, Mathorez, Tourneux, and others; partially on the publications of the Russian Historical Society and the French memoirs of the time. It has seemed advisable, for the sake of unity and completeness, to present here some of the material already published in France and to make a more extensive survey of the French memoirs of the time than has been offered heretofore.

The material for the second part is derived from several

sources: French literary journals of the time, various literary correspondences (Grimm, La Harpe, Métra, Bachaumont, and others), memoirs of travelers and literary works of French writers. Most of the bibliographical data come from Michaud's *Biographie universelle, Catalogue russica,* Petitot's *Répertoire,* and the periodicals of the day.

It is hoped that the present study may bring into relief Russia's rôle in the intellectual cosmopolitanism of eighteenth-century France and that it may throw additional light upon the whole subject of Franco-Russian relations.

I wish to acknowledge my indebtedness to Professor Ernest Hunter Wright of Columbia University for his invaluable criticism of this manuscript with regard to content and style. His continuous interest and generous help have made possible the completion of this work. I am also indebted to Professors Frank Allen Patterson, Henri François Muller, Clarence Augustus Manning and Jefferson Butler Fletcher for reading the manuscript in its entirety and for offering important criticisms. For having suggested the subject of this study and for the initial encouragement in its preparation, I should like to thank Professor Henri Peyre, formerly Professor of French at Yale University.

DIMITRI SERGIUS VON MOHRENSCHILDT

NEW YORK
May 18, 1936

CONTENTS

PART TWO

RUSSIA IN EIGHTEENTH-CENTURY
FRENCH LITERATURE

PART ONE
DIRECT RELATIONS BETWEEN FRENCH AND RUSSIAN SOCIETY

I

EARLY CONTACTS AND DIPLOMATIC BACKGROUND

THE prevalent notion that during the Middle Ages Russia was *terra incognita* to France seems to be no longer tenable.[1] Several recent studies, particularly that of M. Lozinski,[2] reveal the fact that some relations between the two countries existed as early as the eleventh century and that medieval French society had a knowledge of Russia which was by no means negligible.

M. Lozinski confines his study chiefly to the *Chansons de geste* and the chroniclers of the twelfth and thirteenth centuries. He finds that Russia is first mentioned geographically in the *Annales Bertiniani* in 839.[3] A rather precise knowledge of Russia's location is found then in many poems and romances of the twelfth century, such as *Ipomedon*, *Thèbes*, and *Bueve de Hantone*.[4] In these poems and romances Russia does not seem a fantastic, imaginary country, but a great and powerful state situated on the eastern border of Europe. Thus, in *Ipomedon* a proud maiden chooses between three suitors,

[1] Such was the opinion of Gaston Paris in his *L'Estoire de la Sainte-Guerre*, Paris, 1897, p. 563. E. Haumant believes that aside from the introduction of the *Chansons de geste* into Russia by the Byzantines and the Bulgarians, there was, during the Middle Ages, no contact between the two countries. Cf. Emile Haumant, *La Culture française en Russie*, 1910, p. 2.

[2] Gregory Lozinski, "La Russie dans la littérature française du moyen age," *Revue des études slaves*, Vol. IX, 1929.

[3] *Ibid.*, pp. 73-88.

[4] In Ernest Langlois's *Table des noms propres de toute nature compris dans les chansons de geste imprimées*, Paris, 1904, p. 516, Russia is mentioned at least sixty times, whereas a country like Poland is mentioned only four times. Cf. G. Lozinski, *op. cit.*, Introduction.

one of whom is *fiz le rei de Russie;* and in *Bueve de Hantone* we find:

> N'a si fort homme jusqu'es pors de Roussie
> S'il me keurt seure, que je le redout mie.

As to the prevalent names under which Russia was known in the Middle Ages, M. Lozinski's data seem less definite. In the geographical treatises of the twelfth and thirteenth centuries he finds "Scythia" and "Russia" used, though the former seems to be more common. In the Latin texts and in the epic romances "Rossia" and "Russia" are found, exclusively. At the end of the thirteenth and the beginning of the fourteenth centuries "Sarmatie" is also found.

The next definite mention of Russia refers to the famous embassy of Henri I (1044-1048) to IAroslav, Grand Duke of Kiev, for the hand of his daughter Anna, whom Henri I married in 1051. At present, next to nothing is known regarding the circumstances surrounding this marriage, or its consequences.[5]

Regarding the people of Russia, M. Lozinski's study reveals a very curious fact.[6] It seems that in all the *Chansons de geste* Russians are referred to as pagans. The *Chanson de Roland,* for example, mentions *Ros et d'Esclavons.* In *Floovent* (twelfth century) the French massacre some pagans, among whom there is *un roi de Rosie.* In *Otinel* (thirteenth century) a messenger comes to Charlemagne from the king of Garsilie, who holds in obedience *Espaine, Alexandre et Roussie, Tyre et Sydoine, Perse et Barbarie.* In *Maugis* and *Baudouin de Seboure* (fourteenth century) wicked pagans *Corfarin de Rosie* and traitor *Anthiames de Roussie* are mentioned. Why Russians were associated with pagans is not clear. The fact that Russians were Christians was, beyond doubt, known as

---

[5] Cf. Vicomte de Caix de Saint-Aymour, *Anne de Russie, reine de France et comtesse de Valois au XI*e *siècle,* Paris, 1896.

[6] G. Lozinski, *La Russie* . . . pp. 252-258.

far back as the eleventh century. Historical records of the
embassy sent to Kiev to ask for Prince ĨAroslav's daughter in
behalf of the King of France prove sufficiently that Russia
was known to be Christian. The confusion of Russians with
pagans, however, not only appears in the epic romances but
is also shared by the few travelers to Russia in the Middle
Ages, such as Otto, Bishop of Freising, one of the authors of
Gesta Frederici Imperatoris (1156-1158). It seems quite possible, as M. Lozinski suggests, that this confusion was due in
part to the unfavorable impression which the Russians produced on the French when they met during the Crusades in
the Holy Land, and which was subsequently strengthened by
the well-known fact of the Tatar invasion of Russia.

M. Lozinski finds numerous indications in contemporary
chronicles and in the *Chansons de geste* that commercially
Russia was considered to be quite an important country during the Middle Ages.[7] The prosperity and commercial importance of Kiev and Novgorod were widely known. Expressions like *ne le ferai por tout l'or de Roussie*, or *fin or de
Rosie* are commonly found in the writers of the Middle Ages.
Even as early as 973, Lampert de Hersfeld speaks of the
munificence and the fabulous riches of Russia. The *Chansons
de geste* have many references to merchandise attributed to
Russia, particularly skins and furs. Furthermore, the author
of the life of Saint Marien, written about 1185, speaks of a
magnificent gift from the Grand Duke of Kiev to the monas-
tery of Ratisbon.[8]

After the marriage of Henri I to the daughter of the
Grand Duke ĨAroslav, the next indication of a direct contact
between the two countries is in the fourteenth century.
About 1350 there came to Roussillon from the Orient a large

[7] G. Lozinski, *La Russie* ... pp. 258-265.

[8] *Ibid.*, p. 263. Saint Marien is also known as Marianus Scotus (d. 1088),
Abbot of St. Peter's, Ratisbon. His life written by an anonymous monk was
printed in Bolland's *Acta sanctorum.*

number of slaves, mostly women, among whom there appeared to be a number of Russians. Concerning what happened to these women and how they were assimilated by the French no definite information has come down to us.[9] Until the reign of Louis XIV there were no established relations between the governments of the two countries. Politically Russia did not exist for France until about the middle of the seventeenth century, and was usually referred to, contemptuously, as *La Moscovie*. The two countries had, indeed, little in common—Russia was a relatively barbarous state, had no feudal duties, no knightly education, and few cities of importance. Moreover, the religion was strange, and the language totally incomprehensible. Only occasionally there would arrive from Russia special couriers—

... quelques hommes barbus et chevelus, vêtus avec une magnificence barbare et sordide, portant des fourrures au cœur de l'été, traînant une horde de laquais qui ressemblaient à des janissaires, parlant une langue inouïe qu'on ne finissait par comprendre qu'à l'aide d'une série d'interprètes.[10]

Following England, which established regular commercial relations with Russia in 1553, France began, towards the end of the sixteenth century, to send an occasional vessel to Archangel.[11] In 1575 Danzay states that *le commerce de la Russie est aujourd'hui de très grand profit et importance et mesme aux Français...*[12] It seems, however, that the French merchants were not so successful in dealing with the Russians

[9] J. Mathorez, *Les Etrangers en France sous l'ancien régime*, Paris, 1919, p. 296.
[10] Alfred Rambaud, *Recueil des instructions données aux ambassadeurs et ministres de France... Russie...* Paris, 1890, 2 volumes, I, ix. Under Henri IV a few students were sent to France by the Tsar Boris Godunov (1598-1605) but nothing is known about them. Cf. A. Rambaud, *op. cit.*, I, 58, and J. Mathorez, *Les Etrangers en France...* p. 297.
[11] N. Notovich, *La Russie et l'alliance anglaise*, Paris, 1906, pp. 75-77.
[12] A. Rambaud, *Recueil des instructions...* I, ii.

as were the English.[13] Their attitude was contemptuous and suspicious, and even in 1683 Colbert de Croissy complains that *Les humeurs et maximes des Français sont si différents de cette nation, qu'il n'y a point d'apparence que deux nations si contraires s'accordent longtemps, et, par conséquent, leur traité de commerce s'anéantira de lui-même.*[14]

During the reign of Henri IV adventurers like Margeret, Pierre de la Ville, or merchants like Jehan Sauvage, went to Russia. In 1607 Mathieu Guillemot published the story of Margeret's adventures, *L'Estat de l'empire de Russie et grand-duché de Moscovie par le capitaine Margeret.* Margeret was in the service of the Tsar Boris Godunov (1598-1605) and was possibly the first recorded Frenchman to learn Russian. The picture he gives of Russia is not a very flattering one. He deplores Russia's low level of culture and the total ignorance of the Latin language and literature. He seems, however, to like the easy and leisurely life in Russia and admires greatly her military organization.[15] In his Preface he says that the purpose of his book is to *lever l'erreur à plusieurs qui croyent que la Chrestienté n'a de bornes que la Hongrie—tandis que la Russie est un des meilleurs boulevards de la Chrestienté et que cet empire et ce pays-là est plus grand, puissant, populeux et abondant que l'on ne cuide.*[16] His book was probably the most important French source of information about Russia for that time. It went through several editions and was reissued by Jacques Langlois in 1668.[17]

During the reigns of Henry IV and Louis XIII several attempts at a *rapprochement* were made between the two countries, but in every case these were unsuccessful. Russia was at

[13] N. Notovich, *op. cit.*, pp. 78 and 91.
[14] E. Haumant, *op. cit.*, p. 6.
[15] A. Mansuy, *Le Monde slave et les classiques français au XVIe et XVIIe siècles*, Paris, 1912, pp. 429-433.
[16] A. Rambaud, *Recueil des instructions* ... I, 12.
[17] A. Mansuy, *Le Monde slave* ,.. p. 432.

that time completely overshadowed by Poland, both politically and culturally. Moreover, France was preoccupied with religious wars and internal dissensions, and had little time or inclination to further her political and commercial relations with a distant and virtually unknown country. The political situation in Europe from about the middle of the seventeenth century was such that any attempt at a rapprochement between Russia and France was out of the question. The reason was that France's traditional allies, Sweden, Poland, and Turkey, were Russia's natural enemies; and as Russia was gaining in power and prestige, she naturally became more aggressive towards these countries. But aside from this unfavorable political situation, there were additional obstacles to a more amicable understanding between the two countries: first, the personal antipathy of Louis XIV for Tsar Peter; secondly, the very unfavorable impression produced on the French by the Russian diplomats.

The first Russian envoys astounded the French. Their manner and dress were oriental, and they were often mistaken for Turks. Such was the case with Potemkin's mission to Louis XIV in 1668.[18] But the mission which produced the most disastrous impression on the French, an impression which persisted far into the following century, was that of Princes IAkov Dolgorukiĭ and Mescherskiĭ, sent in 1687 by the Princess-regent Sof'ia of Russia to negotiate an alliance against Turkey. The Russian envoys landed in Dunkirk with a suite of one hundred and fifty persons, some armed, and an enormous amount of baggage. After the customs officials sealed the baggage, the envoys broke the seals and started to sell merchandise. Asked to stop this sale, the servants of the envoys refused and insulted an officer of the King. The French foreign office became alarmed and tried to dissuade the Russians from coming to Paris to continue the negotiations. Prince Dol-

18 A. Rambaud, op. cit., I, 54-55.

gorukïï, however, insisted, and finally was allowed to have an audience with the King. Louis XIV flatly refused to enter the proposed alliance. After the audience new difficulties arose. Prince Dolgorukïï claimed the title of "Grand Seigneur" for the Tsar, which Louis XIV did not use in his letter to him. After some argument the French yielded, and the title "Grand Seigneur" was granted. By this time the envoys had made themselves so objectionable that when they asked for passports to go to Spain, the foreign office refused to grant them permission to go through France.[19] The unfortunate impression which these two envoys left in France is recorded by their contemporaries. *Ils parurent,* writes Le Dran, *être plutôt des marchands, qui voulaient être défrayés et vendre leurs marchandises sans payer les droits, que des ambassadeurs qui eussent quelque affaire d'état à traiter;*[20] also an official report of 1721 states:

Le sieur Dolgoruki que les Czars Jean et Pierre envoyèrent à Paris en 1687 avec la qualité d'ambassadeur, se conduisit si mal pendant le séjour qu'il fit en France, et se rendit si peu agréable au Roi et à toute la nation française, qu'il ne serait pas parvenu à conclure le traité de commerce proposé en 1681...[21]

It appears that a certain amount of interest was aroused in the French public by this strange embassy of Dolgorukïï's. An anonymous author, profiting by this momentary interest, published in 1687 *La Relation curieuse de la Moscovie,* republished several times since, for example in *La Bibliothèque russe et polonaise* in 1861.[22] Shortly after the publication of this

---

[19] *Ibid.,* I, 85-87.

[20] *Sbornik* (magazine of the Imperial Russian Historical Society), XXXIV, 3-4.

[21] Ministère des Affaires Etrangères, *Russie. Mémoires et documents,* Vol. III, No. 4, Fol. 4. The inferior quality of Russian envoys who, while acting in their official capacity, frequently sold merchandise, is also recorded in the *Mémoires de Dangeau,* Paris, 1817, I, 65.

[22] A. Rambaud, *Recueil des instructions* ... I, 88.

book, a certain La Neuville visited Moscow by order of the
king and in 1698 issued his *Relation nouvelle et curieuse de la
Moscovie.*[23]

Just as the France of Louis XIV—for reasons mentioned
above—seemed altogether disinclined to deal amicably with
Russia, so France at first had no part whatever, at the end of
the seventeenth century, in Peter the Great's political scheme.
"I need," Peter is said to have declared, "the English on the
sea, Germans on land, and Frenchmen nowhere."[24] Nevertheless, he admired Louis XIV personally and was the first to
make advances. In 1698 a certain Kroh, a Russian musketeer
traveling in France, published a *Mémoire où il est parlé du
voyage que le czar ferait en France s'il était assuré d'y estre
reçu*—in all probability not without the knowledge of Peter
himself.[25]

The possibility of an alliance with France was not seriously
considered by Peter until he victoriously ended his wars with
Turkey. The treaty of Prut was signed in 1711, and the
necessity of consolidating his victories through an alliance
with a first-rate power then became apparent. The France
of Louis XIV was certainly an ally greatly to be desired.
Nothing, however, was accomplished in this direction until
Peter's visit to France in 1717. Postnikov's mission in 1703
and that of Zotov in 1716 had no political significance.
These men were merely unofficial agents in charge of Russian

[23] *Journal de Marais*, 1864, III, 307. La Neuville's account of the Russian
character and *moeurs* is, on the whole, a pessimistic one. Yet he praises Russian
hospitality and the culture of the few nobles with whom he came in contact.
Mansuy arrives at the following conclusion regarding La Neuville's account of
Russia: *Pourtant La Neuville n'a ni l'intelligence déliée de Margeret, ni son
goût pour les Moscovites; il est à plus forte raison très éloigné de l'enthousiasme
excessif que montreront à l'endroit de la Russie ou de ses souverains les plus
marquants la plupart des philosophes du XVIIIᵉ siècle.* A. Mansuy, *Le Monde
slave* . . . p. 470.
[24] E. Haumant, *La Culture française en Russie*, p. 12.
[25] J. Mathorez, *Les Etrangers en France* . . . p. 297.

students, whose business was also to attract to Russia professional men, particularly doctors and barbers.[26]

At the beginning of the eighteenth century two factors contributed to a general awakening of interest in Russia— Russia's victory over the Turks and the personality and reforms of Peter the Great. One of the first to inform the French government of the Tsar's extraordinary character and his projected reforms was Sieur de Baluze, a special envoy of Louis XIV to Peter the Great. His first mission, from 1702 to 1704, is recorded in a series of letters to Louis XIV. De Baluze has nothing to say about Russia in general, however, and his attitude towards Russians is the usual one of superiority and contempt.[27]

In 1705 appeared the first volume of the anonymous *Campagnes de Charles XII, roi de Suède*. Considerable portions of this volume and of the three subsequent volumes, published from 1707 to 1711, were devoted to Peter the Great. A reviewer of this work, in the *Journal des savants* for January, 1708, was particularly interested in the singular character of Peter. *Le caractère du Czar*, he says, *tel qu'on le dépeint ici, a quelque chose de singulier. Il tient au dessous de lui de paraître par sa suite, par sa table, par ses habillements . . .*[28]

In 1716 a certain Moreau de Brasset, who spent some time in Russia, published his memoirs, in which he professed great admiration for the Tsar, but like the majority of contemporary travelers to Russia, had little regard for the nation and its inhabitants, who seemed to him little better than savages.[29]

[26] *Ibid.*, p. 298.
[27] A. Rambaud, *Recueil des instructions* . . . I, 99-108.
[28] *Journal des savants*, January 23, 1708.
[29] *Mémoires politiques, amusants, et satiriques de Mesire J. M. de B . . . comte de Lion*, Paris, 1716. Dangeau was the last of the seventeenth-century Frenchmen to speak about the Moscovites. He saw some of them at Versailles and admired their game of checkers. Dangeau gives an extensive account of Peter's European trip, his political interests, and internal reforms. He does not,

In spite of this generally superior and contemptuous attitude toward Russia, there is no doubt that just preceding Peter's trip to France in 1717 there existed already in France some interest in his personality and reforms. His arrival in Paris forms a new chapter in the political and social relations between the two countries.

It appears, then, that until the first quarter of the eighteenth century there was no serious attempt toward a political rapprochement between Russia and France. Distance, an unfavorable political situation, and the personal antipathies of the rulers were the chief obstacles to a more friendly relationship between the two countries. Ever since the Middle Ages there had been a tendency in France to associate Russia with the Orient rather than with Europe, and this tendency was strengthened by the exotic character of the first Russian envoys. With the exception of Margeret, all the French travelers to Russia, up to the end of the seventeenth century, considered her a totally barbaric state, the inhabitants of which were hopelessly uncivilized. Politically and socially, France showed no interest in Russia until the eighteenth century. The average Frenchman's knowledge of Russia must have been exceedingly scant, probably not exceeding his knowledge of the Orient and the Far East.

As for the French writers of the sixteenth and seventeenth centuries, they were indifferent to local or national characteristics of men and were only interested in the universal concept of Man.[30] There are found in these writers, as in Montaigne, for example, occasional references to *le pays des Slaves* or *La Moscovie*. But these are always cursory and vague. As Mansuy says,

---

however, comment on Peter's character. Mansuy thinks that, on the whole, the most interesting and vital account of Russia was that of Margeret. A. Mansuy, *Le Monde slave* ... p. 472.

[30] A. Mansuy, *Le Monde slave* ... pp. 27 ff., and 423 ff.

Pour Descartes, Corneille, Pascal, Molière, Fénelon, La Bruyère, on peut dire qu'il n'y a ni Anglais, ni Allemands, ni Polonais, ni Russes, ni Français, il n'y a que des hommes ou des Chrétiens: pour Racine, Boileau, Mme de Sévigné, et même pour La Fontaine et Saint-Simon, il n'y a qu'un roi, c'est le roi de France, "Le Roi." Lorsqu'un écrivain s'aventure à parler de la Moscovie, c'est souvent par hasard, c'est presque toujours sans s'engager à fond.[31]

The immediate purpose of Peter's visit to France in May, 1717, was twofold: first, to negotiate a friendly alliance, secondly, to sound the attitude of the French court with regard to the possible marriage of his daughter, Elizabeth, to the young Dauphin, the future Louis XV. He failed to accomplish either purpose.[32] He received a cordial reception, but the answers to his proposals were evasive and indefinite. In 1717 a triple alliance between France, Prussia, and Russia was signed at Amsterdam, but it had no political consequences and was definitely repudiated in 1726 by Peter's successor, Catherine I.[33] Peter's marriage project for his daughter was finally abandoned a few years later. The reasons for this failure were many. In the first place, France had not as yet realized the political importance of Russia; in the second place, the French court, particularly Cardinal Dubois, was suspicious of Peter and contemptuous of Russians in general; finally, Peter himself showed throughout a lack of tact and diplomacy. Yet, in spite of the immediate failure of Peter's visit, it had considerable political and social effect upon eighteenth-century Franco-Russian relations. As an immediate outcome of his visit regular diplomatic relations between France and Russia were established in 1721. Compredon was

[31] A. Mansuy, Le Monde slave ... p. 475.
[32] A. Rambaud, Recueil des instructions ... I, 158 ff.; cf. also Mémoires et lettres du maréchal de Tessé, Paris, 1806, Vol. II, ch. xiii, and Mémoires de Dangeau, III, 150 ff.
[33] Albert Vandal, Louis XV et Elizabeth de Russie, Paris, 1882, pp. 38-39.

appointed ambassador to St. Petersburg and Prince Vasilïï Dolgorukïï to Versailles.[34]

During the last year of his reign Peter continued to negotiate for the marriage of one of his daughters to a member of the reigning house of France with the hope that, should she marry the Duc d'Orléans, she might some day become Queen of France. To the French court, however, this alliance did not seem attractive. The Regent, in particular, thought it would be a misalliance for France because the mother of the Russian princesses was not of royal birth and had a doubtful past.[35]

Compredon, writing to the Foreign Office about Peter's elder daughter, Elizabeth, described her as beautiful and clever. *Les défauts, s'il y en a, seront du côté de l'éducation et des manières, car on m'a assuré qu'elle a de l'esprit, à l'aide duquel il ne sera pas impossible de rectifier ce qui manquera.*[36] The French court, however, delayed answering, partly because of the negligence of Dubois and his general antipathy to Russia. Peter, in fact, never received an official answer. He soon learned of the marriage of the Duc de Chartres to a German princess.[37] Thus ended Peter's fondest hopes of securing succession and seeing his daughter married into one of the most powerful reigning houses of Europe.

Peter's successor, Catherine I, continued the marital negotiations through Compredon. Her hopes were revived, especially when she learned in 1724 that Louis XV had broken his engagement with the Infanta of Spain. Again Compredon pleaded the Russian cause. At this time the Duc de Bourbon had hopes of marrying his own daughter to Louis XV. Conse-

[34] A. Rambaud, *Recueil des instructions* ... I, xxxiv.

[35] A. Vandal, *Louis XV* ... p. 52. Regarding the marriage negotiations of Peter the Great and Catherine I of Russia with the French Court, see Gauthier-Villars, *Le Mariage de Louis XV*, Paris, 1900, ch. viii.

[36] Ministère des Affaires Etrangères, *Russie*, "Compredon à Dubois," March 13, 1723.

[37] A. Vandal, *Louis XV* ... p. 68.

quently, he feared the power and ambition of a Russian princess and opposed the Russian alliance.

The French office continued, therefore, to pay no attention to Compredon's pleadings, and in 1725 the marriage of Louis XV to Marie Leszczyńska, daughter of the former King Stanislaw of Poland, was officially announced—an affront Catherine could never forgive. In 1726 she concluded an alliance with Austria which remained in force until 1756.[38] For thirty years Russia was actively hostile to France and the successors of Catherine I (Peter II, the Regent Biron, and the Empresses Anna Ivanovna and Anna Leopoldovna) were all pro-German, so that during this period Austria and Germany became exclusively Russia's models.

This situation continued to exist until the appearance in Russia of the Marquis de la Chétardie, Louis XV's ambassador to the court of the Empress Anna Ivanovna.[39] A typical "mondain" Frenchman of the eighteenth century, intelligent, gracious, adventurous, and very much aware of his birth and position, the Marquis was especially chosen to show the Russians *en tout sens ce que c'est que la France.* He arrived in Russia at the end of 1739, accompanied by a magnificent suite numbering twelve secretaries, eight chaplains, six cooks, and fifty pages, and at once proceeded to pay court to the Empress and also to Princess Elizabeth, daughter of Peter the Great. He found the Russian court grandiose, puerile, and, naturally, since it was predominantly German, governed by bad taste. Believing that Russia would be irrevocably abandoned to the Germans unless something radical were done, La Chétardie decided upon a court revolution as the only means to save the situation.

Accordingly a conspiracy was formed, the object of which

[38] A. Rambaud, *op. cit.*, II, 15.
[39] For a detailed account of the La Chétardie mission, see A. Vandal, *op. cit.*, pp. 117-195.

was to put Elizabeth upon the throne, since her sympathies were pro-French. Versailles, at first hesitant, finally consented to provide money, credit, and advice. With the help of Lestock, a Hanoverian by birth, but a Frenchman by education, La Chétardie proceeded with his intricate and daring scheme. The plot was entirely successful. Elizabeth was proclaimed Empress of Russia, and Louis XV was assured by his intrepid ambassador of her gratitude and continuing friendship. The immediate result of the *coup d'état* was, as was anticipated, the disappearance of the German party from court and a general gravitation towards France. French language and customs were introduced, and *on vit les Russes s'essayer*, says Vandal, *sous les auspices de l'heureux La Chétardie, aux manières libres et aisées, à l'élégance frivole et aux graces raffinées de la société française.*[40]

Soon, however, complications arose. La Chétardie, emboldened by his success, forgot his rôle of envoy and, after abusing the Empress's confidence, began to intrigue against the prime minister, Bestuzhev. At first very kindly disposed toward the Frenchman, Elizabeth finally tired of his machinations and issued orders to her former favorite to leave Moscow in twenty-four hours. The French court, unable to protest, remained silent. Thus again, an important attempt at a rapprochement between the two countries ended in nothing.[41]

The political situation which followed the La Chétardie episode was tense. In France, about 1744, the head of the Foreign Office was D'Argenson, a man not sympathetic with Russia, though fully aware of her political importance.[42] The ministry of Bestuzhev was definitely hostile to France, and in 1745 Russia signed a treaty of alliance with Austria against France. At the same time D'Argenson considered a permanent

[40] A. Vandal, *op. cit.*, p. 165.   [41] *Ibid.*, p. 195.
[42] Cf. *Journal et mémoires d'Argenson*, Paris, 1862, V, 285.

alliance with Turkey against Russia. Bonneval, French ambassador to Turkey, was chosen to negotiate this alliance.
When, however, the time came to act, D'Argenson's ministry
did not dare to sign this treaty with a non-Christian power.[43]
Bonneval, one of Louis XV's ablest diplomats, insisted upon
the merits of his plan, stressing the fact that the Russians
were also heretics. *Notre très-Saint Père le Pape approuvera
certainement que le Roi se serve des Turcs pour augmenter sa
puissance contre des ennemis qui sont hérétiques et par conséquent aussi bien damnés que les Turcs.*[44]

Though Bonneval's plan did not succeed, friendly negotiations with Turkey continued. French agents led secret campaigns against Russia in Poland, Sweden, and Turkey. For
a while it seemed that open hostility was unavoidable. The
political situation, however, changed almost at once. In 1756
the long Bourbon-Hapsburg struggle came to an end. Russia
became more friendly toward France and, as an ally of Austria, joined France in the Seven-Years War against Russia.
Thus, again, a new opportunity for a closer alliance between
France and Russia presented itself. But the French government, as before, failed to take advantage of it.

Russia's more friendly attitude was due first of all to
Empress Elizabeth herself. In reality she remained always sympathetic toward France, even after the unfortunate La
Chétardie episode. She retained a half-sentimental attachment for the brilliant Frenchman and reproached herself for
being ungrateful to his master, Louis XV.[45] Furthermore, the
new Vorontsov ministry was also well-disposed towards
France.[46] On the other hand Louis XV and his prime-minis-
ter, Bernis, remained unfriendly and suspicious. An alliance
with Russia was thought undesirable. What Louis XV wanted

[43] A. Vandal, *op. cit.*, p. 203; also Marquis d'Argenson, *Mémoires*, IV, 437-
441.
[44] Ministère des Affaires Etrangères, *Turkie*, "Bonneval."
[45] A. Vandal, *op. cit.*, p. 256.   [46] *Ibid.*, p. 258.

was "to disarm Russia without combat" through secret diplomacy—in other words, to put an end to Russia's friendship with powers hostile to France.[47] This friendly attitude of Elizabeth towards France and Louix XV can best be illustrated by her correspondence with the French monarch, which started about 1757.[48] About four or five letters a year were exchanged through their respective ambassadors. The tone, at first formal and ceremonious, became quite personal and free. Elizabeth, for example, would describe her ailments, and Louis XV would send her a special doctor in response. At one time she asked for the two best Parisian actors, Lekain and Mlle Clairon, but this request was not granted. In general she seems to have made all the advances, while Louis XV remained for the most part aloof and uninterested. Occasionally she made extravagant requests; such was, for example, her request for a loan of five million roubles, which was promptly and not very graciously refused.[49] Finally, attempting a closer rapprochement, Elizabeth asked Louis XV to be godfather, with herself as godmother, to the Grand Duchess Catherine's child. The prime minister, De Bernis, answering for Louis XV, refused the request, giving as the reason the fact that the child belonged to the Greek-Orthodox church. He writes to the ambassador, L'Hôpital:

Si l'on vous en parle, vous devez représenter ces raisons et faire sentir que des principes de religion sont seule cause de la peine que Sa Majesté sent à ne point contracter une liaison de plus avec l'impératrice de Russie. Le plus prudent serait d'éluder cette demande sans que l'impératrice de Russie pût en être blessée.[50]

This refusal could not help hurting Elizabeth's feelings, how-

---

47 A. Vandal, *op. cit.*, p. 260.   48 *Ibid.*, pp. 334-339.
49 Ministère des Affaires Etrangères, *Russie*, letter of M. Rouillé, April 24, 1757.
50 *Ibid.*, Bernis to L'Hôpital, October 16, 1757.

ever, and is another example of the weak and short-sighted diplomacy of Louis XV. Toward the end of her reign Elizabeth needed Louis's help. Abandoning the affairs of state to her ministers and herself to the pleasures of court life, she felt desperately in need of moral support. *En s'efforçant de se rapprocher intimement de Louis XV*, says Vandal, *Elizabeth cherchait un guide et un secours contre sa propre faiblesse; elle ne le trouva point.*[51]

A more salutary and forceful policy towards Russia was inaugurated about 1758 by Bernis' successor, the Duc de Choiseul. A typical eighteenth-century Frenchman, a philosopher and wit, Choiseul did not personally like Russia, but he nevertheless realized the necessity of a rapprochement. About 1760 the victorious Russian army was approaching Berlin. France naturally viewed its victories with alarm. Russia was already too powerful, and the acquisition of additional territory was deemed prejudicial to the principle of the balance of power. Choiseul decided to act at once. He sent to St. Petersburg a young and brilliant diplomat to handle the very delicate Russian question; Baron de Breteuil became an additional aide to the old and ineffective ambassador, L'Hôpital. The instructions given to De Breteuil are an interesting example of eighteenth-century secret diplomacy. He was to capture the confidence of Russia's statesmen, flatter and please everybody, and exert at the same time his utmost ingenuity to prevent a further extension of Russia's power. *Le Baron de Breteuil ne doit ni exciter vivement les Russes, ni les retenir ... en être en quelque sorte l'avocat à Pétersbourg ... ralentir, si les circonstances le permettent, les opérations des Russes.*[52] It was thus De Breteuil's rôle to be more of a spy than an accredited envoy. At the beginning he achieved

[51] A. Vandal, *op. cit.*, p. 339.
[52] *Ibid.*, pp. 378-379; cf. also A. Rambaud, *Recueil des instructions* ... II, 139 ff.

considerable success and was soon appointed ambassador in place of the old L'Hôpital. In 1760 the Russian troops took Berlin, and De Breteuil received personal orders from Louis XV to negotiate peace. In the midst of these efforts the Empress Elizabeth died, on January 5, 1762. With the accession of the pro-German Peter III, Russia's policy underwent an abrupt change. Peace with Prussia was promptly concluded, followed by a friendly alliance. In the meantime Peter's wife, Catherine, began to conspire, and looking for support, turned to De Breteuil, believing that her accession would be entirely to the advantage of France. De Breteuil, however, lacked La Chétardie's resourcefulness, and France lost again what was perhaps her best chance to effect, at this point, an undeniably advantageous rapprochement.[53] Catherine's advances were stupidly rejected. The French Foreign Office remained undecided, and avoiding a difficult political situation, decided to recall De Breteuil, thus losing all contact with Russian affairs at a time when such a contact was most essential.[54] Thereupon, realizing that no help from France was forthcoming, Catherine rallied all the forces of the opposition around her. The conspiracy was a complete success, and in July, 1762, Peter III was deposed. Catherine II, in spite of the affront she had received from De Breteuil, showed upon her accession no direct signs of hostility to France. Louis XV, on the other hand, remained uncompromisingly hostile. De Breteuil was sent back to Russia with the following instructions: *L'objet de ma politique avec la Russie est de l'éloigner autant qu'il sera possible des affaires de l'Europe. Tout ce qui peut la plonger dans le chaos et la faire rentrer dans l'obscurité est avantageux à mes intérêts.*[55] At the same time all French envoys in Europe received similar orders. The

[53] A. Vandal, *op. cit.*, p. 415.   [54] *Ibid.*, p. 417.
[55] Ministère des Affaires Etrangères, *Russie*, Instructions to De Breteuil, September 10, 1762.

prime minister Broglie, in his instructions to De Breteuil, was even more uncompromising: *L'utilité des liaisons avec la Russie est de préparer les moyens d'annuler les dispositions de cette puissance, et de la jeter dans une anarchie dont il convient de ne pas la laisser sortir.*[56] Catherine at once perceived the course of French diplomacy and adopted a corresponding attitude. When De Breteuil was taking leave of her to go to his new post in Stockholm she remarked smilingly: "There [i.e., in Stockholm] you will be my enemy."[57] From then on, for the first twelve years of her reign, Catherine waged a continuous diplomatic battle against the influence of France. There was no open hostility, but a series of diplomatic thrusts was directed against France. This political situation contributed to the division of Poland, the dismemberment of Sweden, and attacks upon Turkey. Catherine, says Rambaud, was delighted to hurt France's friends:

. . . c'est qu'en les frappant elle atteint du même coup la France, sa puissance, ses intérêts, son prestige. Le piment de ce festin de peuples et de provinces, c'est le plaisir d'avoir bravé, joué, bafoué le Roi des "Welches," sa politique, ses diplomats, son grand ministre Choiseul, le maladroit "cocher de l'Europe." Elle en triomphe dans ses lettres à Voltaire, à Grimm, à Zimmermann, à tous les correspondants attirés de France et d'Allemagne.[58]

In spite of Russia's waging war against France's allies, amicable relations between the two countries continued, and each sent envoys to the other. The diplomatic correspondence and the instructions of the French court, however, are full of resentment and animosity against Russia from about 1763

[56] Ministère des Affaires Etrangères, *Russie,* Instructions to Broglie, April 9, 1763.

[57] A. Rambaud, *Recueil des instructions* . . . II, 218; for a detailed treatment of Catherine's foreign policy see A. Sorel, *The Eastern Question in the XVIIIth Century,* London, 1898.

[58] A. Rambaud, *op. cit.,* I, li.

to 1772. In the instructions given to De Bausset, for example, we read:

Il ne convient pas aux nations éclairées par une saine politique de voir sans inquiétude la Russie, à peine dépouillée d'une écorce vraiment barbare, profiter rapidement de son nouvel état pour étendre ses bornes et s'approcher de nous.[59]

Catherine was the immediate object of Versailles' hatred. She was accused of *fausseté* and *inconséquence* in her foreign policy, corrupt morals and a *passion effrénée pour le comte Orlof*. Hopes were expressed that *cette princesse ne finisse pas ses jours sur le trône*, and *qu'elle sera précipitée d'un trône où elle n'aurait jamais dû monter*.[60] This unfortunate reputation of Catherine's was created to some extent by Rulhière's account of Tsar Peter's overthrow and death in 1762. The book, not published until 1797, was circulated and read in manuscript form.[61]

A more friendly orientation towards Russia began about 1772, after her completion of conquests in Turkey and Sweden. It was then deemed that Russia was no longer an aggressor, but *une puissance conservatrice*. This new attitude toward Russia is seen, for example, in the instructions given to Durand, Ambassador plenipotentiary to St. Petersburg from 1772 to 1775.

Il [i.e., Durand] tachera de faire comprendre que jamais le Roi n'a mis dans sa conduite aucun ressentiment ni aucune animosité personelle; que Sa Majesté rend justice aux talents et la façon de penser de l'Impératrice, qu'elle n'a cessé de conserver le désir de vivre en bonne intelligence avec elle; qu'elle a souvent regretté, pour le bien général, qu'elle ne fût pas aussi intime que l'intérêt des deux empires de l'Europe l'eût peut-être exigé; et que sa conduite convaincra

59 A. Rambaud, *Recueil des instructions* . . . II, 224.
60 *Ibid.*, I, lii.
61 Claude Rulhière, *Œuvres posthumes*, Paris, 1819; see especially the introduction by Augnis, p. iv.

bientôt cette puissance de la sincérité de ses dispositions, si elle marque de son côté les mêmes sentiments.[62]

The death of Louis XV and the accession of Louis XVI brought the two countries even closer together. The French Foreign Office, impressed by the growing power of Catherine's empire, seems to have realized for the first time the necessity of resigning itself to a more amicable attitude towards Russia. The period between 1775 and 1789 is the golden age of eighteenth-century Franco-Russian diplomacy. The Grand Duke Paul's incognito trip to France in 1781 and the splendid impression he produced at Versailles sealed the growing understanding between the two governments, and the signing of the commercial treaty, negotiated in 1787 by the ambassador Ségur, brought it to a culminating point.[63]

But all these new developments in the Franco-Russian diplomacy, says Rambaud, came too late. France was bankrupt, and the French royalty weak and powerless. The Revolution put a complete end to this more friendly phase in the relations between the governments of the two countries.

Catherine of Russia, at the beginning of her reign, had a great enthusiasm for liberalism and encyclopedic philosophy, but long before 1789 she showed signs of alienation from this youthful idealism.[64] When the Revolution broke out she completely repudiated, outwardly, at least, the last vestige of liberal thinking. She seems to have foreseen rather early the course the Revolution eventually would take. At the end of 1789 when Ségur came to take leave of her, she is said to have expressed her views on the French situation in the following terms:

[62] Ministère des Affaires Etrangères, *Russie*, Instructions to Durand, July 24, 1772; see also P. Oursel, *La Diplomatie de la France sous Louis XVI*, Paris, 1921, ch. viii, pp. 268-311.

[63] A. Rambaud, *Recueil des instructions*, I, lvi.

[64] Charles de Larivière, *Catherine II et la Révolution française*, Paris, 1895, pp. 1-5.

Votre amour de la liberté et de la philosophie vous portera probablement à soutenir la cause populaire. J'en suis fâcheé; car moi je resterai aristocrate, c'est mon métier; songez-y, vous allez trouver la France bien enfiévrée et bien malade.[65]

It was, of course, inevitable that Catherine should declare herself an enemy of the Revolution and a friend of the old régime. Not only did her own security demand such a course, but also her friendship for the king. Perhaps, too, she took a certain pride in protecting the members of a fallen dynasty.

Beginning with the spring of 1790 Catherine forbade the circulation of any literature pertaining to the Revolution.[66] The sale of the Encyclopedia was stopped; even Voltaire was not spared, and a new edition of his works was confiscated. *Il faudra faire jeter au feu tous leurs meilleurs auteurs, et tout ce qui a répandu leur langue en Europe, car tout cela dépose contre l'abominable grabuge qu'ils font.*[67] From 1789 to 1792 all foreigners who spoke French and were established in Russia became suspect and were put under the supervision of the police.[68] Ségur's successor, the head of the legation, Genet, was not recognized by Catherine's ministry. At first he was merely snubbed, then insulted, and finally required to leave the country on eight days' notice.[69]

The execution of Louis XVI was a terrific shock to Catherine. When she heard the news she went at once to bed and ordered six weeks of mourning at court. An official order was issued requiring all Frenchmen in Russia to swear their allegiance to Louis XVI. All French imports were prohibited, and some Frenchmen were sent to Siberia. It was a regular

[65] Léonce Pingaud, *Les Français en Russie et les Russes en France,* Paris, 1886, p. 162.
[66] *Ibid.,* p. 168.
[67] Letter from Catherine to Grimm, June 23, 1790.
[68] L. Pingaud, *Les Français en Russie* ... p. 169.
[69] A. Rambaud, *Recueil des instructions* ... I, p. lvii.

war against French liberal ideas. French culture itself became suspect.[70]

Le prétendu siècle de la philosophie, declared Simon Vorontsov, once an ardent admirer of Voltaire, *est celui des paradoxes et de tous les crimes.*[71] *Siècle de civilisation,* exclaimed Meodor, *je ne te reconnais plus! dans le sang, dans les flammes, au milieu des massacres et des destructions, je ne te reconnais plus.*[72] Thus republican France, and along with her eighteenth-century *philosophie,* seems, for the time being at least, to have been completely repudiated.

In 1791 the French royalists, headed by Comtes de Provence and d'Artois, and Baron de Bombelles, sent from the temporary court at Coblenz their first representative to Catherine. A brilliant courtier and skillful intriguer, Esterházy succeeded in quickly winning her confidence and friendship. He failed, however, to persuade Catherine to join actively the coalition against republican France. Money in large amounts was sent to Nassau's army; even regiments were promised, although they never actually arrived. The Russians provided Condé's army with money and even proposed to Richelieu that it settle upon the shores of the Azov Sea. An agricultural colony was to be formed there with Richelieu as governor and Esterházy as superintendent of works. The plan as a whole failed, for the majority of the *émigrés* refused to go. Isolated individuals, however, went to live in Russia; some, eager to make fortunes and distinguish themselves, entered the Russian army.[73]

In 1793 Comte d'Artois arrived in St. Petersburg and asked for help. He was given all the honors due a prince, was royally entertained, but received very little actual help. More and more émigrés began to come to St. Petersburg. The court,

[70] L. Pingaud, *Les Français en Russie* ... pp. 173-176.
[71] *Ibid.,* p. 168.
[72] E. Haumant, *La Culture française en Russie,* p. 179.
[73] Ernest Daudet, *Mémoires d'Esterhazy,* Paris, 1905, II, 348-351; cf. also E. Daudet, *Histoire de l'émigration,* Paris, 1905-1907, Vol. I, ch. ii.

especially, began to assume a foreign character. *Il n'y aura bientôt plus de noms étrangers à Pétersbourg*, writes in 1793 the Prince de Ligne, *et Mme Vigée-Lebrun va bientôt se croire à Paris, tant il y a de Français dans les réunions.*[74]

In spite of all the desire and willingness of Catherine to help the royalists, little had actually been done for their cause by 1796, the year of her death.

The Emperor Paul's share in the suppression of revolutionary ideas and in the sponsoring of the royalist armies was much greater. All that he did, however, was carried out in such a haphazard "order, counter-order, disorder" fashion that it probably injured the royalist cause as much as it helped. All signs of liberalism were at once suppressed, and many Frenchmen were either conducted out of the country or sent to Siberia. In 1797, after the Austrians had concluded peace with the French republic, the existence of Condé's army on the Rhine became quite futile. Paul ordered the army to disband, swear allegiance to him, put on Russian uniforms and be exiled to the province of Volynia.[75]

About five thousand of Condé's men submitted and were accordingly marched across Europe, many deserting on the way. The question of an agricultural colony came up again, but the soil near Azov was found unfit for cultivation, and the plan had to be abandoned. In 1799 Paul joined the coalition against France, and fighting began in Italy and in Switzerland. Condé's army joined the reserve, and soon afterward the remains of it were transferred to an English pay roll.[76]

The émigrés, whose number at the end of the century was greatly augmented, had a very difficult time in their dealings with the half-demented Emperor Paul. Louis XVIII

[74] L. Pingaud, *Les Français en Russie* ... p. 196.
[75] *Ibid.*, pp. 210-211; cf. also E. Daudet, *Histoire de l'émigration*, Vol. I, ch. ii.
[76] L. Pingaud, *op. cit.*, pp. 211-213, 216 and 218.

was allowed at first to settle at Mittau, but no sooner had he established his court there than he was ordered to leave. Richelieu's command of a regiment was withdrawn without any apparent reason. The brothers Masson, upon mere rumors of liberal thinking, were conducted out of the country. Some émigrés were sent to Siberia. Until his death in 1802, Paul remained loyal to the royalist cause and invincible in his hatred of the Republic.[77]

The accession of Emperor Alexander I begins the era of Napoleonic wars and invasions of Russia, a period which is outside the scope of this study.

From this brief summary of Franco-Russian diplomatic relations in the eighteenth century, several facts stand out clearly.[78] First, with the exception of a very brief period preceding the revolution, the governments of the two countries were hostile throughout the century. Secondly, the French court in its relations with St. Petersburg had two policies from which to choose: either to ally itself frankly with Russia, thus abandoning the old traditional alliance with Turkey, Sweden, and Poland, or, on the contrary, to strengthen these traditional alliances and consequently to bar Russia from contact with the western world. France seemed to lack energy to embrace strongly either of these policies. Indecision was the keynote of her policy with Russia throughout the whole century. Thirdly, both countries seemed to understand that unless France broke away from Sweden, Turkey, and Poland, no alliance between France and Russia was possible. Fourth, in spite of realizing this, several Russian emperors (Peter, Catherine I, Elizabeth, and to some extent Catherine II) tried to break through this wall, largely for romantic and emotional reasons. Finally, the preceding sum-

[77] *Ibid.*, pp. 239, 241, and 242.
[78] See the conclusions in A. Vandal, *Louis XV*...pp. 415-429, and A. Rambaud, *Recueil des instructions* ... I, Introduction, especially pp. xlviii, liv, lv, and lvii.

mation clearly suggests that one should look beyond mere diplomatic relations for evidence of the interest, sympathy, and understanding which existed between Russian and French society of the eighteenth century.

II

RUSSIANS IN FRANCE DURING THE
EIGHTEENTH CENTURY

THE main facts relating to Tsar Peter's sojourn in France are too well known to need treatment in detail here.[1] What remains to be done is to analyze further the impressions left by the Tsar and his suite on contemporary French society. By 1698 the Tsar must have aroused considerable interest at the French court. He had made, writes Saint-Simon, *tant de bruit dans le monde,* and the historian found it necessary to give a complete account of the Tsar's travels and his apprenticeship in Holland.[2] Information about the Tsar, prior to 1717, had appeared in contemporary accounts of Russia, such as La Neuville's, and in the reports of the French envoys to the Russian court. Peter's arrival in Paris on May 10, 1717, was therefore an event of considerable interest, not only to Versailles, but to France in general. All the chroniclers of the time describe at length the Tsar's arrival and sojourn.[3]

During the two-month visit, the activities of the Tsar were varied and many. He visited the Invalides and ate with

[1] For a general account of Tsar Peter's stay in France see: (a) Kazimir Waliszewski, "Pierre le Grand en France," *La Revue de Paris,* October, 1896; (b) Russkiĭ arkhiv, 1865, pp. 63-90, 1881, I, 5-16; (c) E. Haumant, *La Culture française en Russie,* pp. 21-23.

[2] Saint-Simon, *Mémoires,* Paris, 1886, V, 50-54.

[3] Saint-Simon, *Mémoires,* Paris, 1920, XXXI, 356-390. C. P. Duclos, *Mémoires secrets,* Paris, 1829, I, 270-280. P. Dangeau, *Journal,* Paris, 1859, XVII (1717-1719), 52 ff., and XVIII, *passim. Gazette de la Régence,* par E. de Barthélemy, Paris, 1887, pp. 170-188. Jean Buvat, *Journal de la Régence,* 1865, I, 263-277. For a fuller bibliography of Peter's visit see note of the editors in the *Mémoires de Saint-Simon,* Hachette, 1920, XXI, 357.

the old veterans; he called upon a great many nobles; he made several trips to Versailles, Fontainebleau, and Cluny; he hunted with the Comte de Toulouse; he visited Saint-Cyr and examined the stables there; he went to the Gobelin factory, and to the Mint, where a gold medal was struck in his honor; he reviewed troops; he attended a session of the Parliament and a special session of the Academy of Sciences during which he was shown every new mechanical invention;[4] he visited the Sorbonne, where the doctors offered him a project for the union of the two churches;[5] he sat for two painters, Natounar and Rigault; he was present at an operation for trachoma performed by a British surgeon; finally, on several occasions, he joined in the revelries of his suite.

Even from this brief sketch of Peter's activities one can judge how wide were his interests, and how extensive was the section of French society with which he came in contact during his short visit.

The astonishing vitality and unquenchable curiosity of the Tsar did not fail to impress contemporary chroniclers. Saint-Simon, whose memoirs were not generally known until 1760, writes as follows: *Ce monarque se fit admirer par son extrême curiosité*, a curiosity, he adds, which *atteignit à tout et ne dédaigna rien.*[6] Duclos, too, reports that wherever the Tsar went, he gave proof *de ses lumières et de ses connaissances.*[7] Both agree, however, that Peter was chiefly interested in practical things and that, as Duclos puts it, *les choses de pur goût et d'agrément le touchaient peu.*[8]

Especially interesting and impressive were Peter's eccentricities. They manifested themselves in the extreme simplicity

[4] An account of the Tsar's visit to the Academy of Sciences is given in the *Journal des savants*, January, 1730.

[5] Paul Pierling, *La Sorbonne et la Russie*, 1882, pp. 23-52.

[6] Saint-Simon, *Mémoires*, 1920, XXI, 266.

[7] Duclos, *Mémoires*, I, 273, 276.

[8] *Ibid.*

of his dress, in the absence of a powdered wig and of gloves and cuffs;[9] in his familiarity with people of very inferior rank, such as soldiers and servants;[10] and on the other hand, in his *grandeurs* with many nobles of royal blood, particularly with the ladies, such as Mme de Maintenon and Mme d'Antin;[11] in an impulsiveness, brusqueness, and changeability of mood which wore out the officers appointed to accompany him;[12] finally, in the Tsar's and his suite's astonishing capacity for eating, drinking, and general revelry.[13]

In spite of these oddities of character and conduct, which were promptly ascribed to national barbarism, all the chroniclers, particularly Saint-Simon, praised Peter's graciousness, dignity, intelligence, and—above all—his vast stock of information. The *Gazette de la Régence* for May 14, 1717, thus expressed the current opinion: *On commence à ne parler de ce prince qu'avec éloges, étant affable pour tout le monde et paraissant goûter les choses avec esprit et discernement.*[14]

Louville, writing to the Duc de Saint-Aignan, June 17, 1717, says:

Je vous dirai que c'est un prince qui a beaucoup plus de grandes qualités qu'il n'en a de mauvaises. . . Son extérieur n'est pas trop poli, mais son intérieur l'est infiniment. . . Il sait beaucoup, et nous n'avons en France aucun homme aussi habile que lui, ni dans la marine ni dans les fortifications. . .[15]

---

[9] Saint-Simon, *Mémoires*, XXI, 368-369. J. Buvat, *Journal*, I, 270. C. Duclos, *Mémoires secrets*, I, 274.

[10] Saint-Simon, *Mémoires*, XXXI, 364, 366. C. Duclos, *Mémoires* . . . I, 269, 276.

[11] Saint-Simon, *Mémoires*, XXXI, 375, 381, 383. Comte de Barthélemy, *Gazette*, p. 175. This haughtiness with the ladies was, perhaps, due more to Peter's timidity than to pride.

[12] Duclos, *Mémoires* . . . I, 271.

[13] The licentiousness of the Moscovites is particularly stressed by Buvat, *Journal*, I, 271-272, 275; see also Saint-Simon, *Mémoires* . . . I, 275, 277; and Comte de Barthélemy, *Gazette*, p. 187.

[14] Comte de Barthélemy, *Gazette*, p. 175.

[15] Saint-Simon, *Mémoires*, XXXI, 368.

Villeroy, writing to Mme de Maintenon, seems quite surprised to find in Peter traces of civilization:

Ce prince prétendu barbare ne l'est point du tout; il nous fait connaître des sentiments de grandeur, de générosité, et de politesse
auxquels nous ne nous attendions point.[16]

Nevertheless, the Tsar was not an easy guest to entertain.
The constant debauches of his followers apparently became,
towards the end of his stay, quite trying to all concerned.
In the *Gazette de la Régence* for June 11, we find the following complaint:

Ceux de sa suite ont été au cabaret faire de grosses dépenses sans rien
payer, disant que c'était au roi de tout acquitter. Le maréchal de
Tessé est sur les dents. Le duc d'Antin a déserté de la cour: en un
mot il fatigue tous ceux qui l'approchent. Il rebute par ses manières
plus que bourgeoises; nous espérons qu'il partira le 15 ou le 16.[17]

On June 20, 1717, greatly to the relief of the French
court, the Tsar departed to join his wife at Spa. He was well
content with his visit to France, though politically it had
been a failure.

The immediate impressions left by Peter were conflicting.
There were some who, with Saint-Simon, admired *ce prince si
grand, si illustre, comparable aux plus grands hommes de
l'antiquité,* and who praised him for his creative genius and
for his *majesté la plus haute, la plus fière, la plus délicate, la
plus soutenue...*[18] This *majesté,* however, was not, even in
Saint-Simon's estimation, exempt from *une forte empreinte
de cette ancienne barbarie de son pays.*[19] There were others,
no doubt (perhaps the majority), who were shocked by the
debauches of the Tsar and his suite,[20] by their lack of polish

[16] E. Haumant, *La Culture française en Russie,* p. 22.
[17] Comte de Barthélemy, *Gazette,* p. 187.
[18] Saint-Simon, *Mémoires,* XXI, 357, 367.
[19] *Ibid.*
[20] See Buvat's many accounts of scandalous stories, *Journal,* I, 263-277.

and manners, and were wondering with Cardinal Dubois whether the Tsar *n'était qu'un extravagant, né pour être un contremaître d'un vaisseau hollandais.*[21] On the whole, taking the Tsar and his followers as a group, the impression they left was not unlike that created by the seventeenth-century Moscovite envoys: they were conceived to be a people essentially un-European, coarse, and barbaric. There is, however, one essential difference: a new type of traveled and cultured Russian noble had appeared in the Tsar's suite. This was a type until then unfamiliar to the French. Later in the century it became, under French influence, more and more common.

Chief among the representatives of this type in 1717 was the Tsar's official interpreter, Prince Boris Kurakin.[22] Saint-Simon described him as follows:

C'était un grand homme bien fait, qui sentait fort la grandeur de son origine, avec beaucoup d'esprit de tour et d'instruction. Il parlait assez bien français et plusieurs langues; il avait fort voyagé, servi à la guerre, puis été employé en différentes cours.

Nevertheless, he adds, even this polished diplomat *ne laissait pas de sentir encore le Russe.*[23]

As for Tsar Peter himself, whatever the immediate verdict of Versailles was, he unquestionably aroused a general interest and left an imprint upon the French mind more profound, it appears, than that of any other foreign visitor of the entire century. The extent of this interest can be grasped only after an examination of the historical, political, and imaginative literature of the century, which is the subject of the second part of this study. At present, one can notice only the dicta

---

[21] Voltaire, *Correspondance*, Voltaire to Chauvelin, October, 1760.

[22] Prince Boris Kurakin (1671-1727) was Lieutenant-Colonel in the Guards, envoy to Rome, Holland, London, and ambassador to France from 1724 to 1727. Other Russians of the same type were Prince Dolgorukiï, Baron Shafirov, Count Tolstoï, and General Buturlin. Cf. Saint-Simon, *Mémoires*, XXXI, 366.

[23] Saint-Simon, *Mémoires*, XXXI, 359.

of two minds which were conspicuous in the century, Fontenelle and Voltaire. One produced a brilliant *éloge* of the Tsar,[24] and the other a history of his reign. Lesser, though no less representative figures, like La Harpe and Dorat, wrote tragedies with Peter as hero, or like Thomas, spent their lives in the effort to glorify the Tsar in elaborate epics. Furthermore, most political writers of the century from Montesquieu to Mirabeau had something to say about the significance of Peter's reforms. Finally, a great variety of anecdotes based upon the Tsar's personal character were published throughout the century.

From 1717 to the signing of the Franco-Russian alliance in 1756 only isolated representatives of the Moscovite world appeared in France. It was only after the signing of the treaty that the number of visitors increased and something approaching a definite colony began to be formed in Paris.

After Tsar Peter's trip in 1717, visitors like the Princes Dolgorukiï, the Princes Golitsyn, and the Naryshkins became rather frequent. These belonged to the oldest and most distinguished families of Russia. Others of less distinguished ancestry came as special envoys, like Peter Apostol in 1725, or as members of the embassy staff, like Betskiï, in 1728. The latter returned later in the century and became a well-known figure in the Parisian salons. Others, of more humble extraction, but known for their talents—like the poet Trediakovskiï, the translator Karzhavin, and the actor Dmitrevskiï—came to study. The first two entered universities, the latter took lessons from the famous Lekain.[25] A few of the most distinguished among these early visitors were well received at Versailles. D'Argenson, for example, records in his memoirs a dinner given by Louis XV in April, 1745, in honor

[24] Fontenelle's *Eloge du Czar Pierre I* appeared first, together with other *éloges*, in Paris, Chaubert, 1733, in 12°.

[25] For these and others see E. Haumant, *La Culture française* ... pp. 54-56, and L. Pingaud, *Les Français en Russie* ... p. 106.

of Count Michael Vorontsov and his wife.[26] Nevertheless, none of these early Russian visitors seem to have made many contacts with the French, and all appear to have left little impression upon the French society of the time. An important exception to this, however, was Prince Antioch Kantemir, ambassador to France from 1738 to 1744.[27]

A Moldavian prince, born in Constantinople, he early distinguished himself as a diplomatist and man of letters. He translated into Russian parts of Anacreon, Horace, and Justinian and wrote satires, odes, and epistles in imitation of Horace and Juvenal. His works, lacking originality, are today interesting chiefly from the historical standpoint.

Because of his personal charm, fine education, and literary interests, Prince Kantemir, soon after his arrival in Paris, made a great many friends and acquaintances among the chief literary and social lights of the time. Among these were Voltaire, Montesquieu, and Mme de Geoffrin.[28] He died in Paris, April 11, 1744.

Prince Kantemir had perfect command of French, and was one of the first Russians to write verses in French, most of which were addressed to his friend the Duchess d'Aiguillon. These have recently been found by Mr. Lozinski in a collection entitled *Elite de poésies fugitives*, published in London in 1764 in three volumes and edited by the poet Blin de Sainmore.[29]

[26] Marquis d'Argenson, *Journal et mémoires*, Paris, 1862, IV, 440-441. Count Mikhail I. Vorontsov (1714-1767) was chancellor of state under Empress Elizabeth, and the head of this distinguished Gallophile family. His daughter, Princess Dashkova, corresponded with Voltaire, Diderot, and other wits and philosophers of the time. His brother, Count Aleksandr, later became an habitué of many Parisian salons, and was in close contact with the highest nobility of France.

[27] See *Archiv Vorontsov*, Moscow, 1870; letters of Kantemir to Prince Vorontsov, pp. 337-395 (in Russian).

[28] Michaud, *Biographie universelle*, I, 270.

[29] G. Lozinski, "Le Prince Antioche Cantemir, poète français," *Revue des études slaves*, V, 238-244.

Kantemir's relations with Voltaire are especially interesting, for they offer the first instance of a correspondence between a Russian *lettré* nobleman and *le grand philosophe,* who was always so generous in praising the culture and enlightenment of his Russian friends. Voltaire wrote two letters to Kantemir, both from Cirey, dated, respectively, March 13 and April 19, 1739.[30] These letters reply to Kantemir's request that an error which Voltaire had made in his *History of Charles XII* regarding the Greek origin of Kantemir's family be corrected.[31] Voltaire acknowledged the criticism, adding that, although in his estimation there was not much difference between Greek and Moldavian, he would, nevertheless, rectify the error. His promise, however, seems never to have been fulfilled. In his first letter Voltaire stated that he had read with pleasure the *History of the Ottoman Empire* written by Prince Antioch's father.[32] The philosopher also inquired about the area and population of Russia, and concluded the letter with praises of Kantemir's family for abandoning the Turks and joining Tsar Peter in his vast scheme of civilizing an empire.

Upon Kantemir's friendship with Montesquieu the evidence is very scant; it may have been largely a fiction. Certainly, from the few references to Kantemir in Montesquieu's published correspondence one does not receive the impression that a close friendship existed between them. On April 11, 1744, Montesquieu wrote to Guasco[33] to console him on

[30] Published in *Bulletin du bibliophile et du bibliothécaire,* 1860.

[31] A. Kantemir, *Works,* St. Petersburg, 1868, II, 435-440 (in Russian).

[32] This history, originally written in Latin, was translated into English in 1734, and into French by De Jonquières in 1743.

[33] Octavien Guasco, Comte de Clavières, Chanoine de Tournai (1712-1781), friend of Montesquieu and Kantemir, translated the latter's satires into French, and dedicated them to the Duchess d'Aiguillon under the name of "Mad..." It was on her insistence that these satires were translated. Guasco had apparently considerable difficulty in finding a publisher for them in France. They finally appeared in London under the title: *Satires du prince Cantemir, précédées de l'histoire de sa vie,* London, Nourse, 1750, in 12°. Cf. C. Montesquieu, *Correspondance,* Paris, 1914, I, 426, 436.

Kantemir's death. A man of Guasco's personality, he said, surely would find another friend worthy of the deceased. The ambassador's death, he added, would become a loss to Russia: ... *la Russie ne remplacera pas si aisément un ambassadeur du mérite du prince Cantemir*.[34] He himself, however, exhibited no signs of personal affliction over the loss of a friend.[35]

As to Kantemir's other literary connections, notably with D'Alembert, Fontenelle, and Mme Geoffrin, the evidence seems to be chiefly limited to his own cursory references to these individuals in his letters to various Russian friends.[36] After Kantemir's death, the Abbé Venuti, a close friend of Montesquieu's, wrote a long and laudatory preface to the London edition of the Russian's satires. One of the pioneers in the transplanting of French culture to Russia, Kantemir was, at the same time, one of the first representatives of a new Russia, characterized by enlightenment and progress, which was then beginning to attract the interest and admiration of contemporary French society.

The diplomatic relations between Russia and France, interrupted in 1748, were resumed in May, 1756. From that time until the Revolution there came to France a constantly increasing number of Russians. Most of these went to Paris, the eighteenth-century Russian Mecca; a few journeyed to the provinces.[37] The Russian embassy in Paris became the

---

[34] Montesquieu, *Correspondance*, I, 403.

[35] Montesquieu evidently had a higher opinion of Kantemir as a diplomat than as a man of letters. His satires, for example, he considered unoriginal and lifeless; see Montesquieu to Venuti, July 22, 1749, *Correspondance*, II, 212.

[36] Prince Kantemir, *Works*, II, 329-415. See also Marquis de Ségur, *Le Royaume de la rue Saint-Honoré*, Paris, 1897, p. 203.

[37] With the exception of the students, one finds only occasional Russians traveling in the provinces. The most popular place was Montpellier, at the time a very lively resort. The vice-chancellor, Vorontsov, stopped there in 1747; the writer Fonvizin studied French life and manners there, and talked about *illuminisme*, a cult made fashionable then by one of its founders, Saint-Martin. Lyon, too, was visited by a few Russians, notably by Betskiï in 1757. See J.

center of a regular Russian colony, composed chiefly of prominent and wealthy aristocrats, who came for the most part to
spend money and to enjoy life at the metropolis. There was
also a limited number of poor and obscure students.

To follow the activities of these Russians in the second half
of the eighteenth century one has to read not only the memoirs and correspondence of the time, but also the records
of the Paris police and prisons, since Russians seem to have
frequented both the salons and the Bastille. On the whole,
most of our information comes from Russian sources,[38] the
French memoirs of the middle of the century being rather
uncommunicative.[39] More definite, however, are the reports
of the Paris police commissioners of the time.

Among the Russians in Paris soon after 1756 who were
best known to Parisian society were those who either had
connections with the embassy, or held important offices in
Russia. Such for example, were the Vorontsovs, the Golitsyns,
and the General Betskïĭ. The Vorontsov family was completely Gallicized, and every member of it was as well known
in Paris as in St. Petersburg.[40] The Princes Golitsyn were
equally well known and well received everywhere.[41] The

Mathorez, *Les Etrangers en France sous l'ancien régime*, Paris, 1919, II, 308,
324-325; see also V. Veuclin, *Les Lyonnais et la Russie au siècle dernier*, Lyons,
1896, p. 12; and L. Pingaud, *Les Français en Russie . . . p. 98.*

[38] Such as the memoirs of the Princess Dashkova; the *Archives Vorontzov*
and *Kurakin; The Journal of Komarovskïĭ;* the letters of Fonvizin and Karamzin.

[39] Marmontel, for example, who in his memoirs mentions many foreigners,
particularly English, is silent about Russians; so is Mme d'Epinay, and, with
the exceptions of a few cursory references to Betskïĭ and Shuvalov, Mme du
Deffand. In view of the probability that these three must have known many
Russians through Grimm, Diderot, and La Harpe, their silence may be taken
as an indication that comparatively few Russians frequented these salons, and
that those who did made little impression.

[40] L. Pingaud, *Les Français en Russie . . .* pp. 108-109.

[41] The Ambassador Aleksïeĭ Golitsyn was a friend of Helvétius and Grimm,
and corresponded with Voltaire; he was known also as collaborator in the scientific parts of the *Journal des savants* and editor of Helvétius's *L'Homme.* Prince
Dmitrïĭ Golitsyn (1721-1793) was minister to France and later ambassador to
Vienna. His cousin Dmitrïĭ Aleksïeevich (1738-1813) was chargé d'affaires in

two cousins, Dimitriï Golitsyn, were friends of the Comte Cheverny, Voltaire, and Mlle Clairon.[42] According to the Princess of Anhalt-Zerbst, mother of Catherine II, the Golitsyns were very much liked by the French and were received in the most exclusive salons of Paris.[43] General Betskiï was already in Paris in 1728 as an attaché of the embassy.[44] In the sixties he returned as Catherine's personal agent, engaging artists, buying art collections, and frequenting various salons.[45]

First of all among the salons that received these and other Russians was that of Mme Geoffrin. In her youth she was a friend of Prince Kantemir, and in 1763 she began a correspondence with Catherine II which lasted until 1768.[46] It was in her salon that the third reading of Rulhière's *Anecdotes de la révolution en 1762* took place before a large audience—a scene which Grimm describes in his *Correspondance littéraire* for April, 1770.[47] As to the other salons, the evidence is less clear, if not altogether wanting. It would, however, appear probable that salons like that of the Baron d'Holbach (1759-1788)—among the habitués of which were Grimm, Marmontel, and D'Alembert, and in which Grimm is known to have read his sketch of Catherine II [48]—must have had Russians among their guests. No doubt some of the Moscovites frequented also such cosmopolitan salons as that of Mme Necker (1766-1789), where all the distinguished

Paris in 1762-3; Catherine II was displeased because of his frequenting the Choiseuls', and he was compelled to resign. Cf. J. Mathorez, *Les Etrangers en France*, I, 313.

[42] D. comte de Cheverny, *Mémoires*, 1909, Pt. I, pp. 249-250, 286-288.

[43] *Archives Vorontzov*, Letters of the Princess of Anhalt-Zerbst, cited in E. Haumant, *op. cit.*, p. 62.

[44] Cf. correspondence of Diderot and Falconet, *Revue moderne*, XXXIX.

[45] Grimm, *Correspondance littéraire*, VI, 265, and VII, 201.

[46] Marquis de Ségur, *Le Royaume de la rue St. Honoré*, pp. 206-225.

[47] Grimm, *Correspondance littéraire*, VIII, 493-495.

[48] Marie Foucaux, (Summer), *Quelques salons de Paris au XVIII° siècle*, Paris, 1898, p. 100.

foreigners of the day were present at one time or another.
Mlle de Lespinasse's salon (1764-1776) was another in which
Russians are likely to have been found.[49] Grimm, D'Alembert,
and Marmontel, its habitués, no doubt introduced there some
of their Russian friends.

Some Russians, on the other hand, complained of the difficulty of being admitted into French society of the time. The
writer Fonvizin, for example, was quite bitter about this.
Most Russians in Paris, he writes about 1778, had the same
difficulty: their calls were returned, but the acquaintance
was not continued.[50] Alexander Kurakin registers the same
complaint. *On a beau tenter l'impossible*, he writes, *on part
de Paris comme on y est arrivé, sans lumières sur la façon dont
on vit dans les bonnes maisons.*[51]

Individuals in the Russian colony were disliked for various
specific reasons; some because of the scandalous lives they
led, others because of their clownishness and absurdity. Peter
Orlov, for example, interested society chiefly because he could
eat eggs shell and all.[52] Many were disliked for their proud
and haughty airs. This was the case, for example, with Princess Dashkova. She prided herself greatly upon her erudition,
which was considerable, and which Thiébault tells us was a
source of irritation to many a savant of the time.[53] All Paris,
he recalls, was delighted at one time with an answer made to
the Princess in the Tuileries by an old soldier who stood star-
ing at her: *Qu'avez-vous donc, monsieur, à me considérer?*
she asked him irritably. *Ah, Madame, je vous regarde, je ne
vous considère pas.*[54] Nevertheless, the Princess was probably
one of the most widely known Russians in France as well as

[49] Marie Foucaux, *op. cit.*, p. 131.
[50] D. Fonvizin, *Works*, St. Petersburg, 1866, pp. 330-335.
[51] *Archiv Kourakine*, Vol. VI.
[52] *Ibid.*
[53] *Russkii arkhiv*, 1878, XXIII, "Souvenirs of Thiébault."
[54] *Ibid.*

in England.[55] Diderot was her friend and admirer and wrote
a short *éloge* of her life.[56] She visited and corresponded with
Voltaire and was acquainted with Raynal, Malesherbes, and
Mme Necker. Among the philosophers she was thought to be
far in advance of her age. Marie Antoinette granted audience
to her, and Houdon sculptured her bust.[57]

Another prominent family closely identified with eighteenth-century French society was that of the Comtes Shuvalov.[58] Like the Golitsyns, the members of this family were
bred in French classical traditions, had a perfect command
of French, and were equally at home in Paris or in St. Petersburg. The older representative, Ivan, was a regular correspondent of Voltaire, and on several occasions visited him at
Ferney. The younger, André, also in close contact with Voltaire, as well as La Harpe and Diderot, was the author of the
famous *Epître à Ninon*. This poem was for some time ascribed
to Voltaire, who finally published a letter full of praises for
the *jeunes hommes du Nord* and who at the same time re-
stored the poem to its rightful author. André was widely
known as a brilliant wit, but owing to his vanity and pride
he was not very well liked. According to Fonvizin, his wife
went everywhere, but very few of her calls were returned.[59]

[55] Princess Ekaterina Romanovna Dashkova (1743-1810), daughter of the
general and chancellor Vorontsov, was a woman of great intellectual gifts and
was considered to be a rival even of Catherine the Great, whose friend and maid
of honor she was for a number of years. She was an intellectual pupil of Bayle,
Voltaire, and Montesquieu, who admired and respected her gifts. In 1769, after
a period of disfavor at court, she went abroad, visiting Paris twice and Scotland once. In Scotland she met Robertson and Adam Smith, and received a
degree from the University of Edinburgh. In 1783 she returned home and
became president of the Academy of Sciences. In 1795, after the publication of
her *Vadim*, she again fell out of favor at court and retired to the country,
where she wrote her memoirs. Cf. K. Waliszewski, *History of Russian Literature*,
pp. 124-127.

[56] Diderot, *Œuvres*, éd. Assézat, 1875, XVII, 487-495.

[57] Ekaterina Dashkova, *Memoirs*, London, 1840, I, 180-182, 220, 223; II,
193, 194-195.

[58] Grimm, *Correspondance littéraire*, X, 391; XIII, 514.

[59] D. Fonvizin, *Works*, p. 334; E. Dashkova, *Memoirs*, I, 220.

Ivan Shuvalov, besides being known in Paris as a statesman, *lettré*, and wit, had an additional claim to fame as a lover of the Empress Elizabeth. Chamfort, in this connection, records the following anecdote:

Dans une société où se trouvait M. de Schouwalow, ancien amant de l'Impératrice Elizabeth, on voulait savoir quelque fait relatif à la Russie. Le Bailli de Chabrillant dit: "Monsieur de Schouwalow, dites-nous cette histoire; vous devez la savoir, vous qui étiez le Pompadour de ce pays-là." [60]

Besides those mentioned, several other Russian nobles were especially liked and respected by the French. Prince Vladimir Sergîeevich Dolgorukîĭ is an example. A soldier, he had served as volunteer in the French army, and had taken part in three campaigns during the Seven Years' War. As a diplomat and philosopher, he was envoy to Berlin from 1762 to 1787 and, Thiébault tells us, was greatly respected and admired by all the Frenchmen who knew him.[61] He was a life-long friend of Bernardin de Saint-Pierre, with whom in his youth he served in Finland.[62] The Golovkin family also was known to a great many Frenchmen. Count Aleksandr Gavrilovich Golovkin was made envoy to Holland in 1731, where he remained until his death in 1760. His house was a social center for traveling Frenchmen. His son, Count Aleksandr Aleksandrovich, settled in Paris and educated his children there. He was a man of wide culture, somewhat retiring and eccentric. In Paris he was known as *Golovkine le philosophe*. According to Thiébault, one of his daughters, a very charming and accomplished person, amused Paris by wearing men's clothes before noon and women's after.[63] Count Aleksandr Sergîeevich Strogonov (1733-1811) also belongs to this group. Possessor of an immense fortune, he was a perfect type

[60] Sébastien Chamfort, *Caractère et anecdotes*, 1924, p. 72.
[61] *Ruskîĭ arkhiv*, 1877, "Souvenirs of Thiébault," pp. 507-512.
[62] *Ibid.*, pp. 518-522.   [63] *Ibid.*

of the accomplished gentleman of the time—cosmopolitan, traveled, and a *lettré*. He lived for many years in Paris and was widely known for his lavish and extravagant entertainments. His brother, André, a dignitary in a masonic lodge of Neuf-Sœurs, was a friend of Grimm, D'Alembert, and D'Holbach. His son Paul, born in Paris, was educated in the liberal eighteenth-century manner by the famous Gilbert Romme.[64]

Of somewhat less prominent ancestry, but no less liked by Parisian aristocracy, was Count Oginskïï (1731-1803), one-time favorite of Catherine II. Having conspired against Russia, he was obliged to flee and in 1750 established himself permanently in Paris. He spent his time perfecting himself in various artistic accomplishments, particularly music, and, says his friend Comte de Cheverny, *Dès qu'il se crut quelque acquis, il se fit présenter et se répandit dans les meilleurs sociétés.*[65] He and his friend Prince Nicholas Repnin (1734-1801), at one time also a favorite of Catherine II, were equally admired for their social accomplishments and together made the rounds of the Parisian drawing rooms.[66]

These were some of the representatives of the Russian colony in the 50's and 60's, who were befriended by the French aristocracy as well as by the philosophers. Some of them belonged to the type *le Russe-philosophe*. All of them were imbued with French culture, were polished and accomplished in the best eighteenth-century manner, and in their mode of thought, if not of life, were closer to the French aristocracy than any other foreign group of the time.

What has so far been said about the Russian colony in Paris gives only one side of the picture. The other side ap-

---

[64] L. Pingaud, *Les Français en Russie* ... p. 111; Louis Léger, *La Russie intellectuelle*, 1914, pp. 109-110; J. Mathorez, *Les Etrangers en France* ... I, 322-323.

[65] Dufort de Cheverny, *Mémoires*, Pt. I, p. 485.

[66] *Ibid.*, p. 486.

pears only after closer examination of the kind of life led by the majority of the Russian colonists. It is then that *le Russe-philosophe* retreats, and *le Russe-barbare* steps into the foreground.

Mathorez's study of the life of the Russian colonists reveals that their chief preoccupations were *chercher la femme,* gambling, and debauch.

Pour la femme, les Russes du XVIIIᵉ siècle sacrifient tout: fortune, santé, scrupules de morale; ils lui abandonnent même le port de leur barbe qui leur est un bien plus précieux que l'argent.[67]

A few examples will suffice. Count Serge Saltykov, minister plenipotentiary to France in 1762, was a hero of most scandalous adventures:

Bien qu'atteint d'une sérieuse avarie, il court les actrices. La pauvre petite Lucie, de l'Opéra Comique, est contaminée, et l'inspecteur de police écrit: "Elle est gravement malade; c'est en vérité, pour un homme de nom, avoir bien peu d'humanité. Il est vrai que rarement cette qualité est accordée aux gens de son pays." [68]

Saltykov's wife, while her husband is pursuing actresses,

...a pour amant un bon gentilhomme, Aymard de Villemare. Il a jadis payé les dettes du mari, et, dans le carosse de la dame, au coin des rues Saint-Martin et Transnonain, il tient avec elle les plus doux propos.[69]

The household of André Shuvalov was no less noted for its *libertinage.* The conduct there was shocking even to the

---

[67] J. Mathorez, *Les Etrangers en France* . . . I, 314; Mathorez's sources are (1) Pitou, *Paris sous Louis XV; rapports des inspecteurs de police au roi;* éd. du Mercure de France, 5 vols. (2) Loredan Larchey, *Journaux des inspecteurs de police de M. de Sartines,* Geneva, 1863.

[68] J. Mathorez, *Les Etrangers en France* . . . I, 316. Sergieĭ Saltykov is not to be confused with Boris Saltykov, a friend of Voltaire's who left Paris in 1762. Cf. Voltaire, *Correspondance,* letter of June 4, 1762.

[69] J. Mathorez, *Les Etrangers en France* . . . I, 316.

Parisian society of the time, which is saying a good deal. *De telles relations ne sauraient plaire à tout le monde,* wrote Grimm, and Fonvizin later was even more positive in his statements.[70]

A vast amount of money was spent by the Russians on theaters and actresses: *loges, boudoirs, coulisses des artistes de la Comédie Italienne ou de l'Opéra sont fréquentés par l'aristocratie russe.*[71] Being fierce gamblers besides, the Russian aristocrats were often in desperate circumstances. Some refused to pay their debts, others went further and resorted to devious methods of procuring money. Count Bobrinskiï, natural son of Catherine II, lived in Paris in great luxury and ostentation; he borrowed 1,200,000 livres from the Marquis de Ferrières, and Catherine paid the debt.[72] Count Biron resorted to counterfeiting, and was finally sent to the Bastille.[73]

These few examples of the *mœurs moscovites* will be sufficient to show that French society was made equally aware of the unphilosophical side of the Russian character.

Most of the Russian colonists, some of whom have been mentioned above, arrived in Paris between 1756 and 1760. A great number of them were still there about 1780. Fonvizin, who with his wife was in Paris about 1778, gives a very unflattering account of his countrymen, stressing especially their carefree and gay mode of living. In the whole Russian colony, which, he says, is very large, he found only two *philosophes;* the rest were frankly out for pleasure and were leading scandalous lives.[74] His statements are, however, to be taken with caution, especially since his criticism of French

---

[70] *Ibid.,* I, 317.

[71] *Ibid.,* I, 318. Bachaumont also records that the actresses (Clairon, for example) were always surrounded by Russian admirers. Bachaumont, *Mémoires,* September 16, 1764, and May, 1765.

[72] J. Mathorez, *Les Etrangers en France* . . . I, 319.

[73] *Ibid.,* I, 320.

[74] D. Fonvizin, *Works,* pp. 438-444.

society itself seems so extreme, unjust, and to a large extent borrowed from Diderot's *Pensées philosophiques* and Duclos's *Considérations sur les mœurs du siècle.*[75]

Fonvizin was acquainted with many men of letters, particularly with Marmontel, D'Alembert, and Diderot. These he calls charlatans, liars, and mean self-seekers, who would do anything to get a remunerative post in Russia.[76] With such an attitude toward the outstanding men of a country whose culture he had so thoroughly assimilated, he was not likely to make friends. His stay in Paris seems to have passed unnoticed, and in the memoirs of the time his name is not to be found.

One can estimate the growing numbers of the Russian colony from Diderot's letters to Falconet. In 1772 Diderot writes: *Nous avons ici un bon nombre de seigneurs russes qui font honneur à leur nation.*[77] Next year the number increases: *Nos hôtels garnis ne désemplissent pas de Russes.*[78] Paris theaters, cafés, and shops are flooded with Russians, and in 1780 Grimm writes to Catherine:

On ne voit qu'enseignes "à l'Impératrice de Russie," que "café de Russie," "grands Hôtels de Russie garnis," marchands de mode à l'enseigne du "Russe galant."[79]

Many of the wealthy Russians buy up pictures and various objects of art. Wille, the engraver, mentions in his memoirs many Russians, particularly the Golitsyns and Strogonovs, as fine connoisseurs of art. He often takes orders from them and also from the Russian court.[80] Diderot buys up entire art collections for Catherine and writes enthusiastically to Falconet:

[75] D. Fonvizin, *Works*, pp. 330-352. Cf. also K. Waliszewski, *History of Russian Literature*, p. 102.
[76] D. Fonvizin, *Works*, pp. 341-352.
[77] Diderot to Falconet, April 27, 1772, *Revue moderne*, XL, 323.
[78] Diderot to Falconet, May 20, 1773, *Revue moderne*, XL, 325.
[79] Grimm to Catherine, July 10, 1780, *Sbornik*, XXXI, 40 ff.
[80] J. G. Wille, *Mémoires et journal*, Paris, 1857, I, 140, 460, 488, 512; II, 67, 111.

Combien nous sommes changés. Nous vendons nos tableaux et nos statues au milieu de la paix; Catherine les achète au milieu de la guerre. Les sciences, les arts, le goût, la sagesse remontent vers le Nord, et la barbarie avec son cortège descend au Midi.[81]

Voltaire's views are substantially the same. *Ne remarquez-vous pas*, he writes to D'Alembert in 1762, *que les grands examples et les grandes leçons nous viennent du Nord?* [82] In 1760 he wrote a satire *Le Russe à Paris*, which showed a *Russe-philosophe* who came to Paris to be educated but was disappointed in not finding the expected *lumières* there.[83] A great number of Russians visited Voltaire both at Délices and at Ferney, and in his correspondence he frequently praises their education and culture with enthusiasm.

Ce qui vous surprendra [he writes to Mme du Deffand in 1765] c'est que j'ai vu des Russes de 22 ans qui ont autant de mérite [as the best of the English] autant de connaissances et qui parlent aussi bien notre langue.[84]

In 1771 Carmontelle published a collection of plays under the pseudonym of a Russian prince—Clenerzow—and in the 70's and 80's a number of plays with subjects taken from Russian history appeared on the stage. All this goes to show that in Paris between the years 1760 and 1780 Russians were common phenomena and that there existed a certain interest in them as a group. Much of this interest was no doubt due to Catherine II's clever befriending of the philosophers. In 1763 all Paris talked about the Empress' purchase of Diderot's library, and her letter to D'Alembert was made public by the Academy.[85] Rulhière's *Anecdotes sur la révolution en*

81 Diderot to Falconet, April 27, 1772, *Revue moderne*, XL, 323.
82 Voltaire, *Correspondance*, Voltaire to D'Alembert, February 4, 1763.
83 Voltaire, *Œuvres*, Garnier, X, 119-131.
84 Voltaire, *Correspondance*, Voltaire to Mme du Deffand, March, 1765; cf. also Voltaire's correspondence between 1774 and 1776, Vol. XLIX.
85 "Jamais lettré n'honora plus le trône..." writes the Academician Thomas to his friend Barthe, September 27, 1763, "Quel style, mon cher ami, pour le

1762 was circulating in manuscript form and was read many times before large audiences in Parisian salons.[86] The trips of Diderot and Grimm to Russia excited great general interest, and in 1774, when Diderot returned from Russia, all Paris was eager to hear the details of his journey.[87] Grimm was the center of cosmopolitan social activities. He gave large balls to which he invited all the prominent members of the Russian colony.[88] All Parisian papers recorded the arrival of prominent Russians, and in 1781, for example, the journals were filled for weeks with accounts of the Grand Duke Paul's visit.[89]

Glorified by Voltaire and the group of the Encyclopedists, Catherine II and Russia became the fashion of the time. It even appears that in the 80's russomania became a serious rival to the anglomania prevalent up to that time. That, at least, is Grimm's opinion, written about 1782: *En général, la nation russe est considérablement à la mode dans ce moment-ci; elle a succédé à cet égard à la nation anglaise.*[90]

The enthusiasm of some Frenchmen for Russia even led them to think of visiting the country. Some actually went; others, intimidated by the distance, merely contemplated the idea. In 1761 Thomas was on the point of going to Russia as secretary to Baron de Breteuil. *J'ai balancé longtemps le désir naturel de voir des choses nouvelles...* he wrote to Barthe, *de connaître un monde différent du nôtre, de voir le tombeau du Czar Pierre...* He changed his mind, however,

---

pays des anciens Tartares et des Saramates! Il faut avouer que les gens du Nord nous donnent de belles leçons sur plusieurs articles."—*Revue d'histoire littéraire*, 1918, p. 149.

[86] Grimm, *Correspondance littéraire*, VIII, 493-495.

[87] Thomas to Barthe, January 23, 1773, and July 19, 1774, *Revue d'histoire littéraire*, 1927, p. 128, and 1928, p. 405.

[88] Grimm to Catherine, March, 1781, *Sbornik*, 1881, XXXIII, 125-126.

[89] *Ibid.*, Grimm to Catherine, August 8, 1781.

[90] Louis Réau, *Les Relations artistiques entre la France et la Russie*, 1924, Introduction.

because of poor health and the distance.[91] In 1765 Sébastien Mercier, a friend of Thomas, was eager to go to Russia, but Choiseul refused to give him a passport. Mercier was obliged therefore to renounce his plan, *avec la seule satisfaction d'avoir pu le juger de près.*[92] Diderot was the principal agent for those who wished to undertake the trip. He gave letters of recommendation, helped to engage artists and lawyers. A good many young men sought his protection; he himself encouraged others to the adventure. One day, he writes to Falconet, he asked a young man whom he had just met whether he would like to go to Russia. The youth, according to Diderot, replied without hesitation, "Why not?" and left the next morning.[93] All this indicates a general vogue for Russia which the Russians already in Paris naturally tended to foster.

The arrival in 1782 of the Grand Duke Paul and his wife, under the assumed names of Comte and Comtesse du Nord, gave a further stimulus to French society's interest in Russia and Russian affairs.[94] Like the Tsar Peter in 1717, Paul came unofficially, in fact incognito. Like Peter, too, he came in part to learn. Thus he visited various centers of industry, particularly Sèvres and the arsenals of Brest, and attended a meeting of the Academy. Unlike Peter, however, he took a very active part in the social affairs at Versailles.[95] The critic La Harpe, who had been his correspondent since 1774, was his official spokesman in Parisian society. At a special meeting of the French Academy La Harpe read a long poem addressed to the Count and Countess of the North. In this poem, which was found dull and pedantic by his contemporaries, he commented at length upon the remarkable progress in Russia and

[91] Thomas to Barthe, January 31, 1760, *Revue d'histoire littéraire*, 1917, p. 123.

[92] Mercier, *Tableau de Paris*, Amsterdam, 1788, p. 301.

[93] Diderot to Falconet, September 6, 1768, *Revue moderne*, XL, 311.

[94] For a detailed account of Paul's sojourn in France, see Comte Fleury's *Revue de l'histoire de Versailles*, 1902, pp. 53 ff.

[95] Baroness d'Oberkirch, *Mémoires*, 1869, Vol. I, ch. x.

praised the virtues of the heir to the throne (i.e., Grand Duke Paul), stressing particularly his *art d'être aimable*, his *enjouement, urbanité*, and his mixture of the *pompe asiatique* with the refinement of the West.[96]

The impressions left by Paul and his wife were altogether favorable. Both official and unofficial France were, in fact, delighted with them. *Ils ont laissé dans toute la France une excellente réputation et même beaucoup de regrets*, wrote Buffon to his son.[97] Buffon's great grief was to have missed seeing the Grand Duke, but he said that all those who saw him had found in him *non seulement beaucoup d'esprit et d'instruction, mais un grand caractère de fermeté et de bonté...*[98] The Marquis de Valfons, who met the royal visitors on many occasions, admired Paul's wit, graciousness, and simplicity.[99] The Duke de Croÿ praised his *bon ton, beaucoup de politesse et de retenue même respectueuse.*[100] Paul's sole fault was his ugliness, but this was redeemed, it appears, by his graciousness and *bon ton.*

There remain, after Paul, only a few visitors of distinction to be mentioned here. The most prominent of these were the Counts Rumîantsev, who visited France on many occasions and became well known in French social and literary circles. Their education was entirely French; they were talented and possessed great personal charm. In 1774 Voltaire greatly admired a young Rumîantsev's French verses, parts of which he found even more surprising than those of Count Shuvalov.[101] In 1787 Mme de Genlis met at Spa one of the young Rumîantsevs traveling with Grimm and wrote enthusiastically as follows:

[96] La Harpe, *Œuvres*, "Correspondance littéraire," Paris, 1826. Cf. La Harpe's poem to the Grand Duke Paul, letter to Shuvalov, Vol. II, Letter clxvii.

[97] Buffon, *Correspondance*, Paris, 1860, August 18, 1782, II, 146.

[98] *Ibid.*, cf. also his letter to Mme Necker, July 12, 1782, II, 133-135.

[99] C. Valfons, *Souvenirs*, Paris, 1906, pp. 408-412.

[100] E. de Croÿ, *Journal inédit*, Paris, 1907, IV, 255.

[101] Voltaire to D'Alembert, October 29, 1774, *Œuvres*, XLIX.

Je n'ai connu personne dont la conversation fût plus agréable; son esprit s'était formé, il avait acquis beaucoup d'instruction, et sans avoir rien perdu de son amabilité sociale.[102]

She was so taken by him that she dedicated her novel *Chevalier de Cygne* to the young count.[103] About 1789 a brother of this young count acted Alceste in a Parisian salon and was received by Marie Antoinette.[104]

The last prominent Russian visitor who must be mentioned is Karamzin, the father of the Russian sentimental novel and one of the best known historians of the early nineteenth century. Karamzin went to France in 1790 and spent three and a half months in Paris. His letters on France were published in Moscow in 1792 and were translated into French in 1867.[105]

Karamzin did not shine in the few salons which were still open and, he tells us, made no effort to meet the literary and philosophical celebrities of the time. Instead, he spent his time attending the meetings of the National Assembly, visiting museums, libraries, theaters, and cafés, observing everywhere the life of the streets and the various manifestations of the revolutionary spirit.[106] He met the writer Levesque, whose history of Russia he thought the best to date.[107] In his letters on France, Karamzin admired the sympathetic, amiable quality of the French:

On dirait que vous [i.e., the French] avez inventé la société, ou que la société a été inventée pour vous, tant la politesse et l'art de vivre avec les hommes semblent innés chez les Français.[108]

---

[102] Mme de Genlis, *Mémoires*, 1825, III, 201.
[103] *Ibid.*, III, 203.
[104] E. Haumant, *La Culture française en Russie*, p. 63.
[105] A. V. Starchevskiï, *Karamzin*, St. Petersburg, 1849, pp. 55-64; A. Babeau, *Les Voyageurs en France depuis la Renaissance jusqu'à la Révolution*, Paris, 1885, ch. xxx, pp. 388-394.
[106] A. Legrelle, *Revue de la Révolution*, Paris, 1884, IV, 325-333.
[107] A. V. Starchevskiï, *Karamzin*, pp. 58-59.
[108] Albert Babeau, *Les Voyageurs en France* ... pp. 393-394.

It is interesting to note that this quality of sociability which Karamzin admired in the French is precisely the quality which appeals most to the French in their estimates of the Russian character. Karamzin, however, did not care for society, and, as in the case of Fonvizin, it is impossible to ascertain what impression he himself produced upon contemporary French society.

The group of Russian students who came to France in the course of the century deserves special notice. They were important not only because of their large numbers, but also because of their mode of living and their contacts with various sections of French society.

The first group of Russian students to come to France in the eighteenth century was composed of midshipmen sent by Peter the Great to study navigation. Twenty of them arrived early in 1717. Among these were several bearing illustrious Russian names such as Saltykov, Volkonskii, and Bariatinskii. Some of them were sent to Brest, the others to Toulon.[109]

According to the reports of the officers of Toulon who took charge of them, the midshipmen conducted themselves *comme des sauvages*. In August, 1717, De Watton, their instructor at Toulon, wrote to Paris as follows:

Les gentilshommes moscovites sont appliqués aux exercices et assez polis pour les autres, mais, entre eux, ils vivent comme des crocheteurs, et leur manière de vivre tient beaucoup du sauvage; il ne se passe pas de jour qu'ils ne se battent entre eux à coups de sièges et de chandeliers et cela se termine toujours en mettant le couteau à la main; des suites sont à craindre quoi qu'ils soient traités avec toute la politesse possible, et que le commandant de Watton et les officiers de la compagnie ne travaillent uniquement que pour leur

---

[109] The principal Russian source on these midshipmen is the *Journal* of Nepliuev, St. Petersburg, 1893, pp. 36 ff. The French sources are the archives of the Naval Department and of the Ministry of Foreign Affairs. The best recent study based on French sources is that of J. Mathorez, *Les Etrangers en France*, I, 300-303.

inspirer les sentiments de douceur et les manières de vivre en gens de condition.[110]

On September 9, 1717, it was reported to Paris that a certain Sumbukov had killed a French merchant on the road to Toulon. Two friends of Sumbukov gave assurance, however, that it was merely an accident. Nevertheless, wrote De Watton,

la population de la ville étant fort excitée contre les Russes, on dut leur intredire les sorties du soir et confisquer leurs armes. [At the end of his report De Watton added]: Une partie de ces jeunes messieurs n'ont que la figure de l'homme et il n'y a chez eux que l'animal qui agit.[111]

The finances of these midshipmen were, apparently, in a wretched state. Peter's agent neglected to support them, and so did the French government of the Regent. De Watton's reports to Paris from 1717 to 1720 were full of entreaties for money: *Les gardes de la marine moscovites sont dans une misère extrême; l'aubergiste qui les avait reçus chez lui ne veut plus leur donner de quoi vivre.*[112] As a consequence they contracted more debts and got into further mischief. Some of them left before they received their commissions. In 1722 the Regent signed the commissions of the remainder, and the majority of these went back to Russia. A few lingered in France.[113]

In Brest the behavior of the Russians was better. The climate there was colder than in Toulon, and the discipline was stricter. Their instructor, De Nogent, was apparently satisfied with their progress and wrote to Paris: *Les gentilshommes russes assistent aux instructions ordinaires avec tout le succès possible, ils tiennent une bonne conduite et font une dépense*

[110] J. Mathorez, *Les Etrangers en France*, I, 301, cites Archives de la Marine, B3, 245, fo. 292.

[111] Archives de la Marine, B3, 245, fo. 307; cited in J. Mathorez, *Les Etrangers en France*, I, 302.

[112] *Ibid.*   [113] J. Mathorez, *Les Etrangers en France*, I, 303.

considérable qui leur fait honneur.[114] Between the years 1722 and 1725 all of these midshipmen but one (Yusupov died in Brest) returned to Russia.[115]

Except for a few isolated individuals, such as Trediâkovskiï and Dmitrevskiï, no other group of Russian students came to France until after 1757. The majority of those who then arrived came to study the fine arts.[116]

A permanent arrangement for sending Russian students to France was entered upon in 1764. It required the sending every three years of the twelve best pupils of the Academy of St. Petersburg either to Paris or to Rome. This arrangement lasted until 1789.[117]

Upon their arrival in Paris these students were required to report to the Russian embassy. They were then assisted in finding lodgings by Diderot and Grimm. Usually they lived in groups of two or three in small hotels, or boarded with keepers of small shops.[118] From 1760 to 1789 more than forty young Russians were either enrolled in the Ecole des Beaux-Arts, or instructed elsewhere by the best-known artists of the time.[119]

The conduct of the art students left much to be desired.

[114] Archives de la Marine, B28, fo. 125; cited in J. Mathorez, *Les Etrangers en France,* I, p. 304.

[115] *Ibid.*

[116] In the provinces the only important group of Russian students was formed about 1786 in Strassburg. Most of these studied medicine on fellowships given by the Russian government. The principal sources for the study of the formation of the group of Russian art students in France in the eighteenth century are as follows: Archives of the French and Russian Academies; Diderot's correspondence with Betskiï, Falconet, and Catherine II; also his *Rapport sur les jeunes artistes que Sa Majesté Impériale envoie en pays étrangers;* Grimm's correspondence with Catherine II; J. G. Wille, *Journal.*

Some recent studies are: D. Roche, "Liste des artistes russes dont les noms sont inscrits sur les registres de l'Académie Parisienne de Peinture et de Sculpture," *Starye gody,* 1909; Trubnikov, "Pensionery Akedemïi Khudozhestv," *Starye gody,* 1907; L. Réau, "Les Artistes russes à Paris au XVIIIe siècle," *Revue des études slaves,* III, 286-298.

[117] L. Réau, *Les Artistes russes à Paris . . .* p. 286.

[118] *Ibid.,* p. 287.   [119] *Ibid.,* p. 289.

Finding themselves free in Paris, they seem to have indulged to the full their passion for gambling and women. A sculptor named Sokolov, for example, was described in the following terms by the Russian Ambassador:

Socoloff, abandonné par l'Académie des Arts, était tombé dans la misère; un professeur l'avait recueilli et lui donnait de l'ouvrage. La passion pour le jeu l'a porté à s'oublier et à s'emparer des effets qui ne lui appartenaient pas, pour les convertir en argent. Il n'a pas laissé d'être bientôt découvert et d'être détenu dans une prison du district. Pour arrêter une procédure criminelle contre lui, j'ai dû prendre le parti de l'envoyer à Rouen pour y être embarqué sur un vaisseau qui partait pour Hambourg; ayant vendu ses habits, chemises, souliers, chapeaux, et tout ce qu'il avait pour couvrir son corps, j'ai dû lui faire acheter le vêtement le plus indispensable.[120]

Another very gifted student, Bersenev, was a victim of other *entraînements* and died very young in Paris as a result of his debauches in the *Venusberg du Palais-Royal*.[121]

To prevent such happenings, which were by no means exceptional, Diderot was appointed to report to the Academy of St. Petersburg on the progress and behavior of these students.[122] Diderot apparently found the situation hopeless and in 1773 advised Catherine to send the students directly to Rome instead of to Paris. He wrote:

Les élèves livrés à eux-mêmes ont été leur train; ils ont peu travaillé. Les uns ont été paresseux, les autres, libertins, et presque tous sont partis pour Rome . . . Paris est un lieu de perdition pour tout jeune homme non inspecté . . .

Therefore, he concluded, they should be sent directly to Rome, or if they came to Paris, it would be necessary to *les renfermer, les assujettir à une discipline rigoureuse*.[123]

[120] L. Réau, *Les Artistes russes à Paris* . . . p. 288.
[121] *Ibid.*
[122] Diderot to Falconet, May and July, 1768, *Revue moderne*, 1866.
[123] M. Tourneux, *Diderot et Catherine II*, pp. 423-425.

Diderot's advice was disregarded, and the students continued to come to Paris, staying there on the average about two years and then either going to Rome or returning to Russia.[124] Many of these students did distinguished work, as, for example, the painter Losenko and the architect Volkov. The latter, under De Wailly, subsequently built the Odéon.[125]

The art students, having very little money and no social position, naturally made no appearance in the eighteenth-century salons. Their activities were confined chiefly to the ateliers and the night life of the Palais-Royal. What impression, if any, they produced during their quarter of a century in France, is hard to determine. To Diderot and Grimm they were partly a nuisance because of their disorderly and riotous conduct, but also partly interesting as specimens of Russia's growing *lumières*. The instructors under whom these students worked were, it appears, satisfied with their efforts, while the shopkeepers and the landlords were exasperated by their frequent defaulting in the payment of their debts and rent. In general, the art students must have shown eighteenth-century France that the barbarism of the Muscovites was not incompatible with considerable achievement in the arts.

The examination of the numerous and varied representatives of the Moscovite world, from sovereigns to penniless art students who came to France during the eighteenth century, leads to the conclusion that the interest of the French in Russia and the Russians starting with Peter the Great's visit in 1717, continued during the century and culminated in the decade preceding the Revolution. If one is to believe Grimm, the vogue of Russia in the eighties superseded even

[124] J. Mathorez, *Les Etrangers en France*, p. 309.
[125] L. Réau, *Les Artistes russes à Paris* ... pp. 290, 289-297; cf. also J. Mathorez, *op. cit.*, pp. 209-310; J. G. Wille, *Journal*, p. 172.

that of England.[126] However that may be, it is certain that the connection between French and Russian society was, in the second half of the century, as close as, if not closer than, that between the French and the English.[127] The Russians had, in fact, certain advantages over the English, so far, at least, as French society went. There were more of them permanently established in France, they were richer, and they had a better command of French. They were more sociable, and more like the French themselves in temperament. The English had, of course, a great deal to give: their literature, their philosophy, their capacity for "deep thought," and their picturesque eccentricities of character. Besides their money the Russians had little to give to the French, but a great deal to take. Their rôle was that of clever pupils, and that was precisely, it appears, what endeared them most to the eighteenth-century Frenchmen. It was, in short, their capacity to assimilate French culture successfully that appealed most to the aristocratic and intellectual France of that day. The Vorontsovs, Golitsyns, and Golovkins were almost indistinguishable from the French aristocracy of the time. Voltaire, Diderot, and Grimm praise, above all, the cultural and linguistic capacity of the Russian visitors.

To judge from the impressions left by the Russians, the Frenchmen seem to have been aware of two major qualities in the Russian character: first, their gaiety and amiability, which was so much like their own, and second, their extreme proneness to debauch, gambling, and a generally disordered life. Saint-Simon was, perhaps, the first to describe these qualities; Diderot, through his contacts with the students especially, was also aware of it. No doubt the police commis-

---

[126] Cf. for example, Grimm's letter to Catherine II, July 10 (21), 1780, and Diderot's letter to Falconet, April 27, 1772.

[127] For the Franco-English contacts, see C. H. Lockitt, *The Relations of French and English Society* (1763-1793), London, 1920.

sioners of Paris and the instructors of the students were, best of all, acquainted with this peculiarity of the Moscovite temperament. Throughout the century there seems to have been no attempt to understand and to analyze the Russian character beyond appreciating these two qualities.

III

FRENCHMEN IN RUSSIA DURING THE EIGHTEENTH CENTURY

TRAVEL, it is said, is the chief means of acquiring true mutual knowledge and understanding between nations. The aim of this chapter is to determine the nature and extent of such knowledge and understanding acquired by French visitors to Russia during the eighteenth century.

At the beginning of the century there were very few Frenchmen in Russia; their number increased near the middle of the century and reached its peak at the end. Peter the Great was not interested in attracting Frenchmen, especially in the first half of his reign. The foreigners whom Peter invited to Russia came from Germany, Holland, and England.[1] The first group of Frenchmen that came to Russia under Peter the Great was composed of French Protestants. They were given refuge after the revocation of the Edict of Nantes. Some of them entered the Russian army, others became merchants.[2] Besides these, there was the Genevan Le Fort, friend and adviser of the Tsar, and the Frenchman Villebois, whom Peter himself brought to Russia and who remained in the Tsar's service until his death.[3] An architect, Leblond, was also well known. He came to Russia on a contract to build a summer residence for the imperial family (Peterhof) in imitation of Versailles, a task which he duly accomplished.[4]

---

[1] Inna Lubimenko, "Les Etrangers en Russie avant Pierre le Grànd," *Revue des études slaves*, Vol. III, 1923; Vol. IV, 1924.

[2] Charles Weiss, *Histoire des réfugiés protestants de France*, Book VII, ch. iii.

[3] *Sbornik* (*Memoirs of the Imperial Russian Historical Society*), Vol. XXXIV, *passim*. L. Pingaud considers the memoirs ascribed to Villebois to be apocryphal.

[4] L. Pingaud, *Les Français en Russie* . . . pp. 15-16.

Under the pro-German successors of Peter and Catherine I there were practically no Frenchmen of importance in Russia. One can mention, during the reign of Empress Anna Ivanovna, a company of ballet dancers who came under the direction of François Landet,[5] and the Jansenist Jubé de la Cour [6] who tried to accomplish what in the sixteenth century the Jesuit Possevin had failed to do—to reconcile the Greek Orthodox and Roman Catholic churches. Jubé was brought to Russia by the Princess Irina Dolgorukaîa, who embraced Roman Catholicism in Holland and kept Jubé as her private chaplain. For three years Jubé was engaged in spreading propaganda, but in 1735 he was finally ordered to leave the country.[7]

Under the pro-French Empress Elizabeth (1744-1762) more Frenchmen came to Russia. During her reign Russia began to take its first lessons in French culture. French manners, clothes, and language were introduced at court, and the young men of letters became ardent imitators of the French classics. We have already noted the Empress' own sympathies for France and her friendly correspondence with Louis XV.

Between 1741 and 1754 there came to St. Petersburg at the appeal of the Empress a number of French actors, some of whom were associated with the Comédie Française. The most noted among these was Pierre de Belloy (1727-1775), a well-known playwright of the time. He wrote verses to the Empress and seems to have been her favorite actor. It is possible that it was at her suggestion that De Belloy became a dramatist.[8] Besides acting at court De Belloy taught French at the University of Moscow, which was founded in 1755.[9] In spite of the favors he received at court, De Belloy felt lonely and

[5] E. Haumant, *La Culture française en Russie*, p. 78.
[6] Paul Pierling, *La Sorbonne et la Russie*, pp. 57-60.
[7] *Ibid.*, p. 150.
[8] E. Zimmermann, *De Belloy, seine Leben und seine Tragödien*, 1911, p. 9.
[9] *Ibid.*

does not seem to have liked Russia.[10] In his best known play, *Le Siège de Calais*, he expressed this feeling in the following verse:

> Ah! de ses fils absents la France est plus chérie,
> Plus je vis d'étrangers, plus j'aimai ma patrie.[11]

De Belloy left Russia in 1758 to produce his tragedy *Titus*.[12] In his *Pierre-le-Cruel*, it is possible that he borrowed certain traits characteristic of Peter the Great in depicting the ferocious King of Castille; aside from this, neither in subject nor in setting does De Belloy seem ever to have made use of his experiences in Russia.

Other Frenchmen who were in Russia under the Empress Elizabeth and whose names may be mentioned here were the painters Tocqué, Lagrené, and Le Lorrain; the sculptor Gillet; the comedian Morenberg; the doctor Poissonnier, sent by Louis XV to look after the health of the Empress; and the geographer and academician Delisle.[13] There were also a good number of French merchants and adventurers like the famous free-mason Tschudi, known in Russia by the name of "Chevalier de Lussy." Tschudi was in turn private secretary, actor, publisher, and courtier. Losing favor at court he went back to France, where he was promptly arrested and locked up in the Bastille.[14]

All of these Frenchmen came to Russia with the primary motive of making a fortune. A good many of them succeeded, not, however, without endangering their health. Painters like Lagrené, for example, were eminently successful.[15] He and

[10] *Ibid.*, p. 14.

[11] Petitot, *Répertoire du Théâtre François*, 1817, IV, 189-209.

[12] *Ibid.*, and Michaud, *Biographie universelle*, IV, 126-128.

[13] L. Pingaud, *Les Français en Russie* ... p. 20.

[14] *Ibid.*, pp. 19-24; cf. also F. Tastevin, *Histoire de la colonie française de Moscou* ... Paris, 1908, *passim*.

[15] Louis Lagrené (1724-1805), pupil of Vanloo, was asked by Empress Elizabeth to come to Russia to teach painting. He remained in Russia from September, 1756, to April, 1762.

Le Lorrain were directors of the St. Petersburg Academy of
Arts, received very good salaries, and sold a great many of
their pictures. Lagrené mentioned in his letters a sum of 39,700
francs as his net income from his stay in Russia.[16]

Another artist—or rather craftsman—was a Swiss jeweler,
Gérémie Pauzié, who also became very successful. In his
memoirs, partly published in Russian, he described in detail the
splendors of the court, his many friends there, and especially
his great personal affection for the Empress Elizabeth.
Pauzié was in Russia from 1716 to 1764; he died at home in
Switzerland in 1779.[17]

Among the Frenchmen who came to Russia during this
period, attracted more by curiosity than by gain, were a few
travelers, like Mme de Hocqueville,[18] and the semi-official and
official envoys of Louis XV. The most important of these were
the Chevalier d'Eon, La Messelière, and Rulhière.

The unfortunate mission of La Chétardie terminated, as
we saw in the first chapter of this study, in his expulsion from
Russia on June 13, 1744. In the same year Louis XV sent
another agent, the Chevalier de Valcroissant, who was taken
as a spy and was imprisoned for twelve months.

The next secret agent was a British subject, Douglas, who
went first to Russia in the summer of 1745, accompanied by
the Chevalier or Chevalière d'Eon de Beaumont.[19] Their instructions were to observe everything and try to obtain
information as to the attitude of the Empress and the court
towards France. D'Eon's instructions were of a very intimate nature. He was entrusted chiefly with the private
correspondence between Louis XV and Empress Elizabeth

[16] *Russkii arkhiv*, 1891, III, 572-574.
[17] *Russkaia starina*, 1870, I, 41-127.
[18] E. Haumant, *La Culture française en Russie*, p. 72.
[19] One of the most interesting and ambiguous figures of the century. A
brilliant diplomat and wit, one of the best swordsmen of the time, D'Eon spent
forty-nine years of his life as a man, and thirty-four as a woman.

of Russia. Douglas at first aroused suspicion and had to leave Russia for a time. D'Eon remained. He was introduced to the Empress in woman's clothes and became for six months her private reader. When Douglas returned to Russia as a *chargé d'affaires*, D'Eon was known officially as his secretary. His real job, however, was to be an intermediary between Louis XV and the Empress. He made a number of trips between Russia and France, carrying messages from one monarch to the other. Elizabeth grew very fond of D'Eon, and he was repeatedly invited to enter the Russian service but always declined. In ill health and fearing the loss of his sight, D'Eon left Russia permanently in August, 1760.[20]

D'Eon was one of the chief agents in bringing about the Franco-Russian reconciliation and the alliance of 1756. He had remarkable skill and tact in negotiations of a delicate nature. In the collection of documents relating to his negotiations there is a curious note addressed to the Duc de Choiseul which describes the Russian court at the time as completely under French influence:

Si Pierre le Grand civilisa avec autant de rapidité des peuples auxquels on daignait à peine donner un cœur et des organes, s'il leur fit aimer les arts, s'il leur fit comprendre et respecter les vertues factices dont nous nous sommes passionés depuis quinze siècles; si cette nation aujourd'hui a droit de prétendre au premier rang sous le règne de son auguste Impératrice, votre grandeur n'a qu'a vouloir et le Français n'aura plus de rivaux.[21]

According to D'Eon's own testimony he left Russia because of illness.[22] It appears, however, that life there was not

---

[20] Some of the accounts of D'Eon's mission to Russia are: M. E. Boutaric, *Correspondance secrète de Louis XV*, Paris, 1866, I, 81-85. J. B. Telfer, *The Strange Career of the Chevalier d'Eon de Beaumont*, London, 1885, pp. 5-19, 25-26. Frederick Gaillardet, *Mémoires sur la chevalière d'Eon*, chs. ii and iii.

[21] *Pièces relatives aux lettres, mémoires, et négotiations particuliers du chevalier d'Eon*, 1764. Cf. Letter of Treyssac de Vergy to Duc de Choiseul, no date, I, 10.

[22] *Ibid.*, II, 6.

to his liking, and in his memoirs he stressed repeatedly the fact that he would never serve anyone but Louis XV.[23] In D'Eon's published papers there are few general observations upon Russia, and in his later picturesque career there seems to be no trace of his sojourn in Russia.

The next French diplomat at the court of Elizabeth, La Messelière, is of special interest because of his memoirs on Russia.[24] Among the French official envoys of the time, La Messelière was exceptional because of his desire to study and to understand the country and its people. La Messelière went to Russia with the embassy of L'Hôpital in 1757.[25] He was very much liked by the Empress and had many friends at the court.[26]

In the Preface to his memoirs La Messelière stated that his reasons for writing them were, first, to satisfy the general curiosity about Russia, aroused by its extraordinarily rapid progress; secondly, to rectify the errors of previous travelers who were all too severe and unjust in their estimates of the country and its people.

He found the people gay, good-natured, and possessing a certain *élévation d'âme*. They had, he observed, one trait in common with the French: *C'est cette disposition à l'enjouement, qui remplace la philosophie, et vaut mieux qu'elle.*[27] He was enthusiastic about the progress of Russia and was convinced that an able tsar *ferait des Russes un des premiers peuples du monde.*[28] So far as the Russian government was concerned, La Messelière considered it an enlightened monarchy which had nothing in common with the despotism of Asiatic countries. Rousseau, he believed, was unjust to Russia. Had he known more about the Russian government and

---

[23] *Op. cit.*, II, 5; cf. also F. Gaillardet, *Mémoires* . . . p. 73.

[24] M. de la Messelière, *Voyage à Pétersbourg; ou, Nouveaux mémoires sur la Russie*, Paris, 1803.

[25] *Ibid.*, p. 119.   [26] *Ibid.*, p. 243.

[27] *Ibid.*, p. 18.   [28] *Ibid.*

laws, he would never have uttered his severe dicta.[29] But as to religion, he recorded, *C'est une collection de momeries, de signes extérieurs, un culte pour les images, poussé jusqu'à l'idolâtrie.*[30]

La Messelière was especially struck by the magnificence of the receptions at the court and by the fact that French was spoken everywhere.[31] He greatly admired Empress Elizabeth, her kindness, generosity, and *grandeur d'âme.*[32] He repeatedly deplored in his memoirs the hostility of the French government to Russia and urged a friendly rapprochement.[33] Choiseul, however, took no heed. La Messelière was recalled, and his diplomatic career seems then to have ended. He lived in Poitiers, where he remained, to the end, an effective agent of information and propaganda in behalf of Russia.[34]

The last and most important Frenchman at the court of Empress Elizabeth was Claude Carloman de Rulhière (1735-1791). A graceful poet and wit well known in Parisian society, a member of the French Academy, and an eminent historian, Rulhière spent a short time in Russia as secretary to Baron de Breteuil, which is of special interest to the student of eighteenth-century Franco-Russian relations. Unfortunately, most of his letters and papers perished during the Revolution, and all that is known about his stay in Russia is deduced from his own books and from a few letters to his friends, notably J. J. Rousseau. One can conjecture from these that Rulhière spent most of his time in St. Petersburg at the court, that he visited Moscow, and that he was continually interested in observing and studying the country and the people. His account of Catherine's accession to the throne, under the title of *Anecdotes sur la révolution de Russie en l'année 1762,* began to circulate in Paris early in

[29] M. de la Messelière, *Voyage à Pétersbourg*...p. 63.
[30] *Ibid.,* p. 19.   [31] *Ibid.,* p. 123.   [32] *Ibid.,* pp. 226-230.
[33] *Ibid.,* p. 211.   [34] *Ibid.,* p. 330.

1763. The first reading took place at De Choiseul's, the second at Mme du Deffand's, and the third at Mme Geoffrin's. Voltaire, Diderot, and other protégés of the Empress became alarmed and started a regular campaign to protect Catherine's reputation.[35] Owing largely to the efforts of Mme Geoffrin, the publication of this book was postponed until 1797. In a Preface dated August 25, 1773, Rulhière dedicated it to the Countess d'Egmont: *Je crois avoir suffisamment justifié*, he wrote, *à vos yeux un ouvrage qui n'a été conçu que sous vos auspices.*[36] This book, as well as other writings of Rulhière, was unfavorable to Russia. He was hostile to the Empress and pessimistic as to the future of the Russian Empire. Russia, he said in the Introduction, reminded him of Rome in the period of decline.[37] In the same Preface he intimated that Catherine was directly responsible for the death of her husband, but gave at the same time a flattering picture of her talents and charms.[38] The general tone of the book is gay and frivolous. This, says the author, also in the Preface, is unavoidable because:

...la frivolité des intrigues, [which produced the coup d'état] la license des mœurs russes, et les puérilités qui ont perdu le malheureux empereur Pierre III, ne pouvaient être racontées d'un style sérieux et soutenu.[39]

Concerning the character of the Russian people, Rulhière stressed their lack of independence, their slavish worship of the tsars and priests, and their common trait of resignation. In this he followed, almost *verbatim*, the assertions of early travelers to Russia, particularly Herberstein: *Nation d'esclaves et qui ne paraît pas seulement avoir été assujettie, mais qui semble née pour l'esclavage.*[40] *La volonté du Czar*, he said

[35] Marie d'Armaillé, *La Comtesse d'Egmont*, Paris, 1890, pp. 114-130.
[36] C. C. Rulhière, *Œuvres*, 1819, Vol. IV, Preface.
[37] *Ibid.*   [58] *Ibid.*   [39] *Ibid.*
[40] C. C. Rulhière, *Œuvres posthumes*, Paris, 1819, p. 79.

elsewhere, *fut leur unique loi, et son intérêt leur unique morale.*[41]

In the three extant letters from Rulhière to Rousseau between 1762 and 1764, the former's views upon Russia show the strong influence of the latter.[42] In a letter from Moscow, dated February 20, 1763, Rulhière praised Rousseau's attitude toward Russia as expressed in the *Contrat social* and found himself in complete agreement with Rousseau's views:

Avant de vous avoir lu, toutes mes pensées sur les mœurs de ce peuple étaient confuses; depuis que je vous ai lu l'ordre s'y est mis et je vois toutes mes observations dériver du principe que vous avez établi.[43]

He also agreed with Rousseau's ideas concerning the essentially imitative nature of the Russian people:

Le caractère distinctif de ce peuple est précisément le génie, ou plus communément de talent de l'imitation . . . [and] . . . tous les Russes possèdent chacun dans sa médiocrité ce que leur Czar [Peter the Great] possédait en grand; vrais singes à qui ce don national eût sans doute fait faire de rapides progrès dans les arts, si la vanité, défaut non moins national, n'en balançait les effets.[44]

In the same letter, however, Rulhière voices a disagreement with Rousseau concerning the inevitability of a revolution in Russia.[45] In his last letter of July 12, 1764, Rulhière pointed out the contradictions in Montesquieu's theory of climates and advanced instead the Rousseauesque idea: *Les hommes se corrompent par leur perfectibilité, un peuple ancien ne peut être ni libre ni bon.*[46] Applying this idea to Russia he observed:

Avant que l'Europe les connût [i.e., the Russians] ils étaient bien un peuple barbare, mais leur vices n'étaient point ceux de la corruption. La mollesse y régnait dans la crasse, et le luxe dans la grossièreté. L'époque de cette corruption date sans doute de la grande

[41] *Ibid.,* p. 77. [42] *Ibid.,* pp. 89-98.

[43] M. G. Streckeisen-Moultou, *J. J. Rousseau, ses amis et ses ennemis,* Paris, 1864, I, 304-314.

[44] *Ibid.,* pp. 307-308. [45] *Ibid.* [46] *Ibid.,* pp. 311-314.

communication qu'ils avaient eue avec l'empire grec, dans le temps que leur capitale était à Kiev.[47]

In the subsequent historical work of Rulhière, *L'Histoire de l'anarchie de Pologne et du démembrement de cette république*, the author maintained in general the same views upon Russia as those indicated above. As a protégé of Choiseul's, he was a champion of Choiseul's foreign policy and was consistently hostile to Russia and friendly to Poland.[48]

Beginning with the accession of Catherine II in 1762 and continuing until the end of the Napoleonic wars in 1814, France exercised her greatest cultural influence upon Russia.[49] The Russian rulers, Catherine II, Paul I, and Alexander I, who themselves were finished products of eighteenth-century French culture, constantly encouraged this intellectual and cultural conquest of Russia. Every social group of French society had, during this period, its innumerable representatives in Russia. Aristocrats, philosophers, artists, merchants, cooks, and lackeys—all came in large numbers, like Jews to the Promised Land; some, as Haumant says, attracted by gain, *pour traire la vache;* others to seek refuge for themselves and to find assistance for the lost cause of the fallen régime; and still others out of sheer curiosity to see the splendors of the court and its chief attraction, *Catherine-le-Grand.* The knowledge of Russia gained by these Frenchmen naturally varied considerably with the length of their sojourn, their relations with the court, and their reasons for going there. A division into groups of all the Frenchmen who came to Russia in

[47] M. G. Streckeisen-Moulton, *J. J. Rousseau, ses amis et ses ennemis*, Paris, 1864, I, pp. 311-314.

[48] Rulhière wrote this history of the Polish government at the request of the Duc de Choiseul. He made a trip to Poland and worked on this book for almost twenty-two years, leaving it unfinished at his death. It was published in 1807. Cf. Godefroy, *XVIIIe siècle*, Paris, 1879, volume on the *Prosateurs*, pp. 164-167.

[49] For a detailed examination of these influences see the brilliant and penetrating study of E. Haumant, *La Culture française en Russie*, 1913, Books II and III.

the second half of the century, such as men of letters, professional men, diplomats, travelers, may, by taking into account these varying circumstances, help to determine the
general knowledge and impressions of Russia which these representatives of eighteenth-century French society acquired.

One of the earliest representativs of the group of philosophers and men of letters was Bernardin de Saint-Pierre,
who came to Russia as an adventuring idealist. He set out
in 1762, at the age of twenty-five, to seek a fortune, or, in
his own words, to look for a place in the world, *situé sous un
beau ciel, où l'on trouvat à la fois de l'honneur, des richesses,
et de la société.*[50] More specifically, Bernardin de Saint-Pierre
wanted to present to the Empress a project for the foundation
of a Utopian colony on the shores of the Aral Sea, an establishment which was to be of great benefit to Russia as well
as to mankind.[51] Saint-Pierre evidently supposed that Russia,
a new and primitive country, would be most suitable for the
establishment of an ideal community such as his colony was
to be. In this respect he was completely disappointed. The
all-powerful favorite of Catherine II, Orlov, received the
young adventurer with cordiality and promised all possible
assistance; his project, however, was relegated to the waste
basket. When Saint-Pierre was finally presented to the Empress, he became so nervous and confused that he completely

[50] B. de Saint-Pierre, *Œuvres*, Paris, 1818, II, 332. On Saint-Pierre's sojourn
in Russia see: Ferand Maury, *Etude sur la vie et les œuvres de Bernardin de
Saint-Pierre*, Paris, 1892, pp. 16-36. A. Barine, *Bernardin de Saint-Pierre*, Paris,
1891, pp. 19-25. L. Aimé-Martin, "Essai sur la vie et les œuvres de Bernardin de
Saint-Pierre," *Œuvres de Bernardin de Saint-Pierre*, éd., Méguignon-Marvis, Paris,
1818, I, 52-93.

[51] Cf. Saint-Pierre's "Projet d'une compagnie pour la découverte d'un passage
aux Indes par la Russie, présenté à Sa Majesté l'Impératrice Catherine II," *Œuvres*,
1818, II, 329-558. This colony was to be an independent republic, own land,
elect judges, and administer all its internal affairs. It was to be a frontier
society. Its benefit to Russia was for the most part to be derived from commerce with India; its benefit to mankind from the fact that: "Elle adoucirait
les mœurs d'un grand nombre d'hommes, qui ne connaissent ni les fruits de
l'agriculture, ni les douceurs du commerce"; *Projet*, p. 361.

forgot to present his plan to her. Failing to establish his Utopia, Saint-Pierre consoled himself by becoming a social lion in St. Petersburg.[52] There he was patronized by General Du Bosquet, who acquired him as a companion on a trip to Finland. By order of the Empress, Saint-Pierre received a commission as captain in the Guards, with a salary of 18,000 francs (a sum larger, it appears, than any he had received up to that time or was to receive for some time to come). Aside from his visit to Finland (where he was to observe the country with regard to military operations), his short stay in Moscow, and his trip to and from St. Petersburg, there is no evidence of his having traveled to any extent in the interior of Russia. He appears to have made friends among powerful and influential people, such as Du Bosquet, Villebois, the Dolgorukïïs, and the Vorontsovs.[53] Had he chosen, he might have had a brilliant career in St. Petersburg society and at the court. He remained discontented, however, and persistently rejected all the offers of his friends. Du Bosquet's proposal that Saint-Pierre should marry his niece, Mlle de la Tour, seems in fact to have hastened the visionary's departure from Russia.[54] In June, 1764, he was already in Poland resolved to embrace the cause of the Poles against the Russians. In a characteristic letter to his friend Duval he thus expressed his state of mind on leaving Russia:

Dans l'agitation de mon esprit, regrettant ce que je quittais, ne désirant plus ce que je cherchais, désespérant de tout, la vie, mon ami, me parut un poids insupportable... Je suis mécontent du présent, j'espère peu de l'avenir, et ce qu'il y a de pis, je regrette le passé.[55]

---

[52] Cf. F. Maury, *Etude sur la vie ... de Bernardin de Saint-Pierre*, pp. 16-36.
[53] *Ibid.*
[54] Saint-Pierre resigned from the army chiefly, it appears, because he was offended at being offered a position as copyist, F. Maury, *op. cit.*, p. 37. Another reason for his leaving Russia was the disfavor his patrons drew upon themselves at court. These were Münich and Villebois, cf. L. Aimé-Martin, *Essai ... I, 86.
[55] First letter to Duval, 1764; cf. F. Maury, *Etude ... pp. 33-34.

Bernardin de Saint-Pierre was disappointed in Russia. His project of a Utopian colony failed, and Russia, he discovered, was barbaric, but not primitive enough: Russia's sophisticated society had already acquired all the vices of older European states. He also felt, no doubt, that the two years he spent in Moscow had been wasted.

There is no evidence that Bernardin de Saint-Pierre had at any time made an effort to learn the Russian language. Nor does he seem ever to have become interested in studying and observing the life around him. As for his views upon Russia, we have his own *Observations sur la Russie* (written after he left the country).[56] In this essay Saint-Pierre paints a very black picture of the Russian people:

Les Russes sont inconstants, jaloux, fourbes, grossiers, ne respectant que ce qu'ils craignent. Il ne faut jamais se familiariser avec eux; car ils vous méprisent bientôt.... Ils sont sujets à des vapeurs mélancholiques qui font souvent sur les étrangers des effets terribles... D'autres vices rendent la société désagréable.[57]

Among those "other vices" he mentions the absence of good manners and civility, and a corresponding prominence of hatred and scorn for foreigners, who, he says, although asked to Russian houses, were often insulted there by the servants and family jesters. Nevertheless, he thought that the Russians had a few virtues, but these were *sauvages et farouches*. Chief among them was hospitality.[58] But these very virtues he found to be *odieuses et leurs bienfaits insupportables, même aux plus malheureux*. He found, however, a few exceptions to this general rule:

Il faut cependent excepter ceux que l'éducation, un naturel heureux, ou l'adversité a rendu bons; car les voyages ne font qu'ajouter à leur corruption. Les Woronzof, par exemple, les Dolgorouki, si chers aux

---

[56] Saint-Pierre, *Œuvres*, 1818, II, 271-361.
[57] *Ibid.*, pp. 300-301.
[58] Saint-Pierre, *Œuvres*, 1818, II, pp. 300-301.

Français et aux infortunés, et quelques autres qui vivent dans la retraite sont des modèles de vertu.[59]

The qualities of the Russian character which Saint-Pierre seems to have stressed most were inconstancy, coarseness, and servility. The majority of the people were naturally bad and corrupt, only a few exceptions like Dolgorukiï and Vorontsov being inherently "good" and virtuous. Saint-Pierre believed, like other Frenchmen who visited Russia during the century, that education and travel were of no help in improving the Russian character, but on the contrary tended only to make it more corrupt.

Saint-Pierre's biographer, Maury, remarks that this picture of the Russian people,

Me semble faire connaître le peintre bien mieux que le peuple russe. En jugeant les autres, il se juge surtout lui-même, et ce ne sont pas ses meilleurs côtés qu'il découvre.[60]

In these observations, Maury thinks, Saint-Pierre betrays his own melancholy disposition, his lack of cordiality toward colleagues, and his constant pride—all of which resulted, no doubt, in many unpleasantnesses in his contacts with Russians.

So far as the Russian government was concerned, Saint-Pierre showed very little interest in it. Influenced, no doubt, by Voltaire and the Encyclopedists, Saint-Pierre exaggerated the importance of Peter the Great in the process of civilizing Russia.[61] His account of Russian history from Peter to Catherine is anecdotal and superficial. He found that the court revolutions were mostly due to the amorous passions of the sovereigns: *Souvent l'amour est cause de quelque disgrâce éclatante, ou de quelque révolution extraordinaire.*[62] His admiration for the Empress was great. Catherine, he explained,

[59] Saint-Pierre, *Œuvres*, 1818, II, p. 302.   [60] F. Maury, *Etude* . . . p. 29.
[61] Saint-Pierre, *Œuvres*, II, 305, and 312.   [62] *Ibid.*, p. 315.

...a mis dans son gouvernement une modération inconnu avant elle. ...Elle a introduit le goût des spectacles, de la littérature, et des arts, pour adoucir ces esprits farouches...[63] [and he concluded] aucun souverain n'a entrepris un si grand nombre de projets utiles à la Russie. La postérité décidéra de sa gloire; mais celle de Sémiramis, si célèbre en Orient, ne fut ni plus pure, ni plus méritée.[64]

Regarding the Greek-Orthodox religion, Saint-Pierre had practically nothing to say. His was the usual skeptical eighteenth-century attitude. He found the Russians superstitious and over-devout. He was unaware of any deeper meaning in their religious ceremonies and failed to notice the picturesque and sensuous aspects.[65]

The state of culture in Russia was, according to Saint-Pierre, very low:

Les Russes n'ont aucun goût pour les arts agréables: lorsqu'on leur donne quelques-uns de nos modèles à imiter, ils en copient jusqu'aux imperfections... Ils préfèrent une image gothique et enfermée aux tableaux de Rubens et du Titien.[66]

But, at the same time, the absence of taste and creative instinct was beneficial to Russia because: *C'est un grand malheur à un peuple subjugué de cultiver les arts.*[67]

If Saint-Pierre did not like the Russian people and their institutions, what was his impression of inanimate nature? The cities, it appears, produced little impression upon him, though he said of Moscow that...*rien n'est si magnifique que l'aspect de cette ville où s'élèvent près de douze cents clochers, dont quelques-uns sont dorés.*[68] He seems to have liked most the barren and rocky landscape of Finland, where he spent probably the four happiest months of his stay in the East: [69] *Ce pays est si désert, que dans un voyage de quatre*

[63] *Ibid.*, p. 326.
[65] Saint-Pierre, *Œuvres*, II, 295-296.
[67] *Ibid.*   [68] *Ibid.*, p. 302.
[64] *Ibid.*, pp. 327-328.
[66] *Ibid.*, pp. 294-295.
[69] F. Maury, *Etude*...p. 31.

cents lieues, je n'y ai pas vu vingt villages.[70] The descriptions of the northern landscapes, however, are few in Saint-Pierre's works. His peculiar genius seems to have found its best expression in the descriptions of the luxurious tropics. Nevertheless, there are in his works echoes and reminiscences of the Russian landscape, particularly that of Finland.[71]

Aside from Saint-Pierre's short *Observations sur la Russie,* his *Plan,* a few descriptive passages, a Russian character in his drama *Empsail et Zoraïde,* there seem to be no traces of Russia in his published works.

Much has been written concerning Diderot's trip to Russia and his relations with Catherine II. Tourneux's *Diderot et Catherine II* is still the most comprehensive study of the subject. Since its publication in 1879 some new material has come to light, notably Ledieu's edition of the full text of Diderot's *Observations sur l'instructions de Sa Majesté Impériale.*

Early in 1763 Diderot conceived the idea of selling his library. Through Grimm it was offered to Catherine II for 15,000 francs. The library was bought, left in Diderot's possession, and, as the librarian, he received a pension of 1,000 francs. Two years later Diderot received the sum of 50,000 francs as his pension for fifty years in advance.[72] The purchase of the library excited the admiration of all the Encyclopedists and the boundless gratitude of Diderot himself. His enthusiastic eulogies of Catherine, however, were distasteful, in fact scandalizing to some of his countrymen.[73] Diderot,

[70] Saint-Pierre, *Œuvres,* II, 277.

[71] Saint-Pierre, *Œuvres,* "Harmonie de la nature," IX, 103-106; cf. also a long passage descriptive of Russian landscape cited by Maury from Saint-Pierre's posthumous work, F. Maury, *Etude . . .* p. 237.

[72] Diderot, éd. Assézat, XIX, 472; and Mme de Vandeul, *Œuvres choisies de Diderot,* Garnier, I, Introduction.

[73] Cf. Letter of Mme de Choiseul to Mme du Deffand, *Correspondance inédite de Mme du Deffand,* 1859, I, 92; and Turgot's letter to Condorcet, *Œuvres de Turgot,* 1844, II, 197.

nevertheless, ignored the criticism. *Heureux si nous savons faire notre devoir de panégyriste,* he wrote in 1766 to Falconet, *comme elle* [i.e., Catherine II] *le sien de souveraine.*[74] He sought constantly for an occasion to show his gratitude to Catherine.[75] He wrote that he was forced to accept Catherine's generosity because he was the father of a family, but he was afraid at the same time that his praises of Catherine might seem partial and extreme in the eyes of his countrymen.[76] Many, he observed, were jealous of him—particularly Rousseau, the *perfide.*

Les bienfaits de la grande Impératrice font retentir avec transports mon nom, son éloge et le mien. Le bruit en vient aux oreilles du perfide, et il s'en mord les lèvres de rage.[77]

Occasionally, as in a letter to General Betskiï, he burst forth into verse:

> Vous [i.e., Catherine II] qui de la Divinité
> Nous montrez sur le trône une image fidèle...

which do him more honor as a man than as a poet. He continued in the same letter:

Je jure qu'avant de mourrir j'aurai élevé à sa gloire une pyramide qui touchera le ciel, et où dans les siècles à venir les souverains verront, par ce que le sentiment seul de la reconnaissance aura entrepris et exécuté, ce qu'ils auraient obtenu du génie si leurs bienfaits l'avaient cherché.[78]

As early as 1766 Diderot was eager to go to Russia to see the Empress and to continue his edition of the Encyclopedia there.[79] He was reluctant, however, to leave his family. Early in 1773 he wrote to Falconet that he felt too old to do it,

[74] Diderot to Falconet, *Revue moderne,* XXXIX, 308.
[75] *Ibid.,* XXXIX, 318 and 338.
[76] *Ibid.,* XXXIX, 308 and 313.
[77] *Ibid.,* XL, 51.
[78] Diderot to Betskiï, December 29, 1767, *Œuvres de Diderot,* éd. Assézat, XIX, 494-495.
[79] Diderot to Falconet, *Revue moderne,* XXXIX, 305.

yet still wanted to go. He tried to convince himself that earth is as light in St. Petersburg as in Paris, and that worms have as good an appetite there, *et qu'il est assez indifférent en quel endroit de la terre que nous les engraissons.*[80]

Diderot's motive for going to Russia was, it seems, not solely that of gratitude; he was also curious and eager to talk to the Empress-philosopher, whose liberality, tolerance, and skepticism all the Encyclopedists were so wont to admire. As to seeing Russia, he seems to have had no such desire; there is, at least, no indication of it in his correspondence preceding the trip.

Information concerning Diderot's stay in Russia is scant and fragmentary. It comes partly from his letters to his family and friends, partly from Grimm. Nevertheless, the data are sufficient for one to trace a general outline of his activities during his five-month visit.

Diderot left for Russia with his Russian friend, Naryshkin, on May 10, 1773.[81] From the letter to his wife written shortly after his arrival in St. Petersburg we learn about his first disappointments.[82] In poor health and tired after a long journey, he tells with bitterness of his friend Falconet's refusal to put him up.[83] He was obliged to ask his Russian acquaintances, the Naryshkins, for a place to stay. He was well-received there and, it seems, stayed in their house until his departure from Russia. His daughter, Mme de Vandeuil, writes:

Tout ce qu'il m'a dit des bontés de cette famille pour lui, des soins, des procédés obligeants, des marques d'amitié et d'estime qu'il en a

---

[80] Diderot to Falconet, *Revue moderne*, XXXIX, 391, and XL, 325.

[81] Mme de Vandeuil, *Œuvres choisies de Diderot*, I, Introduction.

[82] Diderot to his wife, Saint-Denis's day, 1773; André Babelon, *Lettres inédites de Diderot*, 1931, II, 240-245.

[83] *Ibid.* The vacant room in Falconet's house, which Diderot was to have, was occupied by the sculptor's son who arrived just then, unexpected by his family. Diderot was not received there, as he had imagined, with open arms. This episode furthered the already strained relations between the two friends.

reçues, ont rendu tous ceux qui portent ce nom l'objet de ma vénération et de la plus tendre reconnaissance.[84]

Poor health, bad climate, and the quarrel with Falconet had no doubt contributed to his first unfavorable impression of Russia. *J'aurai fait*, he wrote to Mlle de Volland, *le plus beau voyage possible quand je serai de retour.*[85] Soon, however, he was presented to the Empress, and his whole outlook changed at once. The more he saw of her, the more enthusiastic he became, forgetting the climate, his family, Falconet, and, incidentally, the very fact that he was in Russia.

Elle [i.e., Catherine II] changera la face de cette contrée, [he writes in October, 1773] la nation russe deviendra une des plus honnêtes, une des plus sages, et une des plus redoutables contrées de l'Europe, du monde![86]

He grows lyrical about Catherine's personal charm, her grace and intelligence. Toward the end of his visit he does not show the least regret for having come to Russia. In fact he describes his stay as the most satisfying period of his life.[87] He writes:

Ce voyage que vous avez tous blâmé,—je ne voudrais pas pour la moitié de ma fortune ne l'avoir pas fait. Il me reste la satisfaction d'avoir accompli un devoir, et une puissante protection dans toutes les circonstances de ma vie! J'oserais presque vous dire que j'ai une souveraine pour ami.[88]

He saw the Empress every day and upon each occasion talked to her for two or three hours. He describes these tête-à-têtes as follows:

J'entre, on me fait asseoir, et je cause avec la même liberté que vous m'accordez; et la voyant, je suis forcé de m'avouer à moi-même que

[84] Mme de Vandeuil, *Œuvres choisies de Diderot*, I, Introduction, p. 28.

[85] Diderot to Mlle Volland, December 29, 1773; A. Babelon, *Lettres à Sophie Volland*, 1930, III, 248.

[86] Diderot to Mme de Vandeuil, October 23, 1773; A. Babelon, *Lettres inédites de Diderot*, II, 248.

[87] Diderot to Mlle Volland, April 9, 1774; A. Babelon, *Lettres à Sophie Volland*, III, 254.

[88] *Ibid.*, March 30, 1774; III, 251.

j'avais l'âme d'un esclave dans le pays qu'on appelle des hommes libres, et que je me suis trouvé l'âme d'un homme libre dans le pays qu'on appelle des esclaves. Oh! mes amis, quelle souveraine! quelle extraordinaire femme! [89]

At the same time he is somewhat afraid of a possible misinterpretation by his countrymen of his enthusiasm.

On n'accusera pas mon éloge de vénalité, car je mis les bornes les plus étroites à sa munificence; il faudra bien que vous disiez tous que c'est l'âme de Brutus sous la figure de Cléopâtre! [90]

The behavior of Diderot during his conversations with the Empress must have been quite out of the ordinary. Enthusiastic, heedless, with no sense of reserve or knowledge of court etiquette, he must have produced a sensation.

L'Impératrice en est vraiment enchantée; voilà l'essentiel [writes Grimm], au reste, il lui prend la main, il lui saisit le bras, il tape sur la table, tout comme s'il était au milieu de la Synagogue de la rue Royale [i.e., at Baron d'Holbach's]. [91]

Catherine herself wrote to Mme Geoffrin that in order to prevent Diderot's slapping her on the shoulder in the ardor of his conversation, she had to have a small table put between them. [92] There were innumerable stories circulating in Paris of Diderot's eccentricities at the court of Catherine II; most of them, however, were probably exaggerated.

On débite sur sa conduite près de la Czarine des choses épouvantables [writes Galiani to Thomas], on dit qu'il a osé lui jeter sa perruque au nez, lui pincer le genou, etc.... [93]

Mme de Vandeuil, too, corroborates these stories of her father's extravagances.

[89] Diderot to Mlle Volland, June 15, 1774; A. Babelon, *Lettres à Sophie Volland*, III, 256.   [90] *Ibid.*
[91] M. Tourneux, *Diderot et Catherine*, p. 75. Cf. also Grimm's letter to Mme Necker, February 10, 1774, E. Caro, *La Fin du dix-huitième siècle*, 1880, I, 326.
[92] Diderot, *Œuvres complètes*, Assézat, XX, Appendix, p. 138.
[93] Galiani to Thomas, December 24, 1773, Eugène Asse, *Lettres de l'abbé Galiani à Mme d'Epinay, Voltaire, etc.*, 1881, I, 401.

Il était si peu fait pour vivre à une cour [she wrote], qu'il a dû y faire un grand nombre de gaucheries.[94]

In spite of all these *gaucheries*, Diderot and Catherine remained on good terms to the end. Their correspondence, which started shortly before Diderot's departure from Russia and lasted for seven years, is ample evidence of the Empress' friendship and good will.

Diderot left Russia, it appears probable, because his poor health was aggravated by the Russian climate.[95] According to his daughter it was this circumstance which eventually led to his death.[96] He left St. Petersburg March 5, 1774, and went to The Hague, where he resided for several months at the home of Prince Golitsyn, returning to Paris early in October, 1774.[97]

Outside the narrow circle of the court Diderot saw practically nothing of Russia.[98] So completely was he under the spell of the Empress' charms that he had apparently no desire to observe closely the country he visited. He himself was aware of this fact and acknowledged it in a letter to Mme Necker:

Peut-être aimeriez-vous mieux que je vous entretinsse de la Russie; mais je ne l'ai pas vue. J'ai manqué l'occasion d'aller à Moscou, et je m'en repens un peu. Pétersbourg n'est que la cour, un amas confus de palais et de chaumières, des grand-seigneurs entourés de mougicks et de pourvoyeurs. Je confesserai tout bas que nos philosophes qui paraissent avoir le mieux connu le despotisme ne l'ont vu que par le goulet d'une bouteille. Quelle différence du tigre peint par Oudry, ou du tigre dans sa forêt! Je n'ai guère vu que la souveraine...[99]

[94] Mme de Vandeuil, *Œuvres choisies de Diderot,* Introduction, p. 30.

[95] Diderot to his wife, April 9, 1774, Diderot, *Œuvres,* XX, 51-56.

[96] Mme de Vandeuil, *Œuvres choisies de Diderot,* p. 30.

[97] *Ibid.,* p. 31.

[98] Diderot to Gessner, March 14, 1774, *Revue de l'histoire littéraire de France,* XV, 574.

[99] Diderot to Mme Necker, September 6, 1774, E. Caro, *La Fin du dix-huitième siècle,* I, 331-332.

Besides, he remarks in the same letter, he is disgusted in general with the study of manners; it takes too much time and is always inconclusive.[100]

From a five-month stay in St. Petersburg, Diderot's general ideas on Russia seem to have been confined to a few observations on the winter climate,[101] and some vague and incomprehensible remarks such as this: *C'est ici le pays des grand phénomènes tout au physique qu'au moral.*[102]

On leaving Russia Diderot's mind was full of vast projects for the glorification of Catherine II and Russia. *Je ne mourrai pas sans avoir élevé un obélisque sur lequel on lira: "A l'honneur des Russes et de leur souveraine" et à la bonté de qui il appartiendra.*[103] Among these works was to be a Russian edition of the Encyclopedia and various educational, legislative, and ethnographical treatises. Diderot obtained part of the material necessary for these writings from Catherine herself and part from Russian officials.[104] All of these works, like so many others projected by Diderot, were destined to remain unfinished. Most of them were collected and edited by Tourneux in 1899.

No better picture of Diderot's ignorance of Russian institutions and life may be obtained than from an examination of these theoretical works written after his return from Russia. They contain the essence of the Encyclopedic political theory and were written apparently with the view of actually applying them to Russia.

The *Plan d'une université pour le gouvernement de Russie*

[100] E. Caro, *op. cit.*

[101] Cf. his letters to Doctor Clerc and General Betskiĭ, April 8 and June 15, 1774, E. Caro, *op. cit.*, I, 328.

[102] *Ibid.*, I, 327.

[103] M. Tourneux, *Diderot et Catherine*, 1899, p. 440.

[104] Cf., for example, Diderot's letters to Count Münich (1774), *Russkiĭ arkhiv*, 1878, III, 409; also copies of Diderot's questions and Catherine's answers, *ibid.*, 1880, III, pp. 1 ff.

was drawn up between 1775 and 1776. It was preceded by a short *Essai sur les études en Russie*.[105] The *Plan* develops a complete system of utilitarian education. The chief principle upheld in it is that of professional education as opposed to the old scholastic system. The *Essai* examines three kinds of schools in Germany and, in general, advocates Protestant schools as the best model for Russia. Both works include many brilliant ideas (the method of studying languages, for example) as well as a good many absurdities (such as the advice to get rid of the clergy by refusing to pay their salaries and thus throwing them *dans l'indigence*). Both are characterized by hatred of the clergy and by worship of the state of the enlightened monarchy type. The *Plan* was never put into practice and lay buried in Catherine's library until the end of the nineteenth century.[106]

Diderot's *Observations sur les instructions de sa Majesté Impériale pour la confection des lois* is only now available in complete form.[107] These are comments on Catherine's *Nakaz*, i.e., her instructions given to the deputies for the drawing up of a code of law. Here Diderot is definitely critical of Catherine's ideas, advocating constitutional monarchy and opposing everything suggesting despotism. A good sovereign, he repeats, is not *le maître de la raison*, but *l'économe et l'intendant*.[108] Two things, he argues, should be at the basis of every code of law: property and liberty. He also makes several specific suggestions, such as moving the capital nearer to the center of the Empire and establishing a colony of Swiss

---

[105] Diderot, *Œuvres*, III, 409-413 and 415-529.

[106] For a fuller analysis of the *Plan* see E. Caro, *La Fin du dix-huitième siècle*, I, 246-275.

[107] The *Observations* were already known to Tourneux, but the full text was published for the first time by P. Ledieu in *Revue d'histoire économique et sociale*, under the title of "Une Œuvre inédite de Diderot," Paris, 1920, Nos. 3-4, pp. 263-412.

[108] P. Ledieu, *Revue d'histoire* ... articles 625 and 630, pp. 406 and 408.

or Germans in order to create in Russia a *tiers état*. Finally, he speaks emphatically against the sending of Russian noblemen to western Europe for instruction because:

Ceux des Russes qui ont voyagé ont apporté à leur patrie la folie des nations qu'ils ont parcouru, rien de leur sagesse, tous leurs vices, aucune de leurs vertus, et je crois que les jeunes seigneurs corrompent plus de jeunes gens qu'ils n'en instruisent.[109]

Most of these suggestions were hardly applicable, at least in the Russia of 1774. What is more, Diderot seems to have misunderstood Catherine's intentions; that is, he believed in the earnest desire of the Empress to submit the question of sovereignty to the deputies for whom she wrote the *Nakaz*, which was far from what she wanted to do. Caro says of this:

Naïf philosophe qui pense avoir conquis un esprit tel que celui de Catherine, avec ses tirades sur la tolérence, sur l'égalité des hommes, les préjugés monarchiques de la vieille Europe, le progrès des lumières, la nécessité d'éclairer les peuples pour les rendre heureux! Et cela dans la Russie de 1774![110]

It is natural that when the Empress received Diderot's *Observations*, she saw in them only *un vrai babil dans lequel on ne trouve ni connaissance des choses, ni prudence, ni clairvoyance*.[111] Each belonged to a different world of thought, and each fundamentally misunderstood the other.[112]

The other theoretical writings of Diderot on police, on foreign policy, and on pedagogical theory [113] show, like the *Plan* and *Observations*, the same basic principle: *il faut que partout un peuple soit instruit, libre, et vertueux*—the idea

---

[109] P. Ledieu, *Revue d'histoire* . . . article 59, p. 304.

[110] E. Caro, *La Fin du dix-huitième siècle*, I, 330.

[111] M. Tourneux, *Diderot et Catherine*, p. 520.

[112] For a fuller analysis of Diderot's *Observations*, see a pamphlet by A. Florovskiï, *Nakazy Diderot* . . . published by the Russian Scientific Institute of Belgrade, 1929 (in Russian).

[113] M. Tourneux, *Diderot et Catherine*, pp. 89-142, 258, 327 ff., 568.

with which Diderot went to Russia and with which he returned home.

But even if Diderot did not bring back from Russia many sound ideas and impressions of the country, he became more than before a most enthusiastic friend and admirer of the Russian people.[114] He never tired of praising the virtues of all his numerous Russian friends (Princess Dashkova, the Naryshkins, the Golitsyns, Betskiï, and others). Aside from admiring their sociability and their receptivity to French culture, he seemed to like them temperamentally.[115] Among the eighteenth-century philosophers he was, perhaps, the one who came nearest to understanding the Russian mind.

It is impossible to exclude from this group of eminent representatives of eighteenth-century literary and philosophical France Melchior Grimm, a German by birth, a Frenchman by education and habit of mind, and a Russian through circumstance and predilection—in short, as typical a cosmopolitan as the century produced.[116] His place in French literature depends almost entirely upon his *Correspondance littéraire*. It was Sainte-Beuve who first lifted Grimm from an undeserved obscurity, due in part, perhaps, to the false and spiteful impression of him given by Rousseau in his *Confessions*. Grimm's reputation has gained considerably since then,

[114] *Et puis j'avoue,* he writes in "Ma rêverie," *que je serais transporté de joie de voir ma nation unie avec la Russie, beaucoup de Russes à Paris, et beaucoup de Français à Pétersbourg. Aucune nation en Europe qui se francise plus rapidement que la Russie, et pour la langue, et pour les usages.*—M. Tourneux, *op. cit.,* p. 258.

[115] See especially his laudatory sketch of the Princess Dashkova (1770) Diderot, *Œuvres,* XVII, 487.

[116] At one period of his life Grimm was, at the same time, minister plenipotentiary of the Duke of Saxe-Gotha, Russian councilor of state, and Empress Catherine's private agent, editor of the *Correspondance littéraire,* and an habitué of all the Parisian salons. The best general account of Grimm's life is by Edmond Scherer, Paris, 1887; see also "Etudes sur Grimm par Sainte-Beuve et Paulin Limayrac" in the *Gazette littéraire de Grimm* (1753-1790), Paris, 1854; for an account of Grimm's relations with Catherine II, see *Russkaïa starina* 1893, LXXVII and LXXVIII, *passim.*

though an impression of him as a self-seeking opportunist cannot be entirely overcome.

Bon et sceptique, sensible et railleur, il s'irritait peu contre les évènements et les hommes. Il voyait bien, il s'enthousiasmait rarement, il écrivait avec calme et finesse... Il n'avait ni haines, ni rancunes, ni préjugés... Ami intime de tous les Beaux esprits, le cœur doucement occupé, correspondant de je ne sais combien de princes, et de Catherine le Grand, il disait des méchancetés et n'en faisait point.[117]

This subtle and polished *lettré* was a skeptic and pessimist in philosophy and politics; i.e., he took no stock in the prevalent optimistic views on the general progress of mankind. It was said that the two most important occurrences in Grimm's life were his friendship with Catherine II and the French Revolution. The first determined the whole course of his life and gave it its chief value; the second destroyed everything except his friendship with the Empress, which continued until her death in 1796.

Grimm made two trips to Russia. The first was in March, 1773, when he left Paris with Diderot to part from him later. While Diderot proceeded first to Holland, Grimm went to Darmstadt to take the young Prince of Darmstadt and his mother, Princess Caroline (Grimm's first protectress) to the wedding of the Tsarevich Paul and Princess Wilhelmina of Hesse-Darmstadt.[118]

Grimm arrived at St. Petersburg in September, 1773. Diderot was already there. They were both given a most flattering reception by the Empress, but each in a different way. *Diderot l'étonnait par son éloquence et l'amusait par sa familiarité et ses distractions; Grimm l'intéressait, la charmait.*[119] Catherine, with her keen perception of character, no doubt at once recognized Diderot's superiority over

[117] P. Limayrac, *Gazette littéraire de Grimm*, p. 32.
[118] E. Scherer, *Melchior Grimm, l'homme de lettres*, p. 239.
[119] *Ibid.*, p. 261.

Grimm; yet the German adventurer was more congenial to her; he was, like herself, a German expatriate who had assimilated the culture and spirit of his adopted country; he was, besides, intelligent, adroit, and honest, and his admiration for the Empress was unqualified. When Caroline of Darmstadt died, Grimm had already acquired in Catherine a faithful friend and protectress.

Grimm's first impressions of the court are recorded in his letter to Mme Geoffrin.[120] He describes at length his reception and his talks with the Empress; *Nous avons jasé ce soir comme des pies borgnes.*[121] He admires especially the kindness, simplicity and graciousness of Catherine.

On jurerait qu'elle n'a autre chose à faire au monde que d'être aimable, et l'on ne douterait, pas en mille ans, qu'elle a une empire à gouverner; elle appelle cela son gagne-pain.[122]

In the same letter Grimm writes about his having been elected together with Diderot to membership in the Imperial Academy of Sciences.

C'est la seule occasion [he adds] où je me serais bien dispensé de voir mon nom à côté de celui de Diderot.[123]

Soon after his arrival Grimm became a familiar figure at court. Every day from eleven in the morning to eleven at night he was in the presence of the Empress either in public or in private.

L'hiver de 1773 à 1774 s'écoula ainsi pour moi dans une ivresse continuelle. Les bontés de l'impératrice semblaient s'accroître de jour en jour, et avec elles sa confiance. La mienne était telle que j'entrais dans son appartement avec la même sécurité que chez l'ami le plus

---

120 Grimm to Mme Geoffrin, November 10, 1773; L. Perry, *Une Femme du monde au XVIIIe siècle*, Paris, 1883, and E. Scherer, *op. cit.*, pp. 262-263.
121 E. Scherer, *Melchior Grimm . . .* p. 262.
122 *Ibid.*
123 *Ibid.*

intime, sûr de trouver dans son entretien un fonds inépuisable du plus grand intérêt sous la forme plus piquante.[124] Les bontés dont l'impératrice m'a comblé [he writes to Meister] ne me donnent pas envie de m'en aller si vite.[125]

In due time he was offered a very lucrative position at court; the practical Grimm, however, hesitated. A fortune based on the favors of a monarch could not be entirely secure; besides he was reluctant to leave behind his friend Mme d'Epinay and the Parisian salon. *Les bontés de l'impératrice m'ont rendu fou,* he writes to Count Nesselrode, *si je la quitte, j'en mourrai de douleur, mais comment rester?*[126] A severe fever necessitated his leaving Russia and in April, 1774, he was off, promising, however, to return.

Grimm kept his promise and returned in September, 1776. He received the same welcome as before. The long tête-à-têtes were continued. Grimm was never tired or bored with these conversations. He claims, on the contrary, to have been inspired by them. Grimm gives perhaps the best description of Catherine's personality—her singular combination of charm, keen intelligence, grace, animation, and dignity.

... il faut avoir vu dans ces moments cette tête singulière, ce composé de génie et de grâce, pour avoir une idée de la verve qui l'entraînait, des traits qui lui échappaient, des saillies qui se pressaient et se heurtaient. Je quittais Sa Majesté pour l'ordinaire tellement ému, tellement électrisé, que je passais la moitié de ma nuit à me promener à grands pas dans ma chambre, obsédé, poursuivi par tout ce qui avait été dit, et me désolant que tout cela ne fût que pour moi et dût rester perdu pour tout le monde. L'impératrice à la vérité, ne fut jamais un seul instant absente dans ces tête à têtes, mais elle n'y fut pas non plus jamais de trop. L'art de conserver la dignité qui lui était naturelle, au milieu de l'aisance, de la familiarité même, était un de ses secrets et des charmes magiques de sa société.[127]

---

[124] E. Scherer, *op. cit.*, p. 264.   [125] Grimm to Meister, November 8, 1773.
[126] E. Scherer, *Melchior Grimm* ... p. 265. Grimm's correspondence with Catherine begins about the time of his departure from Russia. Cf. next chapter.
[127] *Ibid.*, p. 276.

During Grimm's second trip he addressed to Catherine a half-humorous, half-serious petition for a post. He adroitly conveyed the idea that it would have to be in Paris, since the climate unfortunately would prevent his staying in Russia. The petition was granted, and he was appointed Catherine's confidential agent with a salary of 2,000 roubles (10,000 francs). He received in addition the rank of colonel. Grimm left Russia in October, 1777.[128] His subsequent relations with Catherine will be viewed in the following chapter, through their correspondence. At present one may add only that on his return to Paris Grimm spared no efforts to glorify his friend. After Catherine's death he published a complete account of his relations with the Empress. This *Mémoire historique sur l'origine et les suites de mon attachement pour l'Impératrice Catherine* II appears now at the beginning of Tourneux's edition of the *Correspondance littéraire*.[129]

As to general observations upon and impressions of Russia, Grimm, it appears, left none. Like Diderot he saw of Russia only the court, which was in spirit as much French as Russian. He never learned the Russian language, and his knowledge of Russian history, judging from his reviews of books on Russia, was quite superficial. What is certain, however, is that no other foreigner, unless it be Diderot, had a more sincere and profound admiration for the genius of Catherine II. Among the philosophers and men of letters who helped to spread her fame, there was none who served her more faithfully than her agent and friend, Melchior Grimm.

The short and ill-fated trip to Russia made by Mercier de la Rivière, the economist, was undertaken chiefly upon Diderot's recommendation.[130] La Rivière belonged to the

---

[128] *Ibid.*, p. 267.

[129] Grimm, *Correspondance littéraire*, I, 1-63.

[130] For a detailed account of La Rivière's trip to Russia see *Russkaîa starina*, 1891, LXXII; also C. Larivière, *La France et la Russie au XVIIIᵉ siècle*, Paris, 1909, ch. II. This study was first published in the *Revue d'histoire littéraire de la*

school of the "physiocrates." His *L'Ordre naturel et essentiel des sociétés politiques* established his reputation, and he was commissioned by the French government to draw up a code of laws in Martinique. Diderot had a very high opinion of La Rivière's abilities. In his letter to Falconet he calls him *apôtre de la propriété, de la liberté, et de l'évidence.*[131] As a political thinker, he considered La Rivière greater than Montesquieu himself. Unfortunately, as he observed in the same letter, La Rivière was not a courtier, as he was by nature direct and incapable of dissimulation.[132] As a result of Diderot's recommendations and with the approval of Prince Golitsyn, the Russian ambassador in Paris, La Rivière was engaged to go to Russia to apply his experience and skill in the drawing up of a code of laws.

From the time La Rivière, his wife, his mistress, and numerous secretaries left France in August, 1767, difficulties began to arise and difficulties continued until the day of his departure from Russia in May, 1768.[133] In the first place, "the future reformer," as he was jokingly called, instead of going directly to St. Petersburg, stopped for a month in Berlin and for two weeks in Riga, thus causing delay and expense to the Russian government.[134] No sooner had he arrived than he began to complain of the quarters assigned to him and his staff. With his superior airs and his *ton d'oracle* he antagonized everybody, including his countrymen. Ségur, in his memoirs, gives an account altogether uncomplimentary to the French legislator, and Falconet wrote a very sharp letter to Diderot describing his protégé's behavior and urging him

---

France, October 15, 1897; cf. also M. Tourneux, *Diderot et Catherine II,* 1899, pp. 16-20.

[131] Diderot to Falconet, no date, *Revue moderne,* XXXIX, 306-307.

[132] *Ibid.,* pp. 307-308.

[133] M. Tourneux, *Diderot et Catherine II,* p. 17.

[134] *En sorte,* writes the vice-chancellor Golitsyn, *qu'étant en chemin, il coûte au delà de quatre mille roubles, sans qu'on sache de quelque utilité il pourra être.*—M. Tourneux, *Diderot et Catherine II,* p. 17.

to be more careful in recommending people for important positions in Russia.[185]

Within a short time La Rivière had given an impression of wishing to run the whole empire without any one's assistance. After a somewhat delayed audience with the Empress, La Rivière received an indemnity of a hundred thousand roubles and was asked to relieve St. Petersburg of his presence.[136] Catherine wrote to Voltaire:

Monsieur de la Rivière est venu ici pour nous législater. Il nous supposait marcher à quatre pattes, et très poliment il s'était donné la peine de venir de la Martinique pour nous dresser sur nos pattes de derrière.[137]

The chief reason for Catherine's prompt dismissal of La Rivière was apparently that she found him uncongenial; that instead of *une souplesse dont elle se serait fort accommodée*, says Charles de Larivière, *elle découvrit un esprit d'indépendance dont elle ne voulait pas faire l'épreuve.*[138] Bil'basov, on the other hand, thinks that La Rivière was a victim of intrigues and that the stories told of him by Ségur in his memoirs were unjust and exaggerated.[139]

La Rivière never seems to have felt sympathetic toward Russia. Soon after his arrival in St. Petersburg he wrote to Raynal of the utter backwardness of the country—*tout est à faire dans ce pays;* and complained bitterly of the despotism of the government, and of the rigors of the climate.[140] On

---

[135] Cf. L. P. Ségur, *Mémoires, souvenirs et anecdotes*, Paris, 1879, I, 442-443; also letter of Falconet to Diderot, *Revue moderne*, XXXIX, 383.

[136] M. Tourneux, *op. cit.*, p. 20.

[137] Catherine to Voltaire, November 2, 1774. Voltaire, Grimm, and Galiani always made fun of the economist. In his letters to Catherine Voltaire referred to him as *le pauvre Solon nommé La Rivière.*

[138] C. Larivière, *La France et la Russie au XVIIIᵉ siècle*, p. 92.

[139] V. Bil'basov, "Nikita Panin and Mercier de la Rivière," *Russkaïa starina*, 1891, LXXII, Introduction.

[140] La Rivière to Raynal, October 30, 1767, C. Larivière, *La France et la Russie . . . p. 99.*

his return to Paris he loudly denounced Catherine and also
her ministers. Thiébault observes in his memoirs that he
was invariably surprised at *la chaleur et la franchise avec
lesquelles il s'en expliquait* concerning the subject of his
journey to Russia.[141]

The last important representative of philosophical and
literary France at the court of Russia was Sénac de Meilhan
(1736-1803), statesman, philosopher, and a man of letters of
some repute in his time.[142] His chief publication, *Considérations sur l'esprit et les mœurs*, 1789-1790, established his
reputation as a moralist and philosopher. He was also well
known in the Parisian salons as a brilliant conversationalist.
Prince de Ligne admired him in his memoirs, and he was
even compared by some of his contemporaries with La
Bruyère. It was said of Meilhan that he was *une brillante
intelligence*, but not *un homme de génie.*[143]

Sénac de Meilhan's relations with the Russian court are
strongly reminiscent of La Rivière's. Both produced unfavorable impressions on the Empress and were dismissed before
the completion of their tasks.[144]

Soon after the revolution Meilhan wrote to Catherine
asking for permission to come to Russia to write a history of
Russia in the eighteenth century. A Russian representative
at Venice was accordingly instructed to become acquainted

[141] Michaud, *Biographie universelle*, XXXVIII, 162-164. Cf. also his letters
to Turgot written six years after De la Rivière's return from Russia, in *Les
Travaux de l'Académie des Sciences*, 1859, II, 159.

[142] Although he was an émigré, it seems more desirable to consider Meilhan
in the same group with Diderot, as a philosopher and man of letters, rather than
in the group of émigrés.

[143] F. Godefroy, *XVIIIe Siècle, Prosateurs*, 1879, pp. 89-93. Meilhan's other
important publication was: *Portraits et caractères des personnages distingués de
la fin du dix-huitième siècle.*

[144] A detailed account of Meilhan's trip with letters of the Russian court
and his own may be found in the *Sbornik*, Vol. XLII. See also an article of
Prince Obolenskiĭ in *Russkiĭ arkhiv*, 1866, pp. 421-459; Maĭkov's article in
Russkaía starina, 1896; also L. Pingaud, *Les Français en Russie* . . . pp. 67-69.

with Meilhan and report on his character and talents.[145] These apparently were found satisfactory, for, on May 6, 1791, Meilhan had his first audience with the Empress. The first impression on both sides seems to have been a favorable one.[146] After seeing the first drafts of Meilhan's history, however, Catherine's enthusiasm for the Frenchman was considerably lessened. He was found to be too casual and superficial, and to be wanting in proper training.[147] Catherine herself drew up a plan for the history, and Meilhan was urged to use the documents in the state archives. For this purpose he went, in the summer of 1791, to Moscow. From there he wrote a very enthusiastic letter to Catherine about the ancient city, which seems to have inspired him to compose a poem.[148] Soon, however, Meilhan gave signs of restlessness and boredom with his work. He went about a great deal in St. Petersburg society and neglected to gather material for his book or to learn the Russian language. The latter was repeatedly urged on him by the Empress, but apparently to no avail.[149] In addition to neglecting his work, he was wont to annoy the Empress with requests for some important post for himself and his sons.[150] For himself he first wanted a diplomatic post in Turkey, and when that was declined, he asked the Empress for a title such as "Librarian to Her Majesty" or "Historiographer to Her Majesty." Catherine declined, explaining that she already had two "Librarians"; and regarding the historiographer title she wrote as follows:

[145] Catherine's letter to Mordvinov inviting Meilhan to come to Russia is found in the *Sbornik*, XLII, 129-130; and Catherine's letter to Meilhan, *ibid.*, pp. 145-146.

[146] *Ibid., passim.*

[147] *Russkiĭ arkhiv*, 1866, p. 449.

[148] *Sbornik*, XLII, 153.

[149] *Ibid.*, pp. 155 ff.

[150] *Ibid.*, pp. 170-174. Meilhan had two sons; the older remained in France after the Revolution; the younger emigrated to Russia. Catherine appointed the latter to a secretaryship in the department of Foreign Affairs, and he was still in Russia in 1795. There seems to be no record of his subsequent career. *Russkiĭ arkhiv*, 1866, p. 425.

Permettez-moi de vous dire qu'il serait bon de voir quelle tournure prendrait votre travail et si ce titre vous conviendrait chez vous, avant que de vous le donner et que vous puissiez l'accepter.[151]

As time went on the Empress became more and more convinced of Meilhan's inability to write the history and proceeded in a tactful way to prepare him for departure. Thus she wrote of the insurmountable difficulty which a foreigner had to face in writing a history of Russia, urged him not to hasten, and to try to understand the Russian conditions before starting to write. *Je veux bien croire que vous ne trouverez pas à la Russie l'air français. Ce n'est pas aussi celui que je lui désirerais.*[152] Finally he was made to understand that the severity of the Russian climate might seriously affect his health. When he himself suggested a short visit abroad, Catherine definitely advised him not to return.[153] Thus honorably dismissed, with his manuscript and a pension of 6,000 francs, Meilhan left Russia never to return.

Of this sterile adventure of Meilhan's practically no trace remains. His history of Russia remained unfinished. But in the second volume of his *Œuvres philosophiques et littéraires*, published in Hamburg in 1795, is found a sketch of Potemkin and a *Lettre à Mad. de ... sur la Russie*, which contains an account of his interviews with Catherine and his bizarre comparison of her to St. Peter of Rome. A passage from it will give its general tone:

Saint-Pierre inspire un respect religieux, il excite cette sorte de sensibilité que fait naître l'aspect de l'immensité; Catherine II inspire le même sentiment.[154]

Closely connected with the group of philosophers and literary men are the various representatives of professional

---

[151] *Sbornik*, XLII, 196-197.   [152] *Ibid.*, p. 200.   [153] *Ibid.*, p. 229.

[154] L. Pingaud, *Les Français en Russie* ... p. 69. This strange panegyric of Catherine seems to have been written about 1791. Catherine found it exaggerated and in bad taste; cf. her letter to Grimm, August 14, 1792, and Obolenskiĭ, *Russkiĭ arkhiv*, 1866, p. 424.

France: artists, actors, teachers, and other professional and semi-professional people who came to Russia in the second half of the century, usually on contracts. They remained in Russia, as a rule, for periods varying from two years to twelve years, and therefore had a better opportunity than the literary men to acquaint themselves with the country and its people.

Among the numerous French artists who visited Russia in the second half of the century, the best known was the sculptor Etienne-Maurice Falconet (1716-1791). A friend of the Encyclopedists, especially Diderot, Falconet himself was somewhat of a philosopher and literary man, as well as a talented sculptor. He was recommended to Catherine by Diderot, and in 1766 was invited to come to Russia to make an equestrian statue of Peter the Great. He accepted the offer, and the contract was signed August 31, 1766.[155] Soon afterward he left for Russia with his pupil, Mlle Collot, who later became his daughter-in-law.[156]

We learn something about the early part of Falconet's stay in Russia from his letters to Diderot. Finding himself in a totally strange and barbaric country the sculptor's spirits were at first very low. His confidence was maintained, however, by the Empress's constant personal interest in him and his work. Soon after his arrival in St. Petersburg he wrote to Diderot,

L'encouragement perpétuel de l'impératrice échauffe mon âme, l'anoblit, l'agrandit continuellement au point que si j'étais venu sans âme à Pétersbourg, cette magicienne auguste m'en aurait créé une...[157]

---

[155] For particulars of Falconet's relations with Catherine II, see A. Polovtsev, *Sbornik*, 1876, XVII. Cf. also a short account by L. Pingaud, *Les Français en Russie* ... pp. 73-74, and Michaud, *Biographie universelle*, 1815, XIV, 125-128.

[156] The son of the sculptor Falconet, Pierre Etienne, painter, came to Russia in 1773; he painted Catherine II and the Grand Dukes, and married Mlle Collot in St. Petersburg in 1777. He died in Paris a few months after his father, on June 25, 1791. Cf. L. Réau, *Correspondance de Falconet avec Catherine*, p. 213.

[157] Falconet to Diderot, no date, *Revue moderne*, XXXIX, 384.

On the other hand the Empress was delighted with the sculptor and so wrote to Mme Geoffrin:

M. Diderot m'a fait faire l'acquisition d'un homme que je crois n'a pas son pareil; c'est Falconet, il va incessament commencer la statue de Pierre le Grand; s'il y a des artistes qui l'égalent dans son état, l'on peut avancer je pense hardiment, qu'il n'y en a point qui lui soient à comparer par ses sentiments, en un mot, il est l'ami de l'âme de Diderot.[158]

In 1767 Catherine began a lively and very informal correspondence with the sculptor which lasted eleven years.[159]

Falconet's kindly but proud, independent, and irascible nature caused him much trouble in Russia, particularly with General Betskïï, superintendent of fine arts for the Empire. Having accomplished his task, the equestrian statue of Peter the Great, Falconet left Russia, tired and disappointed, in August, 1778, without even seeing the Empress. In spite of his long stay in Russia, there is no evidence of his having ever learned the language. Judging from his correspondence with Catherine, his views on Russia were those of Diderot and other Encyclopedists—he admired her rapid progress and, because of the liberalism of the Empress, saw the future of the country in an optimistic light. He called Catherine's code *chef-d'œuvre de la raison et de l'humanité*, and writing to Catherine expressed his enthusiasm for it in the following terms:

Je ne sais si j'aurais voulu être Russe, il y a 60 ou 80 ans; mais je sens en lisant les divines Instructions de Votre Majesté Impériale, que je voudrais l'être à présent et vivre assez pour jouir des heureux fruits du code Catherinien.[160]

---

[158] A. Polovtsev, *Sbornik,* XVII, xv.

[159] This correspondence will be treated in the next chapter.

[160] Falconet to Catherine, September 29, 1769, L. Réau, *Correspondance de Falconet avec Catherine,* Paris, 1921, p. 101. Falconet's general correspondence was published for the first time in Lausanne in 1781; his *Œuvres choisies,* Paris, 1785; and his *Œuvres diverses,* Paris, 1787.

Equally renowned as an artist was the painter of Marie Antoinette, Mme Vigée LeBrun (1755-1842). Before the Revolution she already knew many Russians in Paris and had painted the portraits of Orlov and Shuvalov.[161] After the Revolution Mme Vigée LeBrun established her residence in Vienna and there met many Russians. It was there, also, that she met Prince de Ligne, who persuaded her to come to Russia.[162] In the first part of her *Souvenirs*, composed of twelve letters addressed to the Princess Kurakin, Mme Vigée LeBrun describes her childhood and early career; in the second part, her stay in Russia.[163]

Mme Vigée LeBrun arrived in St. Petersburg July 25, 1795, and remained there for six years until early in July, 1801, leaving Russia, as did so many of her countrymen, because of poor health.[164] She had in Russia an immediate and conspicuous success as a portrait painter and as a social figure. She made numerous friends in the court circles and had a good opportunity to observe life in the Russian court and in the homes of the aristocracy. She painted portraits of the Imperial family as well as of many dignitaries of the time. Both Catherine II and Paul I were friendly to her, and in 1800 the St. Petersburg Academy of Fine Arts made her an honorary member.[165] She was one of the first of the eighteenth-century French visitors to Russia to be definitely attracted by the picturesque aspect of the country. In St. Petersburg she admired the grandeur of the monuments, the river Neva, and the national costumes.[166] In Moscow she was impressed by the oriental aspect of the city. *Je crus entrer*

---

[161] Michaud, *Biographie universelle*, 1842, LXXI, 66.

[162] *Ibid.*, p. 72.

[163] Mme Vigée LeBrun, *Souvenirs*, Paris, 1835, 3 vols.

[164] Michaud, *Biographie universelle*, 1842, LXXI, p. 74; also *Souvenirs of Mme Vigée LeBrun*, New York, 1879, p. 310.

[165] Michaud, *op. cit.*, 73. Cf. also Vigée LeBrun, *Souvenirs*, ch. xxiii.

[166] *Souvenirs of Mme Vigée LeBrun*, ch. xv.

*dans Ispahan, dont j'avais vu plusieurs dessins, tant l'aspect
de Moscou diffère de tout ce qui existe en Europe.*[167]

Mme LeBrun gave a most enthusiastic and flattering account of the Russian aristocracy. She emphasized especially its politeness, charm, gaiety, hospitality, prodigality, and a gallantry which, she says, was often of a most *recherché* kind.[168] She admired especially the Russian women, who have not only *cette politesse bienveillante qui fait le charme de la bonne société, mais encore qu'elles n'ont pas cette morgue que l'on peut reprocher à quelques dames françaises.*[169]

Mme LeBrun was also one of the first foreigners to observe the common people. She found them religious and backward, but gentle and kind. She observed that the Russian people were as a rule ugly; but they had a straight-forward honest bearing and were the best people in the world.[170] She seems to have developed a real sympathy for Russia and, on leaving, felt as though she were leaving her native country.[171]

Among other artists who came to Russia one may mention the French actors who were engaged to perform at court and who usually stayed in Russia for periods of one to five years. Two such actors, De Belloy and Desforges, who came during the reign of Empress Elizabeth, have already been mentioned. During the reign of Catherine II the number of these players increased, and we find among them at least two well-known names—Aufrêne and Fastier. These two artists appeared in plays composed by the Empress in collaboration with her literary courtiers. A collection of these plays was edited by J. H. Castéra and published in Paris in 1799.[172] It is difficult to determine what part these and other actors played in the

[167] F. Baldensperger, *Le Movement des idées* ... 1924, I, 102.
[168] Cf. *Souvenirs of Mme Vigée LeBrun*, chs. vii and xi.
[169] Vigée LeBrun, *op. cit.*, 1835, II, 310.
[170] *Souvenirs of Mme Vigée LeBrun*, p. 241.
[171] *Ibid.*, p. 310.
[172] J. Castéra, *Théâtre de l'Hermitage de Catherine II*, 2 volumes, Paris, 1799. Cf. especially the Introduction.

spreading of a vogue for Russia upon their return to France. It appears probable, however, that they knew personally playwrights like Morand and Desforges and may well have helped them in the production of their plays on Russian subjects.

Besides the prominent artists mentioned above, there came to Russia after 1762 a constantly increasing number of other professional men.[173] Among them were lawyers, journalists, and second-rate writers. They all came primarily to make fortunes, *pour traire la vache*. Some of them became secretaries to Russian nobles, others private tutors and teachers. This profession, in fact, was completely monopolized by the French. A typical and well-known example of this last group was Gilbert Romme, for many years tutor of the Strogonov family.[174] Most of these professional men remained obscure and returned to France before the Revolution; a few gained prominence and left records of their Russian experiences. The most important of these were Villiers, Charles Masson, Levesque, and LeClerc.

Charles de Villiers, a lawyer, has left nothing of importance. He was a typical representative, however, of the French bourgeois professional man residing in Russia in the latter half of the century. De Villiers was a member of the Parlement of Paris and a student of law and legislation. He came to Russia as one of the secretaries of Mercier de la Rivière.[175] When he arrived at St. Petersburg, his patron, having incurred the Empress' disfavor, had already left, and Villiers then became a protégé of the sculptor Falconet. In a letter of June 16, 1768, Falconet recommended Villiers to Catherine as a modest, industrious *légiste* and not, as La Rivière called himself, a *légis-*

[173] L. Pingaud, *Les Français en Russie* . . . pp. 87-96.

[174] Cf. P. J. Bartenev, "Gilbert Romme and Count P. Strogonov," *Russkiĭ arkhiv*, 1887, I, 5 ff.

[175] For an account of Villiers' stay in Russia see an article by A. Florovskiĭ, "Un Légiste français au service de la Tsarine," *La Revue historique* (a pamphlet), 1922.

lateur.[176] As a result, De Villiers was appointed legal adviser to Prince Vïazemskïï with the understanding that he would devote his time to research in legal and legislative questions. His services were, it seems, completely satisfactory to the Empress and were interrupted only by his sudden death in St. Petersburg on April 4, 1774.[177] His works include a translation into Latin of Catherine's *Nakaz*, which appeared in France in 1769. Tourneux thinks that he was also the author, or co-author, of Catherine's famous *Antidote*.[178] The question, however, is at present not definitely settled.

The extracts from De Villiers' works on serfdom, on the clergy, and on various Russian institutions, which are found in Florovskïï's article, seem to indicate that though Villiers knew the Russian language, his knowledge of Russian history and institutions was very scant. Moreover, his point of view was prejudiced. Like Diderot and so many other eminent French visitors to Russia, De Villiers remained a typical product of the age of enlightenment. He hated inequalities of all kinds, especially caste systems and the privileges of the clergy. Like Diderot, he failed to realize that the doctrines of the encyclopedic philosophers could hardly be applied to the Russia of 1770.

Charles-François Masson (1762-1807) spent ten years in Russia, partly in military service, partly as tutor and secretary to various Russian nobles.[179] He came from a middle-class family and in his youth had been apprentice in a watchmaker's shop. He had literary ambitions, however, and started to write poetry at a very early age. His elder brother was an officer in the Russian army and, in 1786, invited Charles-

[176] *La Revue historique.*
[177] *Ibid.*
[178] "Antidote, ou examen d'un mauvais livre, superbement imprimé..." *Journal encyclopédique*, December, 1771, pp. 375-386. Cf. also M. Tourneux, *Diderot et Catherine*, pp. 22-23.
[179] For a short biographical sketch see Michaud, *Biographie universelle*, 1820, XXVII, 428-430.

François to join him, promising him a lucrative career. Masson left for Russia at the end of 1786. Upon his arrival in St. Petersburg he entered the army, and soon became tutor in the family of Count Saltykov. He received several promotions in the army, and was welcomed in St. Petersburg society. In 1795 he married a Russian, Baroness Rosen, and became secretary to Grand Duke Alexander. In 1796 his good fortune came to an end. The Emperor Paul, suspecting the Masson brothers of revolutionary sympathies, gave orders for their arrest and transportation to the Polish frontier. Charles Masson wrote his memoirs of Russia in Poland, after his deportation.[180] Upon his return to France in 1799 he became a member of several academies and spent the remainder of his life in scholarly and literary pursuits. In addition to his memoirs of Russia he left unedited a translation from Russian, *Description des jardins de Tsarskoe Celo,* a philological treatise on the Russian alphabet, and material for a history of Russian literature.[181]

Masson's *Mémoires sur la Russie* show evidence of a varied and extensive knowledge of the country and its people. His point of view was bitterly hostile to the Russian government (i.e., the Tsar Paul I). There were, of course, many exaggerations, hasty judgments and inaccuracies, but on the whole the *Mémoires* gave a fairly impartial picture of Russia and the Russian court at the end of the century.[182]

In the Preface to his memoirs Masson explained his position and criticized his predecessors in the following terms:

---

[180] Masson, *Mémoires sur la Russie,* Paris, 1800-1803, 4 vols., in 8 °.

[181] Michaud, *Biographie universelle,* XXVII, 428-430; A. J. Beuchot, *Décade philosophique,* LIV, 565.

[182] The memoirs of C. Masson were criticized by Kotzebue in his *L'Année la plus remarquable de ma vie,* and by Fortia de Piles in his *Examen de trois ouvrages sur la Russie.* The memoirs were translated into English and German, cf. J. Michaud, *op. cit.,* XXVII, 430. For a more recent Russian criticism of Masson's memoirs cf. Riabinin, *Russkaia starina,* XVI, 384-387.

On a, dans ces derniers temps, beaucoup écrit sur la Russie: les Français l'ont fait très superficiellement, les Anglais, en voyageurs qui notent tout ce qui se trouve sur leur chemin, et les Allemands, en flagorneurs. Je me sens, moi-même, je l'avoue, une grande prévention en faveur des Russes; elle m'est inspirée par leurs bonnes qualités, par l'hospitalité, l'estime, et l'amitié qu'ils m'ont accordées pendant dix ans: mais j'ai d'un autre côté, j'en conviens, des préventions profondes contre leur gouvernement; elles sont fondées sur ce que j'ai vu ou éprouvé.[183]

Regarding the court of Catherine II Masson stressed especially its French character.[184] The country as a whole he considered backward, especially from the political point of view, but among the nobility there was culture and enlightenment.

Cependant il y a parmi la noblesse, et même à la cour de Russie, des âmes généreuses et fières, qui sans être éprises d'un système d'égalité et de liberté parfaites, sont indignées pourtant de l'abnégation honteuse que l'on exige d'elles; car le despotisme ne convient qu'à des barbares; et les gentilshommes russes ne le sont plus.[185]

The dominant characteristic of the Russian noble, according to Masson, was his flexibility.

Le noble Russe, le seul Russe qu'on puisse voir dans l'étranger et bien connaître dans son pays, a effectivement une grande aptitude à s'identifier avec les opinions, les mœurs, les manières, et les langues des autres nations.[186] [Unfortunately] ... il a reçu de l'étranger des arts, des sciences, des vices, et peu de vertus... On peut dire du Russe que son gouvernement l'avilit, que sa religion le déprave, et que sa prétendue civilisation l'a corrompu.[187]

The Russian peasant, who was not affected by Western influences, was, however, naturally good:

Le paysan russe sans propriété, sans religion, sans morale, sans honneur, est hospitalier, humain, serviable, gai, fidèle, et courageux: plus on s'enfonce loin des villes, plus on le trouve bon.[188]

---

[183] Masson, *Mémoires sur la Russie*, Paris, 1863, pp. 45-46.
[184] *Ibid.*, p. 93.   [185] *Ibid.*, p. 165.
[186] *Ibid.*, p. 170.   [187] *Ibid.*, pp. 170-171.
[188] *Ibid.*, p. 171.

Thus the peasant had certain "natural," "patriarchal" virtues; his vices—coarseness of manner, servility, lack of honor— were the results of serfdom and of the bad example of the clergy.[189]

Masson showed no mercy to the Greek Orthodox religion. He considered it the most degenerate of Christian sects and its clergy the most contemptible specimens of humanity.[190]

Like all Frenchmen who recorded their impressions of Russia at the end of the century, Masson noticed the ascendancy of French culture in Russia, particularly the importance of French tutors.

A commencer par le célèbre Le Fort qui inspira à Pierre I le désir de s'instruire, et à finir par un petit clerc de procureur français, qui enseigne à conjuguer quelques verbes de sa langue, ce sont ces out-schitéli [i.e., tutors] qui ont donné aux Russes ce goût, ces connaissances, et ces talents que plusieurs d'entre eux firent admirer dans l'étranger.[191]

It is their influence, too, that fostered a natural predilection of the Russians for the French.

Les Russes presque tous élevés par des Français, contractent, dès leur enfance, une prédilection marquée pour cette nation.[192]

The last two representatives of professional France to be treated here—Levesque and LeClerc—spent extended periods in Russia with significant results.

Pierre Charles Levesque (1736-1812) was the author of an extensive and authoritative history of Russia.[193] He came to Russia in 1773 upon the recommendation of Diderot and stayed there for seven years, teaching literature at a military school in St. Petersburg. In France he was chiefly known for

---

[189] Ibid., p. 175.
[190] Ibid., pp. 185-188.
[191] Ibid., pp. 221-222.
[192] Ibid., p. 222.
[193] Michaud, Biographie universelle, XXIV, 372-375.

his moral and historical works, as well as for translations from the classics.

Levesque was the first serious scholar of Russian history and culture. He not only learned the Russian language but also mastered Old Slavonic and so was able to use original sources for his history. Upon his return to France in 1780 and the publication of the *Histoire de Russie,* Levesque became professor at the Collège Royal, collaborated in the *Biographie universelle,* particularly on Russian subjects, and made several translations from Russian.[194] His history of Russia will be discussed in one of the following chapters of this work.

Nicholas-Gabriel LeClerc (1726-1798),[195] a physician by profession and author of a pedagogical novel *Yu-le-Grand et Confucius, histoire chinoise,* held various professional posts in Russia, finally becoming connected with the Corps of Pages in St. Petersburg. LeClerc visited Russia twice—in 1759 and 1769—and, according to his own testimony, spent about ten years there altogether.[196] During his second trip to Russia in 1769 he started to collect material for the history, and upon his return to France in 1777, he began this work in collaboration with his son. His history, although very elaborate and extensive, is inferior to Levesque's, from the standpoint of scholarship and presentation. LeClerc's sources apparently were secondary, and his judgment in selecting them was not always infallible.[197] Catherine II was displeased with the work, and a refutation of it appeared in St. Petersburg in 1787, under the title of *Remarques sur l'histoire de la Russie ancienne et moderne.* LeClerc published also a short *Histoire de Pierre III, empereur de Russie,* which was mutilated by the

[194] Michaud, *Biographie universelle,* XXIV, 372-375.
[195] *Ibid.,* IX, 78-80.
[196] N. G. LeClerc, *Histoire physique, morale, civile, et politique de la Russie ancienne,* Paris, 1783-1785, Preface, I, viii.
[197] Much of LeClerc's material seems to come from his Russian friends.

editor, made several translations from the Russian, and left a number of unedited manuscripts in the Department of Foreign Affairs in Paris.[198] LeClerc's work will also be treated at some length in a subsequent chapter dealing with eighteenth-century sources of information on Russia.

The three representatives of professional France last mentioned—Masson, Levesque, and LeClerc—were as yet the only visiting Frenchmen who had lived in Russia with definite intellectual results. They had learned the language, had acquainted themselves with the history and culture of Russia, and had tried to express in works of some importance the information they acquired at first hand.

The next group to be examined is composed of representatives of official France, that is, the accredited ambassadors, envoys, and agents sent to Russia by the governments of Louis XV and Louis XVI. The prevalent views on and attitude toward Russia of these official representatives of France can best be seen in their letters and reports to the Ministry of Foreign Affairs. We shall first examine these official reports, and consider later the two most important memoirs of Russia —one by the chargé d'affaires, Corberon, the other by the ambassador, Ségur.

Three representatives of the French government have already been mentioned—D'Eon, Rulhière, and La Messelière. The first two, as we have seen, were on the whole not interested in Russia, though Rulhière wrote a sensational book on the coup d'état of 1762, of which he was a witness. La Messelière, although quite sympathetic with Russia in his memoirs, gave a rather impressionistic and superficial account of the country. Yet even he was critical of the Russian government and pessimistic as to its future.

In 1754, we find an anonymous envoy expressing his views on the Russian people in the following terms:

[198] Michaud, *Biographie universelle*, IX, 80.

Tout ce que l'on leur attribue d'avantageux est combattu et même anéanti par des défauts et des vices dont la plus grande partie prend sa source dans l'intempérance, dans l'inconstance, et particulièrement dans l'ingratitude.[199]

In 1758 Ambassador L'Hôpital wrote:

Tout est ici prestige et fumée, les rangs sont des vertus.[200]

In 1763 Breteuil, envoy to the court of Catherine II, likewise expressed very unfavorable views on Russia:

Cette nation, qui n'est que d'hier sur la scène des nations policées, n'y mérite encore aucune place du côté de ses mœurs, ni de ses lumières.... Le Russe est aujourd'hui plus livré à la dissipation qu'aucune nation de l'Europe; un luxe insoutenable et sans le moindre ordre augmente l'avidité naturelle à cette nation.[201]

Breteuil's successor, Corberon, in 1778 states in a report to the minister of foreign affairs, Vergennes, that the institutions of Catherine II had no future, that her academies were without pupils, and that her teachers were depraved, and her laws arbitrary and unjust.[202]

The envoy, Sabatier de Cabres, in 1771 sent to Vergennes a crushing refutation of all the optimistic views on Russia and Catherine II. He stressed the ruin of commerce, the famines, and the brigandage, and denounced the whole nation in the following terms:

Il est moralement impossible que les Russes parviennent à former ce qu'on appelle une nation: l'avarice alliée à la prodigalité, la bassesse servile et rampante, l'insolence et la vanité seront les productions éternelles de ce sol ingrat... Ils ont au moral l'agitation trompeuse et perfide du singe... On m'a souvent voulu persuader que les gentilshommes et surtout les paysans de l'intérieur sont naturellement bons, vertueux, et hospitaliers. La crainte, la servitude, et l'absence de besoins les montrent tels; ils ont à peu de choses près les mœurs

[199] Ministère des Affaires Etrangères, *Russie, Mémoires et documents,* Vol. IX.
[200] *Ibid., Russie, Correspondance,* LVIII, dispatch of October 27, 1758.
[201] *Ibid., Russie, Mémoires et documents,* Vol. IX.
[202] *Ibid.,* Vol. XXXI.

des Tartares. Appelez-les à Pétersbourg ou à Moscou, changez leur état, montrez-leur les objets du luxe, habillez-les, en vingt-quatre heures ils ne vous offrent plus rien de leur première allure... L'amitié, la vertu, les mœurs, la probité sont ici des mots vides de sens.[203]

Nothing, he observed, can be expected from education, as everything in Russia is cant and show. As to the Empress herself, Cabres has nothing to say except that while praising French art, culture, and philosophy, she at the same time bitterly hates the French, *notre cabinet* and *notre monarchie*.[204]

This very black picture of the Russian government and people is shared by the majority of the French diplomats of the second half of the century and likewise by many occasional travelers in Russia. Such an attitude seems indeed to have been characteristic of most Frenchmen who came to Russia uninvited by the court. In part, it is no doubt due to the hostility between the two governments; in part also to the inherent difficulty which prevented the eighteenth-century Frenchmen from viewing impartially the *mœurs barbares* and general backwardness of the country. Moreover, the French diplomats came to Russia with preconceived notions of the Russian government and people and were unwilling or unable to change their point of view. Corberon and Ségur seem to be the only two exceptions in this group.

Burée de Corberon spent five years, from 1775 to 1780, in Russia.[205] He came first as secretary to the envoy Marquis de Juigné. From 1779 to 1780 he was chargé d'affaires. Corberon spent a great deal of his time in Russia studying the court, the government, the commerce, and the people. His observations on Russia are recorded in a journal which begins

[203] Ministère des Affaires Etrangères, *Russie, Mémoires et documents*, Vol. V.
[204] *Ibid.* Fragments of Sabatier de Cabres's correspondence were published in *La Cour de Russie il y a cent ans*, and in a memoir, *Catherine II, sa cour et la Russie en 1772*, Berlin, 1869.
[205] For a biographical sketch of Corberon see Introduction by L. Labande to *Un Diplomate français à la cour de Catherine II*, Paris, 1901, Introduction, p. xix.

January 1, 1775, and continues until October 12, 1778.[206] His judgments, at first, are severe and unsympathetic. Upon his return to France, however, he seems to have repudiated to a large extent his early and severe impressions and to have changed to more favorable ones. *Ces Russes*, he wrote in 1781, *qu'on traite trop de barbares à Paris, ont meilleurs choses que nous, à soixante-dix ans qu'ils ont, lorsque nous en avons douze cents.*[207]

At first Corberon was shocked by the insufficiency of culture and the superficiality of manners in Russian society, which aped everything French without discrimination.

Au lieu de notre urbanité ils ont adopté nos grimaces et pris la licence et les sottises pour l'aisance et le ton plaisant de la société.[208]

Regarding the endless intrigues at court, its empty ceremonial and pomp, he observes:

Je ne connais pas de nation plus singe que celle-ci, et de plus grands courtisans qu'à la cour de Russie... [209] [and again] la politesse russe ne consiste qu'en révérences, compliments d'usages, repas, etc...[210]

The court bored him, though he found a congenial circle of friends among a few Russians.[211] He seemed particularly annoyed at certain Oriental usages at the court, such as kissing the Empress' hand on one's knees.[212]

Tu n'imagines [he wrote to his brother towards the end of his stay in Russia] combien la société russe est difficile: du froid et de la politesse, mais voilà tout, et si on se livre à elle, vous êtes déchiré.[213]

---

[206] On Corberon's diplomatic mission and his journal see P. Oursel, *La Diplomatie de la France*, 1921, ch. viii, especially pp. 280-281.

[207] Chevalier de Corberon, *Un Diplomate français à la cour de Catherine II*, Paris, 1901, Introduction, p. xix.

[208] *Ibid.*

[209] *Ibid.*, "Journal," February 27, 1776.

[210] *Ibid.*, March 21, 1776.

[211] *Ibid.*, November 25, 1776.

[212] *Ibid.*, March 12, 1779.

[213] *Ibid.*, August 19, 1780.

At the same time Corberon praised the *esprit* and *sensibilité* of the Russian aristocracy, as well as their graciousness and simplicity. *C'est un talent que les Russes possèdent singulièrement, et c'est la nation qui nous imite davantage pour les manières.*[214]

Analyzing the Russian character in general, Corberon emphasized especially the instability, malice, and the pride which *laisse voir l'empreinte de l'esclavage qui partout et dans tout le suit et le décède...*[215] Yet, and this seems a new note, Corberon realized the complexity of the Russian character and the difficulty of analyzing it:

Plus j'étudie cette nation, plus je la trouve difficile à définir. C'est un composé d'êtres si peu assortis les uns aux autres, entre lesquels on ne trouve point la gradation des nuances, et où vous ne pouvez saisir le progrès et la marche de leurs idées, de leurs principes, de leurs systèmes![216]

Following Rousseau, Corberon believed that the sudden civilization introduced into Russia had corrupted the masses of the people.

Enclins à tous les vices qu'amène le luxe, corrompus sans avoir passé par les différentes gradations de la maturité, ils ressemblent à des fruits verts et pourris, qui n'ont ni sève ni douceur et qui ne pourront jamais parvenir à la perfection.[217]

Like Rousseau also, Corberon was pessimistic regarding the future of Russia. The introduction of Western culture into Russia was contrary, he believed, to the fundamental nature of the people. The only remedy for Russia, in his opinion, was to safeguard the present generation, which was already corrupted, from the coming one, in order to preserve the latter from *la gangrène qui le ronge maintenant*. When this

[214] *Ibid.*, September 3, 1775.
[215] *Ibid.*, September 27, 1780.
[216] *Ibid.*, May 12, 1776.
[217] *Ibid.*, December 19, 1776.

had been accomplished and the nation had returned to its "original simplicity," several enlightened monarchs could gradually lift Russia to perfection, but only *avec le temps et sans crise, sans mouvements forcés et contre nature.*[218]

Catherine II, he found, was a great monarch but she had weaknesses; chief among them was her desire to rule over Europe rather than over her own country.[219] He was skeptical of Diderot's and Voltaire's enthusiasm for the Empress because the first *sait bien ce qu'il fait; il a une édition de l'encyclopédie à soutenir, et les coffres de sa Majesté Impériale lui serviront;*[220] the second is nothing but *un journaliste à la solde de Catherine II.*[221] On the other hand, he considered Rulhière's work on the coup d'état of 1762 inadequate; *c'est un ouvrage dans lequel beaucoup de gens admirent plus l'imagination que le savoir et la politique.*[222]

These, then, are Corberon's conclusions in his study of the Russian character, manners, and government. They are not original; like Rulhière's they represent a point of view strongly reminiscent of Rousseau. Although Corberon later became less severe to Russia and more optimistic as to her future, his *Journal* is of special interest because his observations were drawn from the author's immediate contacts with Russian society.

In spirit and conclusions Ségur's memoirs on Russia are quite different from the *Journal* of Corberon. The similarity between the two men lies only in the fact that they were both diplomats of the *ancien régime* and both tried to study and observe Russia at approximately the same time.

Louis-Philippe, Comte de Ségur (1753-1830), minister

[218] Chevalier de Corberon, *Un Diplomate français* ... "Journal," December 19, 1776.
[219] *Ibid.*
[220] *Ibid.*, June 9, 1776.
[221] *Ibid.*, October 30, 1776.
[222] *Ibid.*, August 1, 1775.

plenipotentiary to Russia from 1785 to 1789, was by birth, training, and temperament a brilliant example of the eighteenth-century statesman, diplomat, and man of letters. He was handsome, elegant, and witty, and his life was an extraordinary succession of the most varied activities. Godefroy says of him:

Le hasard ayant voulu qu'il fût successivement colonel, officier, général, voyageur, navigateur, courtisan, fils de ministre, ambassadeur, soldat, électeur, poète, auteur dramatique, collaborateur de journaux, publiciste, historien, député, counseiller d'Etat, sénateur, académicien, et pair de France.[223]

Upon his arrival in Russia, Ségur at once favorably impressed the court and Catherine II. With the latter he formed a friendship which lasted to the end of his sojourn in Russia. It was due to his adroit diplomacy that a friendly treaty was signed between Russia and France in 1787.

Most of Ségur's works relating to Russia were published during the last decade of the century. His *Pensées politiques* appeared in 1795. In 1798 he edited the *Théâtre de l'Ermitage,* a collection of plays written by himself, Catherine II, and a few other intimates of the court. The first collected edition of his works appeared in thirty-three volumes in 1824. The account of his stay in Russia is found in the *Mémoires, souvenirs et anecdotes* in this collected edition of his works.[224]

Unlike Corberon, Ségur seems to have enjoyed the social life of the court. For him it had all the *douceurs* of Versailles. He found the Russians kindly and hospitable: *La Russie a d'ailleurs un droit réel à la bienveillance des étrangers: nulle part ils ne trouvent une plus courtoise hospitalité.*[225] He felt,

---

[223] F. Godefroy, *XVIIIᵉ siècle: Prosateurs,* 1879, p. 225.

[224] Michaud, *Biographie universelle,* 1847, LXXXII, 58-59. The entire Ségur family was devoted to Russia. The Count's son, Philip de Ségur, was taken prisoner in Russia in 1807. He left memoirs of his Russian experiences. A nephew of the old Count married a Russian, the daughter of the Count Rostopchin. Cf. A. Rambaud, *Instructions . . . Russie,* II, 385 ff.

[225] L. P. de Ségur, *Mémoires, souvenirs et anecdotes,* Barrière, 1879, II 345.

in fact, quite at home in Russia—*En peu de temps les liaisons que je formai avec les hommes d'un vrai mérite et des femmes les plus aimables purent me faire oublier que là j'étais un étranger.*[226] He was especially enthusiastic about the women. *Elles sont bonnes musiciennes, savent plusieurs langues, ont lu ce qui est intéressant en chacune d'elles.*[227] Like Mme Vigée LeBrun, Prince de Ligne, and other foreign visitors to Russia at the end of the century, Ségur repeatedly expressed his admiration for the culture and amiability of the Russian aristocracy. To be sure, he remarked on one occasion that there were still a good many nobles at the court of Catherine II who belonged in spirit and manner to the Middle Ages; nevertheless, he added, some of the greatest families of Russia, like the Saltykov, Ostermann, Dolgorukïï, Bariatinskïï, had already reached a high level of culture and civilization, and *annonçaient déjà à la Russie que sa gloire et sa civilisation ne reculeraient plus.*[228]

So attached to Russia did Ségur become that many years after his return to France he could not think of his stay there without emotion.

Je ne puis penser [he wrote about 1820] aux jours heureux que j'ai passés dans ce pays, qu'avec une émotion qui tient un peu de celle qu'on éprouve quand on est éloigné de sa propre patrie.[229]

Ségur had only unqualified praise and admiration for the Empress. He seemed, in fact, completely enthralled by her charm and drew a brilliant picture of her as a woman of genius, as a great sovereign, and as a matchless wit and companion.[230] Among the many sketches of Russian nobles

[226] L. P. de Ségur, *Mémoires, souvenirs et anecdotes*, Barrière, 1879, II, 345.
[227] L. P. de Ségur, *op. cit.*, Paris, 1824, II, 235.
[228] L. P. de Ségur, *op. cit.*, II, 347.
[229] *Ibid.*, II, 346.
[230] See especially the account of the famous trip to Crimea which Ségur took with the Empress, as one of her unofficial suite; L. P. de Ségur, *Mémoires . . . 1824*, III, 1 ff.

whom Ségur described in his memoirs, that of the famous
Potemkin is the most vivid. It is a masterpiece of subtle analysis. The characteristic which he stressed most in the great
favorite of the Empress and which he also emphasized to
some extent in portraying other Russian nobles was the combination of most contradictory qualities, both European and
Asiatic.[231]

It is doubtful if Ségur was ever interested in observing the
life of the common people. He dismissed the peasantry as
completely uncivilized, inarticulate, and ignorant of the *bonheur moral* of Western Europeans. Nevertheless, during his
Crimean trip he admired the picturesqueness and simplicity
of rustic life and manners. He was, in fact, one of the first
Frenchmen to observe the picturesque contrasts of Oriental-
ism and Western civilization in Russian architecture, religious
art, and the national costumes of the people.[232]

There is no evidence that Ségur had actually studied Russian history and institutions. He seems, however, to have
had a better grasp of the development of the country than
most of his countrymen. He was one of the few eighteenth-
century Frenchmen who approved of the absolute form of
government and found that even *dans ce pays soumis à un
pouvoir absolu on jouissait cependant d'une liberté refusée à
beaucoup de nations libres.*[233]

The Russian clergy he considered superstitious and ignorant but a necessary evil for the Russia of that time. On the
whole, it would appear, Ségur had a rather optimistic view
of the future progress of Russia.

So far we have examined two kinds of Frenchmen who
came to Russia in the second half of the century—those who
came upon direct invitation of the Empress and her ministers

---

[231] L. de Ségur, *Mémoires* ... II, 348-350.
[232] *Ibid.*, 1824, II, 230-231, and III, *passim.*
[233] *Ibid.*, II, 368; cf. also ed. of 1824, II, 196-218.

(Diderot, Falconet, Levesque, and others), and those who came as official representatives of the French government (D'Eon, La Messelière, Corberon, et al.). The next group to be considered represents unofficial France—isolated travelers who either went out of curiosity or were sent on unofficial missions. Their opinions on Russia, uninfluenced either by the French government or by the Russian court, may thus represent a more unbiased attitude towards Russia, though perhaps a more superficial one, as their stay in Russia was usually short. The number of these visitors must have been very large, especially in the seventies and eighties, but only a few of those who left memoirs of their sojourns will be treated here.

The earliest representative of this group was Abbé Chappe d'Auteroche (1722-1769), an astronomer, sent to Siberia in 1761 to observe the passage of the planet Venus.[234] He reached St. Petersburg in November, 1761, and left Russia in the spring of 1762.[235] While in St. Petersburg he was apparently well liked by Empress Elizabeth, for he received from her a gift of one thousand roubles.[236] Upon his return to France he added to the scientific account of his trip many observations on the soil, people, and government of Russia. His *Voyage en Sibérie* appeared in 1768.[237] Its publication provoked a lively controversy, and for a time fixed general attention upon Russia. Chappe's book was first attacked in the famous *Antidote ou examen d'un mauvais livre, superbement imprimé* ... published anonymously in 1770, and purporting to be written by Catherine herself.[238] The author of the

[234] On Abbé Chappe see M. Tourneux, *Diderot et Catherine*, pp. 21-24, and L. Pingaud, *Les Français en Russie*, p. 60.

[235] Chappe d'Auteroche, *Voyage en Sibérie*, Amsterdam, 1769, II, 550.

[236] M. Tourneux, *Diderot et Catherine*, p. 21.

[237] The original edition of the *Voyage* appeared in Paris, de Bure, 1768, 3 vols., in 4º.

[238] The *Antidote* had two editions: the first edition, 1770, was in two parts, 15 and 232 pages, respectively, in 8º. A third part was promised, but never appeared; the second edition appeared in Amsterdam in 1771, also in two parts

Antidote called the *Voyage* a calumniation of Russia and the Russian government and accused its author of hasty judgments, of ignorance of the Russian language and customs, and of a willful intention to misinterpret and vilify Russia. Another anonymous refutation, shorter than the *Antidote* but not less violent, appeared in 1771 under the title of *La Lettre d'un scythe franc et loyal à M. Rousseau de Bouillon, auteur du Journal encyclopédique,* and caused, like the *Antidote,* considerable discussion in the French literary and social circles which were interested in Russia.[239]

In the preface to the second edition of the *Voyage en Sibérie* Abbé Chappe states that before the beginning of the eighteenth century Russia was completely uncivilized and unknown to Europe.

On savait à peine qu'il existait dans ces climats glacés un peuple ignorant et grossier.[240]

At the time of his writing the book, however, the picture had changed:

L'influence actuelle de la Russie dans le système politique de l'Europe montre assez les avantages qu'on peut tirer de la connaissance de ce peuple et du pays qu'il habite.[241]

He then gives a short sketch of the history of Russia, using Voltaire as a source.[242] He dwells at length on the coarseness and ignorance of the people and the debauches of the clergy, and repeatedly denounces the total absence of political liberty.[243] Of Catherine he has a flattering opinion: *Elle porte l'encouragement dans les sciences, dans les arts, dans*

---

and under the same title. Both editions are very rare now. Cf. M. Tourneux, *Diderot et Catherine,* pp. 22-23, note. An abstract and review of the *Antidote* appeared in the *Journal encyclopédique* for December, 1771.

[239] M. Tourneux, *op. cit.,* p. 23 n.

[240] Chappe d'Auteroche, *Voyage en Sibérie,* Preface, p. ii.

[241] Chappe d'Auteroche, *Voyage en Sibérie,* p. ii.

[242] *Ibid.,* I, 177 ff.

[243] *Ibid.,* see especially I, 204-233, 261, and 315.

toutes les parties de l'administration.[244] Regarding the Russian people in general, Chappe agrees with Montesquieu that *il faut écorcher un Russe pour lui trouver du sentiment.*[245] The Russians are, moreover, gay and sociable, but lack imagination, having instead a real talent for imitation.[246] Progress, he finds, is possible in Russia, but there are many obstacles in the way —the climate, serfdom, national pride, and a despotism which *détruit l'esprit, le talent, et toute espèce de sentiment.*[247] He has some hopes, however, for the future of Russia, based chiefly upon the enlightenment of Catherine II.[248]

Chappe saw very little of Russia. As Pingaud remarks, he simply recorded with naïveté what came into his head while he rode in a sleigh across Siberia.[249] His book, *Voyage en Sibérie*, was widely read in France, however, partly because of the controversy it started, partly because of its popular character. It served as a source for many other superficial accounts of Russia and was severely criticized by LeClerc and Levesque.

In 1775 a certain Lescallier, an under-secretary of the navy, came to Russia partly to investigate the state of the Russian navy, partly to satisfy his own curiosity about the country, and especially its court *que l'on faisait sonner si haut en Europe.*[250] In the introduction to his book he warns the reader not to expect the usual opinions about Russia; his account, he claims, will be quite different from those of his predecessors.[251]

Lescallier's description of Russian cities, of which he had

[244] Chappe d'Auteroche, *Voyage en Sibérie*, I, 197; also I, 196.
[245] *Ibid.*, II, 356.
[246] *Ibid.*, II, 357, 358.
[247] *Ibid.*, II, 359-361.
[248] *Ibid.*, II, 363-364.
[249] L. Pingaud, *Les Français en Russie* . . . p. 60.
[250] Daniel Lescallier, *Voyage en Angleterre, en Russie et en Suède* . . . Paris, Firman Didot, 1800, Introduction, p. iii.
[251] *Ibid.*, Introduction, p. vii.

visited a great many (Moscow and Novgorod among others) is very dry and matter of fact. They are very much like other European cities, he believes, only a little more primitive and dirty. In Moscow he is struck by the number of churches and compares the great bell in the Kremlin to that of Georges d'Amboise, observing that both are records of an age of barbarism.[252] He seems to have been disappointed in the court. Its splendors are *faux brillant,* he finds, for everything is purely imitative and its fame is vastly exaggerated.

Je compare ce pays [he adds], à une perspective peinte grossièrement, qui perd tout son effet lorsqu'on la voit de près, et qui ne fait illusion que de bien loin.[253]

His praise of Catherine is quite reserved:

La czarina a un extérieur agréable, doux et honnête, et c'est peut-être un de ses talents de savoir mitiguer l'expression de ses traits.[254]

The state of culture in Russia is, Lescallier finds, very low. *Cette nation paraît avoir peu d'aptitude à la perfection des arts.*[255] This, he believes, is partly due to Peter the Great's desire to effect too many things in too short a time. *Il semble,* he adds, *qu'on ait pris une mauvaise route pour leur civilisation.*[256]

Lescallier was one of the first Frenchmen to be interested in the Russian language.

Cette langue est peut-être un peu, comme celles des peuples sauvages, pauvre d'expression, et incapable de rendre ces nuances de sentiment et de goût qui ne sont connues que des peuples policés.[257] [Yet] Cette langue paraît susceptible de grandes beautés; [in many years to come] elle pourra devenir belle et intéressante.[258]

[252] *Ibid.,* p. 83.
[253] Daniel Lescallier, *Voyage ... en Russie ...* p. 88.
[254] *Ibid.*
[255] *Ibid.,* p. 91.
[256] *Ibid.*
[257] *Ibid.,* p. 92.
[258] *Ibid.,* pp. 92-93.

The Russian language, he thinks, is not difficult for a Frenchman to learn; he himself in a month learned enough to be understood.[259]

The government of Russia, according to Lescallier, is a red-tape bureaucracy, which governs a nation composed of two classes: *les nobles et leurs esclaves*.[260] Both classes show vestiges of barbarism and have no fixed idea of honor.[261]

This is the substance of Lescallier's observations. Except for his remarks on the language, there is nothing new or original in them. They represent, in fact, an average French bourgeois point of view.

In the same group of visitors may be mentioned Prince Charles-Joseph de Ligne (1735-1814). Of Belgian extraction, in the service of Austria, Parisian in spirit, and Russian by predilection, the Prince was a perfect example of an eighteenth-century *grand-seigneur cosmopolite*. His reputation rests chiefly on his brilliant conversational powers (like that of Chamfort and Rivarol) and upon his thirty volumes of *Mélanges*.[262]

The Prince de Ligne's motive for taking his first trip to Russia was not altogether a disinterested one. He came in August, 1780, with the object of recovering from the Russian court 400,000 roubles due to the family of his daughter-in-law, Mme Mosal'skaĭa.[263] He never recovered the money, but this did not prevent him from becoming an intimate friend of the Empress and of a great number of Russians. Before his departure for Vienna in 1780 he received the hon-

---

[259] Daniel Lescallier, *Voyage ... en Russie ...* p. 93.

[260] *Ibid.*, p. 90.

[261] *Ibid.*, p. 95.

[262] The first collected editions of his works appeared in Vienna and Dresden in 1807, 30 vols., in 12°.

[263] Marthe Oulié, *Le Cosmopolitisme du prince de Ligne*, Paris, 1926, p. 121. For a very complete account of De Ligne's relations with the Russian court, see V. Bil'basov, *Russkaĭa starina*, LXXIII and LXXXIV.

orary rank of colonel in the Russian Guards and endeared himself to the entire court. He began a regular correspondence with the Empress which continued until her death in 1796. In 1787 he came again to Russia, this time to accompany the Empress on her journey to the southern provinces of the country. During this four-month trip the Prince was a constant companion of Catherine's, a sort of *extra* or *jockey diplomatique* as he called himself in his memoirs. He had a keen sense of the picturesque, and it is from this point of view that the Russian countryside appealed to him most. *Les civilisations moins civilisées conservent mieux leur caractère pittoresque,*[264] and in Russia he admires *tout ce qui peut paraître piquant par le changement des mœurs, des usages, de l'esprit.*[265] De Ligne's memoirs are full of enthusiastic descriptions of Kiev, Moscow, Crimea, and especially the Azov Sea, where at one time he considered settling down and growing a vineyard.[266] But it was not only the picturesque aspect of the country that attracted De Ligne to Russia; it was his genuine fondness for the Russian people. *Le Prince,* says General Löwenstern, *aimait beaucoup les Russes, et l'hôtel De Ligne leur était toujours ouvert.*[267]

In 1790 De Ligne entered the Russian service and took part in Suvorov's campaigns in Bessarabia together with Langeron, Richelieu, Damas, and other French émigrés.[268]

During De Ligne's two trips to Russia in 1780 and 1786 the Empress herself was for him the principal attraction. He had a boundless admiration for her, and he was responsible, perhaps more than any other foreigner, for the spreading of her fame over Europe. In his letters to the Marquise de Coigny,

---

[264] M. Oulié, *op. cit.,* p. 131.
[265] *Ibid.,* p. 103.
[266] *Ibid.,* pp. 102, 131.
[267] General Löwenstern, *Mémoires,* Paris, 1903, I, 95.
[268] L. Perry, *Une grande dame au dix-huitième siècle,* Paris, 1887, pp. 390 ff.

De Ligne's feelings for *Catherine-le-Grand*, as he called her, found almost lyrical expression.[269] In 1780, when presented to her for the first time, De Ligne was struck by the expressiveness of her face and wrote: *On y lisait comme dans un livre: génie, justice, justesse, courage, profondeur, égalité, douceur, calme, et fermeté.*[270] He found the Empress *populaire et généreuse* like Henri IV and *fière, tendre et victorieuse* like Louis XIV, combining the great and the weak characteristics of the two monarchs.[271] In his memoirs De Ligne frequently compares Catherine with Louis XIV and considers her superior to the French monarch in learning, in common sense, and in practical level-headedness. *Tout était chez elle,* he wrote, *mesuré et méthodique...*[272]

De Ligne's attitude toward Russia comes nearest to that of the ambassador Ségur, with whom he had a good deal in common, in temperament, background, and worldly position. Both maintained throughout their long and varied careers a lifelong interest in Russia and were equally instrumental in arousing European interest in Russia and in the Empress.

Two other French visitors to Russia at the end of the century deserve to be treated in this group: Fortia de Piles and Abbé Georgel.

The first of these, Comte Fortia de Piles (1758-1826), author of a great variety of miscellaneous writings, was an officer in the French army until 1790, when he left France and started on a long tour of Northern Europe, including Russia, accompanied by his friend, Chevalier de Boisgelin.[273]

---

[269] H. Lebasteur, *Lettres du prince de Ligne à la marquise de Coigny*, Paris, 1914; see especially introduction, pp. v ff.

[270] Princess Charles de Ligne, *Les Lettres de Catherine II au prince de Ligne,* Paris, 1924, p. 18.

[271] *Ibid.,* p. 30.

[272] C. J. de Ligne, *Mémoires et mélanges,* Paris, 1827, II, 316; see also Vol. II, pp. 163 ff., and Vol. III, *passim.*

[273] For a short biographical sketch of A. Fortia de Piles see Michaud, *Biographie universelle,* LXIV, 276-278.

An account of their trip appeared in 1796.[274] Two out of five volumes of this work were devoted to Russia. In the Preface De Piles states that his aim in the *Voyages* is a practical account for travelers. The work is, in fact, a sort of Baedeker, full of charts, itineraries and prices. In the introduction to Volume III of the *Voyages* De Piles gives a critical bibliography of earlier works on Russia. He finds, with the exception of Levesque's history of Russia, which he praises moderately, that most of his predecessors are either superficial or partial, or both. On the other hand he praises highly the works on Russia by foreigners like Gmelin, Strahlenberg, and Manstein. These authors are his principal sources for geographic and historic topics.

De Piles keeps his promise to give a practical account of Russia for travelers and not for general readers. In Volume III he provides a thorough account of the state of manufacturing, of commerce, and of the private collections of Russian nobles. He also gives precise descriptions of St. Petersburg and Moscow, including statistics concerning population, and so forth. He seems totally unimpressed by the picturesque aspect of these cities.

He finds the state of education in Russia at a very low level. The clergy, who are responsible for this condition, are as a class immoral, ignorant, and altogether incapable of educating the young.[275] The general backwardness of the country he ascribes, like other authors, to certain national characteristics—pride, indolence, and in the case of the peasantry, laziness, avidity, and dishonesty.[276] For the Empress he has

---

[274] A. Fortia de Piles, *Voyage de deux Français en Allemagne, Danemarck, Suède, Russie, et Pologne, en 1790-1792*, 5 vols., Paris, Desenne, 1796. F. de Piles' other works on Russia are *Examen de trois ouvrages sur la Russie* (Chantreau, Rulhière and Masson), 1802, and *Quelques mots à M Masson, auteur des mémoires secrets sur la Russie*, 1803.

[275] A. de Piles, *Voyage de deux Français* ... IV, 72-75.

[276] *Ibid.*, IV, 76, 79, 81, and 326.

nothing but praise, believing that her enlightened genius will lead the country out of the darkness.[277]

In his judgments of Russia, which are often severe, De Piles seems, on the whole, to be impartial and to weigh carefully the evidence on both sides. He found and rectified many errors in previous accounts of Russia and urged repeatedly a more objective and impersonal method of studying the country. In this sober, conscientious, and matter-of-fact attitude lies the chief value of De Piles's *Voyages*.

The last of the unofficial visitors to Russia to be treated here is Jean-François Georgel (1731-1813), Jesuit, Bishop of Strassburg, Grand Almoner of the Prince Louis de Rohan, chargé d'affaires in Vienna, and so forth. He executed, in the course of his life, a number of important ecclesiastical and political missions.[278]

After the Revolution Georgel went to live in Switzerland and in 1799 was sent to Russia as one of the delegates of a German chapter of the Maltese Order to offer to Emperor Paul I the Grand Mastership of the Order. On his return from Russia he wrote his memoirs, devoting one volume to his trip to Russia.[279]

Georgel spent six months in St. Petersburg. He met the Emperor Paul and all the dignitaries of the court, where he seems to have spent most of his time. The trip apparently left a very vivid impression on his mind. He is struck by the beauty and the picturesque character of St. Petersburg, and gives a detailed account of the city.[280] In this respect he shares the feelings of De Ligne, Ségur, Mme Vigée LeBrun, and many émigrés at the end of the century who admired certain aspects of Russia from an aesthetic point of view.

---

277 A. de Piles, *Voyage de deux Français* ... IV, 190 ff.
278 For a biographical sketch of Abbé de Georgel see his *Mémoires*, 6 vols., Paris, 1818, Vol. I, Introduction, pp. i-xxx.
279 *Ibid.*, VI, *Voyage à Pétersbourg.*
280 *Ibid.*, VI, 238.

The Abbé had a keen and inquisitive mind and observed everything with which he came in contact. He visited Russian churches and monasteries and was impressed by the solemnity and beauty of the religious services.[281] At the same time his attitude toward the Greek Orthodox clergy is the conventional, mocking eighteenth-century attitude. He finds it, as a body, ignorant, immoral, and superstitious. The religion itself is mere form and superstition,—

Jeûner, réciter des litanies, se courber devant les images, faire des signes de croix, voilà toute la religion du Russe.[282]

As to the common people, they are, like their clergy, corrupt and immoral,—

D'après ce que j'ai vu à Saint-Petersbourg on peut dire que l'ivrognerie, le vol, et le libertinage sont des vices nationaux.[283]

Georgel's verdict on the Russian people is again in conformity with the view prevalent among French visitors to Russia. He epitomizes one definite eighteenth-century conception of Russia in the following lines:

Comment trouver des mœurs dans un peuple privé d'instruction et de lois répressives des vices du cœur et de l'âme? La religion russe n'étant qu'un tissu de momeries extérieurs, qui laisse un libre essor aux passions les plus dépravés, il ne doit pas être étonnant que la moralité soit si peu respectée.[284]

Again, like so many other eighteenth-century Frenchmen, Georgel stressed one outstanding virtue of the Russian character—hospitality, a virtue which partakes more of Asia than of Europe.[285] In describing the Russian government Georgel emphasized its un-European character. The absolute autocracy of Russia, he found, is purely Asiatic, and the Tsar is more

[281] Abbé de Georgel, *Mémoires*, VI, 262.
[282] *Ibid.*
[283] *Ibid.*, VI, 270.
[284] *Ibid.*
[285] *Ibid.*, VI, 271.

comparable with an Oriental despot than a European monarch.[286] Emperor Paul, he believed, exemplified this. Nevertheless, he praised in him as well as in some of the Russian nobles certain positive qualities, especially amiability, graciousness, culture—all results of the civilizing influence of France.[287]

The last group to be examined here is that of the émigrés. Haumant, in his *La Culture française en Russie*, considers the period 1789-1815 as one during which France exercised through the émigrés its greatest cultural influence on Russia.[288] It would likewise appear that through the same medium France had acquired a better knowledge and understanding of Russia. Many representatives of this group remained for years in Russia, lived on Russian country estates, married into Russian families, and served in the Russian army. Some of them later returned to France and, through personal contacts and memoirs, became important sources of information concerning Russia. An examination of the rôle of these émigrés as centers and purveyors of russophile interests in France, however, is outside the scope of the present study. Their influence becomes apparent only after the Napoleonic wars and is connected more with the Romantic movement than with the eighteenth century proper. At present a general sketch of the émigré group with a few examples of the more typical representatives will suffice.[289]

In general, the Frenchmen who settled in Russia after 1789 were obliged either to enter the Russian army, to become

[286] Abbé de Georgel, *Mémoires*, VI, 271.

[287] *Ibid.*, VI, p. 361.

[288] E. Haumant, *La Culture française en Russie*, ch. iii, "L'Apogée des influences françaises (1789-1815)."

[289] For a detailed study of the destinies of the French émigrés in Russia see E. Daudet's *Histoire de l'émigration*. For a more general survey see E. Haumant, *La Culture française en Russie*, pp. 189-191; L. Pingaud, *Les Français en Russie* . . . pp. 179 ff.; and F. Baldensperger, *Le Movement des idées dans l'émigration française*.

tutors and teachers, or, if fortunate, to remain at the court. A few, like the Polignacs, settled on Russian estates, which were in some cases offered to them by their Russian owners.[290] Except for Richelieu, Langeron, Damas, and a few others who distinguished themselves in the Russian army, few of the émigrés rose above obscurity. The chief reason for this was, no doubt, the inherent incapacity of the old-régime aristocracy to adapt itself to entirely new conditions of life. Most of these aristocrats were courtiers by profession and training, and in Russia this sphere of activity was already overcrowded. Another difficulty was, of course, the language. Few of the émigrés made any efforts to learn it. Langeron, for example, after spending thirty years in Russia, could say only a few words in Russian to his dogs. Others achieved a certain knowledge of the language but mutilated it, and their accent was frequently ridiculed by contemporary Russian writers.[291]

One of the most distinguished, certainly the most constructive, of the émigrés was Duc Emmanuel du Plesis Richelieu (1766-1821).[292] A direct descendant of the cardinal, Emmanuel received the best of educations, traveled extensively, and held several official posts at the court of Louis XVI. About 1790 he made the acquaintance of the Prince de Ligne in Vienna, and with him entered the Russian army and took part in the campaigns against the Turks. He rendered distinguished service and was decorated by the Empress for his bravery during the capture of the fortress Ismaïl. In 1792 he joined the suite of the Prince de Nassau and Comte d'Artois. He was to be appointed governor of the colony of royalists to be founded on the shores of the Azov Sea, but the plan failed, and Richelieu re-entered the Russian army with the

[290] E. Haumant, *op. cit.*, p. 188.
[291] E. Haumant, *La Culture française en Russie*, p. 189.
[292] For biographical data on Richelieu cf. L. Pingaud, "Le Duc de Richelieu en Russie," *Le Correspondant*, May and June, 1882,

rank of colonel. In 1799, losing the favor of Emperor Paul I, he was demoted and deprived of his regiment. With the death of this emperor Richelieu's fortunes changed for the better, and it was then that he began his important administrative and educational work in Russia.[293] In 1803 he was appointed governor of Odessa by the Emperor Alexander I and held this post until the restoration of Louis XVIII, returning to France in 1814. He seems to have maintained an active interest in Russia and Russian affairs until his death in 1821.

Richelieu's *Journal*, dealing chiefly with his campaigns against the Turks, was published by the Russian Historical Society in 1866.[294] In this *Journal* Richelieu gives a vivid picture of military life in Russia, praises the Russian soldier, and arraigns Russian officials for their negligence and mismanagement of the army.[295] There are in the journal no other general observations of importance. Like many of his fellow-countrymen in Russia at the end of the century Richelieu seems to have been attracted by the scenery and landscapes of Southern Russia, and he showed an unmistakable feeling for the picturesque aspects of Russian life and art.

Like Richelieu, his friend Comte Andrault de Langeron (1763-1831) rendered distinguished service in the Russian army. He fought against the Swedes, the Turks, and the Revolutionary French.[296] He commanded Russian regiments at Austerlitz, Berezina, and Leipzig, and in 1814, at the head of his regiment, was the first to enter Montmartre. He remained in the Russian service until his death in 1831. His

---

[293] Stempovski, "Notice sur les travaux administratifs de M. le duc de Richelieu dans la Russie méridionale," *Journal asiatique*, 1882.

[294] *Sbornik*, LIV, papers and documents regarding the life and activity of the Duc de Richelieu, edited by A. Polovtsev.

[295] *Ibid.*, cf. especially, pp. 111-198.

[296] On Langeron see Mme Vigée LeBrun, *Souvenirs*, ch. xi; and Countess Golovin, *Memoirs*, London, 1910, p. 16.

memoirs, dealing chiefly with the Napoleonic campaigns, are found in the archives of the French Ministry of Foreign Affairs. They were edited and published by the Société d'Histoire Contemporaine in 1902.

Two other émigrés who served in the Russian army and who, like those just mentioned, left records of their Russian experiences, should be mentioned here—Comte Roger de Damas and Baron Ange de Damas.[297] The family of the Comte François-Emmanuel de Saint-Priest (1735-1821) was perhaps even more typically russophile than the preceding émigrés.[298] The old Comte François had semiofficial relations with the court of Catherine II long before and after the Revolution. He had three sons who were all closely connected with Russia. The eldest, Emmanuel (1776-1814), was colonel in the army, fought against Napoleon, and died on the battlefield. The second son, Armand (1782-1863), married a Russian, was governor of a province in Podolia, and after the restoration returned to France. The third son of the old Comte, Vicomte Louis-Antoine (1789-1881), also fought in the Russian army and had, after the restoration, a long and successful diplomatic career in France. The father, Comte François, left memoirs of his life as a diplomat and was author of an opera and a few plays, some of which were translated into Russian.[299]

Among the émigrés who were closely connected with the Russian court the philosopher Sénac de Meilhan and the painter Mme Vigée LeBrun have been treated elsewhere. The majority of this group, however, were composed of old

[297] *Mémoires du comte Roger de Damas*, published by Jacques Rambaud, Introduction by Léonce Pingaud, 2 vols., Paris, Plon, 1912; also *Mémoires du baron de Damas* (1785-1862), published by his grandson, Comte de Damas, 2 vols., Paris, Plon-Nourrit, 1922. These memoirs give a vivid picture of the life of some of the most prominent émigrés in Russia at the end of the century. Cf. especially I, ch. i (1785-1800), and ch. ii (1800-1801), of the last-mentioned work.

[298] Cf. Michaud, *Biographie universelle*, XL, 68-88, 88-89.

[299] *Ibid.*

courtiers of Versailles now transported to St. Petersburg. Contemporary memoirs give an adequate picture of the better known among them—Choiseul-Gouffier, Chevalier d'Augard, the Marquis de Bombelles, the Princesse Tarente, and Comte Esterházy.[300] The latter is perhaps the most typical representative of this group and one of special interest because of his writings on Russia.

Comte Valentin Ladislas Esterházy de Galántha (1740-1805), member of an ancient and illustrious Hungarian family, was born and educated in France.[301] As a close friend of Marie Antoinette and the royal princes he was sent to Russia in 1791 to represent them.[302] In a short time he became a favorite of the Empress, who showered favors on him in the form of money and land, refusing, however, to start a war against revolutionary France. The count was very successful at court and in St. Petersburg society, where he seems to have been completely at home. *Au fond*, says Comte Fleury, *Esterhazy était de la race de ces grands seigneurs cosmopolites qui à l'école du prince de Ligne, se créaient une patrie là où on les traitait bien.*[303] Some contemporary émigrés like Mme Vigée LeBrun were less charitable to him, accusing him of perpetual intriguing. Like De Ligne and Ségur, Esterházy took great pleasure in the life of Russian society. In his letters to his wife he gave a vivid picture of the magnificence and gaiety of the court.[304]

In 1791 he wrote a vivid sketch of Russian life under the

---

[300] See *Mémoirs of Countess Golovine* and *Vie de Catherine* by J. Castéra, especially II, 415-424.

[301] On Esterházy see Ernest Daudet's introduction to *Mémoires du comte Valentin Esterhazy*, and C. Larivière, *La France et la Russie au XVIIIe siècle*, ch. iii.

[302] For an account of Esterházy's mission to St. Petersburg, see his own *Mémoires*, published by Ernest Daudet, Paris, 1905, chs. x and xi.

[303] C. Larivière, *op. cit.*, p. 218.

[304] See E. Daudet, *Lettres du comte Valentin Esterhazy*, 1905, Vol. I, *passim*.

title of *La Vie russe en 1791*.[305] In this sketch he expresses the usual eighteenth-century views of Russian character, stressing its imitative nature: *Le Russe est très adroit, peu inventif; il copie avec exactitude, et apprend avec la plus grande facilité les métiers les plus difficiles.*[306] He praises also the hospitality and amiability of the Russian nobility. He seems especially impressed by the contrasts in Russia: great poverty and want side by side with extraordinary luxury; complete ignorance and illiteracy side by side with the height of refinement and culture: *La Russie, ou du moins Saint-Pétersbourg, ressemble quelquefois à une maison meublée dont les murs ne sont pas faits.*[307] His attitude toward the Church is the usual mocking and critical one. Like a few other writers on Russia at the end of the century, Esterházy shows a certain interest in the common people, particularly in the peasantry, and is enthusiastic about the picturesque aspect of the Russian country and of Russian cities.

It is advisable to summarize briefly here the characteristics of each of the social groups treated in this chapter and the general ideas concerning Russia as expressed in memoirs and letters of the various French visitors to Russia.

The group of eminent French philosophers and literary men brought back, as we saw, a very meager supply of ideas and impressions of the country they visited. They were all in close contact with the court and had little opportunity to study and observe the country itself. Diderot, Grimm, and Sénac de Meilhan had been, moreover, friends and admirers of Catherine II, which may account in part for their lack of interest in the country itself. With the exception of Saint-Pierre's unsympathetic observations on Russia, Diderot's theoretical works, and Meilhan's unfinished history of the

[305] *Ibid.*, II, Appendix, pp. 359-391.
[306] *Ibid.*, II, 360. [307] *Ibid.*, II, 364.

country, their sojourns in Russia seem to have left no marked traces in their subsequent works.

The representatives of professional France returned from Russia with more definite intellectual results. Thus we have Mme Vigée LeBrun's memoirs, Desforges' play *Feodor et Lyzinka*, the very informative memoirs of Charles Masson, and the extensive cultural and historical surveys of Russia by LeClerc and Levesque. Many of these professional men learned the Russian language and attempted to study and observe the country they visited.

The official representatives of France were, as a group, unsympathetic with Russia. Nevertheless, we have La Messelière's friendly though superficial account of his trip, and the hostile but more penetrating journal of Corberon. Ségur's memoirs evince a marked sympathy for Russia and a degree of understanding of the people which was unusual.

Most of the accounts of Russia by unofficial, isolated travelers, beginning with Chappe d'Auteroche's *Voyage en Sibérie*, seem hasty, superficial, and on the whole unfavorable to Russia and the Russian people. An exception to this group of travelers, however, is the Belgian Prince de Ligne, who maintained throughout his life an active interest in Russia and a deep admiration for Catherine II.

The émigrés seem to have achieved, after their prolonged sojourn in Russia, a more sympathetic and friendly attitude toward the country and the people, an attitude which is prominent in the life and activities of the Duc de Richelieu, or of such families as those of Saint-Priest and Damas. Moreover, the émigrés observed new aspects of Russia which had not been perceived by previous visitors to the country.

There is, however, a marked similarity in the general ideas about Russia expressed by these French visitors during the eighteenth century. In the first place, beginning with Saint-Pierre, every one of them observed with pride and satisfaction the ascendency of French culture and the special capacity of the Russian upper classes to assimilate it.[308] At the same time many deplored the general backwardness of the country, the insufficiency of its culture, and its barbaric, Oriental nature.[309] The national character of the people impressed the majority of the French visitors as imitative, proud, unstable, and indolent, but also hospitable and sociable. The absence of a clear concept of honor, especially among the peasantry, was also frequently emphasized. The Russian clergy was found to be without exception corrupt, superstitious, and ignorant; and the Greek Orthodox religion a mere empty form. Opinion as to the social and political progress of Russia was, however, divided. There were some men who like Diderot, Grimm, Ségur, and De Ligne, considered Russia capable of progress and development. These tended to place their hopes in the enlightenment of Catherine II and, with Voltaire, exaggerated the importance of Peter the Great's rôle as the initiator of western ideas and culture. Others, like Rulhière, Corberon, and Cabres, were pessimistic as to Russia's future. They denied the salutary effect of Peter the Great's reforms on the ground that they were unsuited and unnatural to the people.

Toward the end of the century there was a marked tendency among the French visitors to Russia to search out some new aspect of the country. Lescallier discovered the Russian language, Ségur and De Ligne the Byzantine architecture, Mme Vigée LeBrun the picturesqueness of the peasant, and Georgel the aesthetic side of the Russian church services. This feeling for the picturesque element of the Russian landscape and life runs through almost all the memoirs of the end of the century. At the same time the typically eighteenth-century skeptical and rather hostile attitude towards Russia becomes less and less apparent. With Mme de Staël and Joseph

[308] See especially the memoirs of Abbé Chappe, Masson, Ségur, and Georgel.
[309] See especially Corberon's journal.

de Maîstre it is altogether gone, and a more sympathetic insight into the spirit of the country and its people is at last achieved.[310]

[310] "Jusqu'à mon dernier soupir," wrote Joseph de Maîstre in the conclusion to *Les Soirées de Saint-Pétersbourg,* "je ne cesserai de me rappeler la Russie, et de faire des vœux pour elle. Naturalisé par la bienveillance que j'ai rencontrée au milieu de ses habitants, j'écoute volontiers la reconnaissance lorsqu'elle essaye de me prouver que je suis russe."

IV

THE PRINCIPAL CORRESPONDENTS WITH
THE RUSSIAN COURT

A GENERAL survey of the direct points of contact between French and Russian society of the eighteenth century would not be complete without an examination of the French correspondents with the Russian court. Some of these correspondents, such as Diderot, Grimm, and Falconet, have been treated in the preceding chapter as visitors to Russia. The majority of the eminent representatives of literary and social France never went to Russia, however, and their contacts with that country were confined chiefly to an exchange of letters with the Russian sovereigns and with officials of the Russian court. The present chapter will attempt to show, through the published correspondence, the personal relations between these eminent Frenchmen and their Russian correspondents.

Most of the correspondence to be treated here was published at the end of the nineteenth century in various Russian historical publications [1] and was known to Rambaud, Pingaud, Haumant, and other students of Franco-Russian relations. Some new material bearing on the subject has come to light within recent years. The present chapter, by including all such material, aims to give a complete and up-to-date presentation of the subject.

---

[1] Especially the following: *Russkaia starina* (The Russian Antiquity), 1870-1896. *Russkii arkhiv* (The Russian Archive), 1863-1892. *Sbornik Imperatorskago Rossiiskago Istoricheskago Obshchestva* (The Memoirs of the Imperial Russian Historical Society), 1867-1912. The earliest general survey of the eighteenth-century Franco-Russian correspondents, based partly on the above publications, was an article by A. Rambaud entitled "Catherine II et ses correspondants français," *Revue des deux mondes*, January and February, 1877.

We shall consider first such French correspondents as had personally visited Russia. Chief among these were Diderot, Grimm, Falconet, Meilhan, and De Ligne. As we saw in the preceding chapter, these were all personal friends and admirers of Catherine the Great, although the nature and results of their relations with the Russian Empress were different in each case.

Only a few of Diderot's letters to Catherine II have been preserved.[2] The first, dated February 11, 1774, was full of regrets for leaving Russia and the Empress: *Je m'en retourne comblé des bontés de Votre Majesté et rempli d'admiration pour ses rares qualités.*[3] She was greater than Cæsar and Peter the Great, and Diderot was burning with the desire to exalt her glorious reign. *Toute ma vie je me féliciterai du voyage de Pétersbourg.*[4] The tone of this and other letters was free and informal. There were jokes and badinage. At the same time a deep admiration for the Empress pervaded them all. It was, in fact, more than admiration. As someone has observed, Diderot's style was at times reminiscent more of a lover writing to his beloved, than of a philosopher writing to a great monarch, his patron. *Toute ma vie,* he wrote on leaving Russia, *je serai jaloux de celui qui aura la prétention de parler de vous mieux que moi.*[5] He may, indeed, have had reason to be jealous, for there were many who competed with him. Nevertheless, none of his countrymen had ever written to the Russian Empress with as much ardour and enthusiasm as characterized the letters of Diderot. What Diderot seems to have admired in Catherine, aside from her personal charm and brilliant intelligence, was her legislative genius and the liberality of her reforms.

[2] Seven letters of Diderot to Catherine II were published by J. Grot in the *Sbornik*, XXXIII, 503-532.

[3] *Ibid.*, XXXIII, 504.

[4] *Ibid.*, XXXIII, 507.

[5] Diderot to Catherine II, *Sbornik*, XXXIII, 513.

Lycurgue [he said in one of his letters to her] forma des bêtes féroces... vous travaillez à former des citoyens honnêtes et des défenseurs de la patrie.[6]

He was frequently enthusiastic about Catherine's foreign policy.

Quelle glorieuse paix! [he exclaimed regarding the peace of 1774] Je m'en réjouis comme homme, comme philosophe, et comme Russe, car je le suis devenu par l'ingratitude de mon pays et par vos bontés.[7]

Back in Paris in the fall of 1774, Diderot had to satisfy a general curiosity about the *Sémiramis du Nord*. The philosophers, especially, were eager to find out more about the Empress' reforms and educational work.[8] *Les talents et les vertus de Votre Majesté sont devenus l'entretien de nos soirées. On veut tout savoir.*

Gratitude for the many benefits conferred by the Empress was a frequent theme in Diderot's letters. *Je tenais de Votre Majesté,* he wrote in 1779, after receiving through Grimm a gift of 2,000 roubles, *le bonheur de vivre en repos; et je tiendrai d'elle celui de mourir en paix.*[9] His very genuine devotion and gratitude to the Empress were attested by many of his contemporaries and characterized his correspondence from the beginning to the end.[10]

Grimm's correspondence with Catherine II was longer than that of any other Frenchman. It began in 1774 and continued without interruption until the Empress' death in 1796.[11] Grimm's letters to the Empress were first collected and pub-

[6] *Ibid.,* XXXIII, 514-521.

[7] *Ibid.,* XXXIII, 520.

[8] *Ibid.,* XXXIII, 521-530.

[9] Diderot to Catherine II, *Sbornik,* XXXIII, 531-532.

[10] Such, for example, was D'Escherny's estimate: "Diderot était très reconnaissant des bontés dont l'avait honoré l'impératrice; elle formait le fond de ses récits sur la Russie, de ses observations et d'un grand nombre d'anecdotes intéressantes." Diderot, *Œuvres,* éd. Assézat, Appendix, XX, 137.

[11] E. Scherer, *Melchior Grimm,* Paris, 1888, p. 265.

lished in 1880 by Grot in the *Sbornik* (*Memoirs of the Imperial Russian Historical Society*).[12] The circumstances of this correspondence were as follows: every three months a special messenger would come from St. Petersburg with a package and a letter from the Empress and would take back Grimm's answers. These answers were a sort of diary, full of business transactions, Parisian gossip, reflections, and accounts of all the happenings at the principal European courts. The tone was very familiar, yet never presuming—*Ce ton est celui d'une plaisanterie, disons mieux, d'une cocasserie qui ne se dément pas.*[13] Grimm, says Scherer, *est tout autre que nous ne le connaissions encore, infiniment plus libre, plus déboutonné, plus bavard, plus plaisant, plus souple, plus familier, plus important.*[14] French was mixed with German, the various monarchs were given nicknames, such as "Maman" for Marie-Thérèse, "Hérod" for Frederick the Great, "Falstaff" for Gustave III.

So far as flattery goes, Grimm had a genius for it, and in this respect surpassed even Voltaire. He called this correspondence his *seul bien, l'unique ornement de ma vie, le pivot de mon bonheur,* and cried *comme un veau* upon the receipt of her letters.[15] He wanted to be counted among Catherine's dogs and considered himself a mere worm, created only *pour ramper à ses pieds.*[16] In spite of these extravagances Grimm's letters, like Diderot's, give the impression of a genuine attachment to his Russian correspondent. He wrote in his *Mémoire historique* in 1797,

[12] *Sbornik*, XXXI, 1-422; Grimm's letters are complete from 1779 to 1783; from 1783 to 1790 a few are missing; no letters are found for the period 1791 to 1793. For a more detailed account see Grot's article in the *Memoirs of the Imperial Academy of Sciences*, Vol. XXXIV.

[13] E. Scherer, *Melchior Grimm*, p. 275.   [14] *Ibid.*

[15] *Ibid.*, p. 277; cf. also A. Rambaud, "Catherine II et ses correspondants français," *Revue des deux mondes*, 1877.

[16] *Ibid.*

Dominé par le prestige d'une puissante illusion, j'étais parvenu à fondre, pour ainsi dire, mon existence dans la sienne, à passer ma vie avec elle au pied de la lettre, et, quoique j'en vécusse séparé à une distance immense, à m'en rendre vraiment inséparable.[17]

Catherine's letters to Grimm preserved by the Russian Historical Society,[18] show personal attachment for and complete confidence in her half-German, half-French correspondent. In her letters to Grimm she is more informal, less on her guard, than with any other foreign correspondent—*elle fait moins de frais de coquetterie intellectuelle*—than, for example, in her letters to Voltaire or even to Diderot. Her tone is light, witty and semicomic. She is never the Empress speaking to her favorite, but a woman speaking to an intimate friend. She abandons herself completely in describing the affairs of state, her private chagrins and joys, small court gossip, and her impressions of people who chance to come into her life. She frequently makes fun of Grimm and admonishes him in a half-joking manner. He is given various commissions to perform, including the purchase of candy, rouge, dresses, books, pictures, occasionally whole libraries and collections. Sometimes his commissions are of a confidential nature, such as finding husbands for the Empress' granddaughters.[19] Through Grimm, too, Catherine helped various people, e.g., D'Epinay and the Bueil families.[20]

The French Revolution and the death of Catherine II in 1796 were the greatest tragedies in Grimm's life. Ruined by the Revolution and deprived of his best friend and protector, he spent the last years of his life in obscure retirement at

[17] See "Mémoire historique sur l'origine et les suites de mon attachement pour l'impératrice Catherine II," in *Correspondance littéraire*, I, 1 ff.

[18] For a complete account of the relations between Grimm and Catherine II see V. Bil'basov, *Russkaïa starina*, LXXVII, *passim*.

[19] E. Scherer, *Melchior Grimm*, p. 289.

[20] *Ibid.*, pp. 311, 367.

Gotha, kept alive chiefly by the memories of his great friendship with the Russian Empress.

Next to Grimm's the longest correspondence conducted between Catherine II and a Frenchman was that with the sculptor Falconet.[21] Altogether about two hundred letters were written during the twelve years of Falconet's stay in Russia.[22] The correspondence began in a lively and friendly fashion. A variety of subjects was discussed—art, politics, literature, and philosophy. In the eyes of Catherine Falconet was a "philosopher," a representative of the intellectual life of France, and for a time he was her friend and confidant, until Grimm definitely supplanted him.

At the beginning of the correspondence Catherine consulted Falconet about everything. She wanted to know his opinions of various Frenchmen, such as Rulhière and La Rivière, who visited Russia, of pictures, of politics, and of philosophical ideas. But even in this she was more reserved with Falconet than with Grimm or Diderot.

Falconet's answers were always frank; perhaps a bit too naïve and direct. *Je ne sais aucun à qui je puisse parler avec autant de franchise qu'à Votre Majesté* . . . he wrote in 1768.[23] Like those of other foreign correspondents, Falconet's letters are full of flattery in the usual vein: the Empress is greater than Peter the Great and Henri IV, her code *est le chef-d'œuvre de la raison et de l'humanité*, she is the most enlightened and the most *philosophe* ruler of Europe.[24] In 1769, he wrote:

[21] Falconet's correspondence with Catherine II was first published in 1876 by A. Polovtsev in Vol. XVII of the *Sbornik*. It was known to A. Rambaud (cf. his article in the *Revue des deux mondes*, 1877), and to M. Tourneux (*Diderot et Catherine*, 1899). The most complete edition of this correspondence was published recently by Louis Réau, *Correspondance de Falconet avec Catherine II*, Paris, 1921.

[22] From February 18, 1767, to September 1, 1778, L. Réau, *Correspondance de Falconet* . . . Introduction, pp. v-vi.

[23] *Ibid.*, p. 66.

[24] L. Réau, *Correspondance de Falconet* . . . pp. 97-98.

Je ne sais si j'aurais voulu être Russe, il y a 60 ou 80 ans; mais je sens, en lisant les divines Instructions de Votre Majesté, que je voudrais l'être à présent et vivre assez pour jouir des heureux fruits du code Catherinien.[25]

Informal and friendly at the beginning, the correspondence between Falconet and Catherine II became less and less so as time went on. The reason for this estrangement was partly Falconet's direct and irascible character, partly his long enmity with General Betskiï, Superintendent of Fine Arts for the Empire. In the course of Falconet's execution of the statue of Peter the Great he had frequent clashes with the general, who was wont to interfere in his work. About 1770 Falconet's letters to the Empress began to be filled with complaints about the encroachments of the general. At first the Empress paid no attention to these, but as they became more and more frequent and bitter, she obviously grew tired of them. Her letters to the sculptor became fewer in number,[26] shorter and more business-like and formal in tone. Owing also, perhaps, to Betskiï's intrigues, she finally completely lost her confidence in her former favorite. When in the fall of 1778 Falconet's statue was finished and was acclaimed unreservedly as a masterpiece, the Empress allowed the tired and discouraged sculptor to leave the country without even a final audience.[27]

Nevertheless, as late as 1783 (in letters to his future daughter-in-law, Mlle Collot, who was then in Russia) Falconet still spoke with affection of his former patron.[28] Catherine, on the other hand, dismissed the announcement of the sculptor's death with the following lines to Grimm: *Avec de telles dispositions vous jugez bien que la mort des Gillet, des Falconet n'a presque pas attiré mon attention.*[29]

[25] *Ibid.*, pp. 101-102.
[26] From an average of twenty to thirty a year, the number of letters fell to four in 1775, and finally to one in 1777.
[27] L. Réau, *Correspondance de Falconet* . . . p. 268.
[28] *Ibid.*, p. 271.
[29] *Ibid.*

Regarding Sénac de Meilhan's and Prince de Ligne's correspondence with Catherine II there is little to be added to what has already been said in the preceding chapter of this work. The few letters of Sénac de Meilhan have been preserved and published by the Russian Historical Society.[30] The relations between the brilliant émigré and the Empress were, as we saw, of short duration. At first well disposed toward him, the Empress soon perceived that he was not fitted to write a history of Russia. Annoyed at Meilhan's superficial attitude toward his work and by his constant requests for titles and posts, she tactfully dismissed him.[31] Meilhan was permitted to leave the country and to finish his history abroad. Catherine's last letter advising him not to return to Russia because of the severity of the climate apparently ended the relationship between the philosopher and the Empress.[32]

The Belgian Prince de Ligne's correspondence with Catherine scattered throughout the period 1780-1796, was published in his *Mémoires et mélanges*.[33] De Ligne's letters attest a genuine admiration and affection for the Empress. He paid her the most elaborate compliments which were never, however, lacking in refinement and grace. The tone of both correspondents was always light, witty, and familiar. These friendly relations continued until Catherine's death.

We shall turn now to those eminent Frenchmen who, although they did not visit Russia, maintained personal relations with the Russian Empress through correspondence. Chief among these was Voltaire. The rest were, for the most part,

[30] *Sbornik,* XLII, 129-230. Cf. also Prince Obolenskii's article on Sénac de Meilhan's stay in Russia in *Russkii arkhiv,* 1866.

[31] *Sbornik,* XLII, 145-146, 153, 196, 197.

[32] Letter of July 8, 1792.

[33] C. J. de Ligne, *Mémoires et mélanges* ... Paris, 1827, 5 vols., *passim.* For a detailed account of Prince de Ligne's relations with Catherine II see V. Bil'basov, *Russkaia starina,* 1892, LXXIII-LXXIV, *passim.* Cf. also a recent collection of Catherine's letters to De Ligne by Princess Charles de Ligne, *Lettres de Catherine II au prince de Ligne* (1780-1796), Paris, 1924.

his friends and associates, like D'Alembert, Mme Geoffrin, Buffon, and Marmontel.

Voltaire's interest in Russia dates from 1717 when, at the age of twenty-three, he saw the Tsar Peter walking in the streets of Paris.[34] Peter the Great already figured prominently in his *History of Charles XII*, which appeared in 1731. In 1748 he published anonymously a collection of anecdotes on the Tsar's eccentricities, and in 1757 he began the history of Peter's reign.

Throughout his life Voltaire corresponded with many Russians,[35] and of these Count Ivan Shuvalov, Chamberlain of the Empress Elizabeth, and Catherine II were the most important. The circumstances which led to his correspondence with Count Ivan Shuvalov were as follows: Early in 1757 Voltaire was invited by Empress Elizabeth to come to Russia to write a history of Peter the Great's reign. In a letter to the Russian ambassador Bestuzhev-Riumin he declined the offer on the ground of ill health, but he agreed to write the history provided Count Shuvalov would send him the necessary material.[36]

The correspondence with Count Ivan Shuvalov began in 1757 and continued until the end of 1762.[37] The relations between the writers remained to the end most cordial and friendly. At first rather formal in tone, the letters became

[34] *Quand je le vis*, Voltaire wrote to Thieriot, *il y a quarante ans, courant les boutiques de Paris, ni lui ni moi ne nous doutions que je serais un jour son historien.*—Letter to Thieriot, June 11, 1759. Cf. also Voltaire's *Œuvres*, Garnier, XXIII, 290.

[35] He exchanged several letters with Prince Kantemir, as we saw in the second chapter of this work, and also wrote on various occasions to Russian ambassadors in Paris (Bestuzhev-Riumin, Panin, Saltykov, and others) as well as to his many Russian friends who visited him at Délices and Ferney (Count André Shuvalov, Rumiantsev, and others).

[36] Voltaire, *Correspondance*, Voltaire to Count Bestuzhev-Riumin, February, 1757.

[37] The Chamberlain Count Ivan Shuvalov is not to be confused with his nephew, Count André Shuvalov, author of the *Epître à Ninon*. André visited Voltaire at Ferney and was also in correspondence with him.

gradually more informal and personal. Voltaire seems to have become more and more enthusiastic about Tsar Peter and about Count Ivan as well. He spared no praises or flatteries of either, writing to Shuvalov in 1758:

J'apprends que vous n'avez que vingt-cinq ans et je suis étonné de la profondeur et de la multiplicité de vos connaissances. De tels exemples redoublent la reconnaissance qu'on doit à Pierre le Grand d'avoir amené tous les arts dans un pays où les hommes naissent avec tant de génie.[38]

Voltaire continually stressed the fact that the real author of the history of the Tsar was Shuvalov and that he himself was merely the Count's secretary or copyist. His aim, he insisted, was *bâtir pour vous la maison dont vous m'avez fourni les matériaux*.[39] Now and then he would be annoyed at the delays in receiving material; he was getting old, he wrote to Shuvalov, and must hurry to finish the work lest it should be necessary to inscribe on his tomb: *Ci-gît qui voulait écrire l'histoire de Pierre-le-Grand*.[40]

As in most of Voltaire's letters to Russians, in his correspondence with Shuvalov he frequently applied his praises of the individual to Russians in general and to the nation itself:

Je n'ai point encore vu de vos compatriots qui ne m'aient convaincu du mérite de votre nation et de l'éducation heureuse qu'on reçoit par vos soins et par votre propre protection dans les deux capitales de votre empire.[41]

He seems to have greatly admired Shuvalov's culture, particularly his rôle as a patron of the arts, and was grateful for the information which the Count provided. Voltaire's interest

---

[38] Voltaire, *Correspondance*, Voltaire to Shuvalov, February 5, 1758.
[39] *Ibid.*, letters of May 29, 1759, and of June 8, 1761.
[40] *Ibid.*, letters of March 4, 1759, and of April 20, 1758.
[41] *Ibid.*, letter of April 1, 1760.

in and zeal for the history of the Tsar seems to have increased steadily during the correspondence with Shuvalov.

Mon zèle ne se ralentira point; vous m'avez fait Russe, vous m'avez attaché à Pierre le Grand. Nous avons en France une comédie dans laquelle il y a une fille amoureuse d'Alexandre le Grand, je ressemble à cette fille.[42]

Shuvalov, it appears, succeeded in stimulating and sustaining Voltaire's interest in Peter the Great. In addition, this was no doubt augmented by Empress Elizabeth's repeatedly expressed satisfaction, which she supplemented by frequent gifts.[43]

Voltaire did not correspond with the Empress; but indirectly acknowledged her tokens of benevolence through Shuvalov. When the news of her death reached him, he seems to have been genuinely afflicted. *J'ai fait une très grande perte dans l'impératrice de Russie,* he wrote to the Marquis d'Argence de Dirac, *et je ne la réparerai pas; elle m'accablait de bontés.*[44] Nevertheless, he consoled himself with the fact that he had already acquired a new friend in Catherine II. *Il faut toujours,* he explained to Mme de Fontaine, *avoir une reine pour soi.*[45]

The news of Catherine's accession to the throne, followed shortly by her husband's death in July, 1762, quickly reached Paris and caused a wave of indignation against the Empress, particularly in circles identified with the foreign minister, Choiseul. At first Voltaire seemed undecided as to which side to take. A letter from Catherine's secretary, the Genevan Pictet,[46] giving him all the details of the coup d'état and absolving the Empress of complicity in her husband's death,

---

[42] Voltaire, *Correspondance,* letter of August 2, 1760.

[43] Voltaire was especially grateful to the Empress Elizabeth for her gift of 8,000 livres for his edition of Corneille's work; cf. *ibid.,* Voltaire's letter to Tronchon, January 6, 1762.

[44] *Ibid.,* Voltaire to Marquis d'Argence de Dirac, February 26, 1762.

[45] *Ibid.,* Voltaire to Mme de Fontaine, February 16, 1762.

[46] Voltaire, *Correspondance,* Pictet to Voltaire, August 4, 1762.

seems to have convinced Voltaire of her innocence. For a while, however, he remained uneasy. But the news which next reached him completely won him to her side. This was the report of Catherine's purchase of Diderot's library, of her intention to continue the Russian edition of the Encyclopedia, and of her letter to D'Alembert inviting him to become tutor to the heir of the Russian throne. *En quel temps sommes-nous* . . . he wrote enthusiastically to Diderot, urging him to accept the offer, *c'est la France qui persécute la philosophie, et ce sont les Scythes qui la favorisent.*[47]

From then on Voltaire became an untiring and unflinching champion of the Russian Empress. In spite of severe criticism directed against him, especially by Mme de Choiseul and Mme du Deffand, for his calling the murder of Peter III *démêlés de famille,*[48] and for his excessive praise of the Empress, he remained loyal to the new patron of the *philosophie.*

Voltaire's correspondence with Catherine II began in November, 1763, and continued until the end of 1777. The first letters from the Empress evoked repeated expressions of admiration from the seventy-year-old philosopher, who was then living at Ferney. These appear especially in his letters to D'Alembert.[49] *J'admire Catherine, je l'aime à la folie. Les Scythes deviennent nos maîtres en tout; voilà pourtant ce que fait la philosophie*[50] is a sentiment he reiterated to all his friends.

What Voltaire admired most in the Russian Empress was her spirit of tolerance and enlightenment, her *philosophie,* and her creative genius.[51] He felt, moreover, personally grate-

[47] Voltaire, *Correspondance,* Voltaire to Diderot, September 25, 1762.
[48] Mme. du Deffand, *Correspondance,* Paris, 1866, I, 110-122.
[49] See especially Voltaire's letters to D'Alembert of November 13, 1762, and February 4, 1763. D'Alembert seemed, however, skeptical regarding Catherine's rôle as protectress of the *philosophie*—cf. his letters to Voltaire of February 12, 1763, and October 4, 1764, Voltaire, *Correspondance.*
[50] *Ibid.,* Voltaire to Damilaville, December 22, 1766.
[51] *Ibid.,* Voltaire to Catherine, January 24, 1766.

ful to her for the benevolent protection she extended to him and to his friends: *Tous les gens de lettres de l'Europe doivent être à vos pieds,*[52] and again, *Nous sommes trois, Diderot, D'Alembert, et moi, quo vous dressons des autels...*[53] He was in raptures over her generosity, culture, and intelligence and on several occasions expressed a desire to see her in person.[54]

The first years of Voltaire's correspondence with Catherine are concerned a good deal with her *Instructions*, addressed to the members of the council, which was convoked for the purpose of making a new legal code designed to remodel the laws of Russia in accordance with the principles proclaimed by eighteenth-century freethinkers, particularly by Montesquieu. Voltaire proclaimed the *Instructions* (a French translation of which appeared in 1767) to be the finest monument of the century.[55]

Between 1770 and 1775 the letters were particularly frequent and lively. Voltaire's tone became more and more informal and even daring.[56] He multiplied compliments and flatteries, signed his letters *le vieux malade de Ferney,* and frequently expressed a desire to come to Russia. During this period the letters deal chiefly with Catherine's victories over the Turks. *Votre Majesté Impériale me rend la vie, en tuant les Turcs,* he wrote in 1769,[57] and each victory of the Russian army brought forth a new outburst of enthusiasm.

There is little ground to doubt that Voltaire's admiration for Catherine's genius was, on the whole, sincere. To him the Empress was the embodiment of an ideal and enlightened monarch. Although his letters lacked the note, found in

[52] Voltaire to Catherine (no date), 1765 (No. 6123, *Correspondance* éd. Garnier frères).

[53] *Ibid.*, December 22, 1766.

[54] *Ibid.*, letter No. 6123, and letter of January 24, 1766.

[55] W. F. Reddaway, *Documents of Catherine the Great* ... Cambridge, 1931, Introduction, pp. xxiii-xxiv.

[56] Voltaire, *Correspondance,* cf. for example, the letter of December 16, 1774.

[57] *Ibid.*, Voltaire to Catherine, October 30, 1769.

Diderot or Grimm, of personal attachment to and affection for the Empress, he seemed genuinely grateful to her for the benefits conferred on him and his friends. *Comblé des bontés de l'impératrice,* remarks Condorcet in his life of Voltaire, *sans doute la reconnaissance animait son zèle; mais on se tromperait si on imaginait qu'elle en fût l'unique cause.*[58]

The tone of Catherine's letters to Voltaire, although light, witty, and informal, was yet somewhat "literary" and studied. She never abandoned herself so completely as she did, for example, in her letters to Grimm or Prince de Ligne. Although imbued with great personal admiration for Voltaire's genius, Catherine did not seem eager to have him come to Russia. "Advise the octogenarian to remain in Paris," she wrote to Grimm in 1778, "what would he do here? He would die by the wayside of cold, weariness, and bad roads... Tell him that 'Cateau' is only good to see from a distance." [59] She felt, perhaps, that closer acquaintance might result in mutual disillusionment and she preferred to keep her illusion. *Depuis que Voltaire est mort,* she wrote to Grimm in 1778, *il me semble qu'il n'y a plus d'honneur attaché à la belle humeur; c'était lui qui était la divinité de la gaieté.*[60]

The correspondence between Catherine and D'Alembert was less friendly and cordial. Soon after Catherine's accession to the throne D'Alembert was invited to come to Russia as tutor to the young heir. He declined on the ground that he did not wish to leave his friends and that he was already a recipient of a pension from the king of Prussia.[61] Catherine then wrote him her famous letter of November 13, 1762, which was published by the French Academy and reproduced

[58] Voltaire, *Œuvres,* Condorcet's "Vie de Voltaire," éd. Garnier frères, I, 269.

[59] W. Reddaway, *Documents...* Introduction, p. xiv.

[60] Catherine to Grimm, August 11, 1778 (Voltaire, *Œuvres,* I, 454). Regarding Catherine's purchase of Voltaire's library, cf. *ibid.,* I, 454-455 and 464.

[61] D'Alembert, *Œuvres et correspondances...* Paris, C. Henry, 1887; cf. letter of Odar to D'Alembert and D'Alembert's reply, pp. 193-197.

in the *Journal encyclopédique* for February, 1763. This letter began a correspondence which did not end until 1772.[62]

Catherine's first letter to D'Alembert was, in reality, addressed to all the philosophers in France; it urged D'Alembert in the name of *philosophie* to accept her offer. She wrote:

Votre philosophie est fondée sur l'humanité; permettez-moi de vous dire que de ne point se prêter à la servir tandis qu'on le peut, c'est manquer son but... Venez avec tous vos amis, je vous promets, à eux aussi, tous les agréments et aisances qui peuvent dépendre de moi et peut-être vous trouverez plus de liberté et de repos que chez vous.[63]

These arguments were, however, in vain. D'Alembert remained firm in his refusal to come to Russia, but to show his regard for the Empress he dedicated his *Mélanges de littérature* and *Eléments de musique* to her.[64]

Catherine never forgave him for his refusal and interpreted it as evidence of his pride and vanity. Her letters to him were always short, formal, and sarcastic in tone. D'Alembert defended himself as best he could. *Ma philosophie et ma vanité même seraient plus flattées de contribuer au bonheur d'un grand peuple que de m'en défendre.*[65] He paid frequent compliments to the enlightenment and *esprit de tolérance* of the Empress, compliments for the most part awkward and forced. *Il démontre*, says Larivière, *il déclame, il multiplie les formules de respect.*

D'Alembert was, in fact, always suspicious of Catherine's professed liberality and interest in philosophy. He wrote to Voltaire after Catherine's offer to finish the Encyclopedia in Russia:

[62] This correspondence was first published in the *Sbornik*, Vols. X and XIII. A study of C. Larivière's based on the above publications formed ch. i of his *La France et la Russie au XVIIIᵉ siècle*, Paris, 1909.

[63] C. Larivière, *La France et la Russie*... p. 14.

[64] *Ibid.*, p. 21.   [65] *Ibid.*, p. 27.

Il faut espérer que la cour de Pétersbourg sera plus fidèle au traité qu'elle fait avec la philosophie, qu'elle ne l'a été à ceux qu'elle a faits avec le cardinal de Bernis.[66]

Writing to Voltaire two years later he definitely accused Catherine of disposing of Prince Ivan as, he contended, she had disposed of her husband:

Je conviens avec vous que la philosophie ne doit pas trop se vanter de pareils élèves; mais que voulez-vous? il faut aimer ses amis avec leurs défauts.[67]

With her keen perception Catherine sensed, no doubt, that D'Alembert's attitude toward her was suspicious and hostile despite his elaborate compliments. Her letters to him are full of bitter and sarcastic retorts to all his professions of friendship. When D'Alembert, to ingratiate himself, asked for a criticism of his works, she replied,

Deux raisons m'ont empêché de vous répondre jusqu'ici; la première c'est qu'encore toute étonnée de votre refus je n'y pensais qu'avec chagrin, la seconde, c'est la tâche audessus de mes forces que vous me donnez de vous dire mon avis sur vos ouvrages.[68]

When, on another occasion, D'Alembert complained of the attacks upon his works made by the French government, Catherine wrote, *Au Nord, on ne permet pas aux souverains d'ignorer quels sont les esprits distingués qui ont droit à leurs bienfaits.*[69] In 1767 D'Alembert wrote again asking for criticisms and professing friendship. This time he received no answer.[70] Five years later he wrote again requesting the empress in the name of philosophy to pardon several French

---

[66] Voltaire, *Correspondance*, D'Alembert to Voltaire, February 12, 1763.

[67] *Ibid.*, October 4, 1764.

[68] C. Larivière, *La France et la Russie* ... p. 31, Catherine to D'Alembert, April 23, 1764.

[69] C. Larivière, *La France et la Russie* ... p. 45, Catherine to D'Alembert, November 21, 1765.

[70] *Ibid.*, p. 50.

officers who were taken as prisoners of war near Cracow.[71] This time Catherine's answer came promptly. She did not refuse flatly but said the officers were quite well-off where they were and needed protection from neither "philosophy" nor D'Alembert.[72] The Frenchman then wrote another letter pleading for the liberation of the captive officers. Catherine's reply was short, sarcastic, and almost insulting in tone.[73] There was no further correspondence between them.

Mme Geoffrin was in correspondence with Catherine II for a period of five years.[74] Their relations, very friendly at the beginning, ended in a complete rupture. As we saw in the second chapter of this work, Mme Geoffrin's salon was always open to Russians. Kantemir, Betskïï, and many unofficial representatives of the Russian aristocracy frequented it. About 1758 Mme Geoffrin became acquainted with the Princess of Anhalt-Zerbst, mother of Catherine the Great.[75] Through her the correspondence with the Russian empress began.

Mme Geoffrin wrote the first letter, dated 1763.[76] Catherine's reply, most cordial and friendly, was somehow made public in Paris. This almost brought about a quarrel between the two correspondents.[77] A reconciliation soon followed, however, and the friendly and familiar tone was resumed. Catherine's letters especially were frank and unrestrained, with no trace of literary affectation. It was a different Catherine from the woman who wrote to D'Alembert and to

---

[71] D'Alembert, *Œuvres et correspondances*, Paris, 1887, p. 250; D'Alembert to Catherine, October 30, 1772.

[72] *Ibid.*, p. 255.

[73] *Ibid.*, p. 256.

[74] The correspondence was published by A. Hamburger in the *Sbornik*, 1867, pp. 253-291. Marquis de Ségur's *Le Royaume de la rue Saint-Honoré*, Paris, 1897, was based, in part, on the above.

[75] Marquis de Ségur, *Le Royaume* . . . p. 203.

[76] *Ibid.*, p. 206.

[77] *Ibid.*, p. 209.

Voltaire. In her letters to Mme Geoffrin, Catherine was addressing an older and more experienced friend. *Vous n'aimez pas à être contrariée*, she wrote at the beginning of the correspondence, *je m'accommoderai le plus que je pourrai à votre humeur.*[78] She described her domestic life, her various problems and difficulties, and not infrequently asked for advice. The latter was freely given. Sometimes, indeed, Mme Geoffrin seems to have been a bit too generous with it. Her elaborate instructions as to how Catherine might improve her reputation in France, a reputation impaired by rumors of her implication in the death of Peter III and in that of Prince Ivan of Brunswick, may serve as an example.[79]

At the outset Catherine was eager that Mme Geoffrin should come to Russia to pay her a visit. The Frenchwoman, however, showed no great desire to undertake this trip and in her letters avoided the issue. Catherine deeply resented this indifference, especially when she heard of Mme Geoffrin's journey to Warsaw and Vienna to visit the Polish and Austrian courts. In 1766 she complained bitterly of this to D'Alembert:

Je ne lui ai proposé et ne lui proposerai jamais de venir ici, pour deux raisons: l'une, du climat; l'autre, c'est que je savais bien d'avance que cette raison l'en empêcherait.[80]

The tone of Catherine's letters to her friend became more formal and reserved. The final break between them was occasioned by the Rulhière episode.[81] Catherine, as we saw in the second chapter, was eager to stop the publication of Rulhière's account of the coup d'état of 1762. This version of the affair indirectly accused her of complicity in the murder

[78] Marquis de Ségur, *Le Royaume* . . . p. 209.
[79] *Ibid.*, p. 212.
[80] *Ibid.*, p. 220.
[81] *Ibid.*, pp. 220-225. Cf. also Grimm's *Correspondance littéraire*, April, 1770, and Bachaumont, *Mémoires*, April 18, 1773.

of her husband. Not wishing to be outshone by her rival, Mme du Deffand, Mme Geoffrin consented to give a public reading of Rulhière's manuscript in her salon. This indiscretion was promptly reported to Catherine. From then on there was nothing that Mme Geoffrin could do to win back Catherine's favor. She interviewed Rulhière at the Countess d'Egmont's house and tried to persuade him to destroy his manuscript or at least to withhold its publication.[82] The interview failed at the time, and Mme Geoffrin's attempts to conciliate her royal correspondent were in vain. Catherine wrote in reply to Mme Geoffrin's tearful apologies:

Je croyais que les soupirs n'étaient propre qu'aux Russes; on m'a dit que dans les pays étrangers on les reconnaissait à cela sous le masque, mais comme vous les recevez chez vous, c'est un mal que vous aurez pris d'eux.[83]

This was Catherine's last letter. On it, in Mme Geoffrin's own hand, was written: *J'ai répondu. Point de réponse.*[84]

The naturalist Buffon was another of Catherine's correspondents.[85] Only a few letters were exchanged between them, but the correspondence deserves to be noticed. Catherine was a great admirer of Buffon's works. About 1780 the latter sent them to her and received in return some medals, a snuff box with Catherine's portrait in diamonds, and a golden chain which had been found by archeologists in Siberia. *Tout Paris vient chez moi pour les admirer* [i.e., these gifts], Buffon wrote to Catherine in his long and extravagantly flattering letter of thanks, *et chacun s'écrie sur la noble magnificence et les hautes qualités personelles de ma bienfaitrice.*[86]

[82] M. d'Armaillé, *La Comtesse d'Egmont*, Paris, 1890, pp. 114-130.
[83] *Sbornik*, 1867, pp. 289-291, letter of August 11, 1768.
[84] *Ibid.*, p. 291.
[85] A. Rambaud in his article on Catherine's French correspondents in the *Revue des deux mondes*, 1877, does not mention Buffon.
[86] Buffon, *Correspondance*, Paris, 1860, II, 113; letter of December 14, 1781. Cf. also regarding these presents and Buffon's letter, Bachaumont, *Mémoires*, February 5, 1782.

In April, 1782, Buffon's son, a young officer of the Guards, went to Russia, taking a bust of his father which was to be given to the Empress.[87] He received a hearty welcome and was very much liked at court. Catherine wrote to Buffon praising his son, and the old naturalist was in raptures over this letter, which he called *mon plus noble laurier*.[88] Eager to show his appreciation to Catherine for her gifts and her kindness to his son, he wrote to her promising to express his gratitude publicly in one of his works.[89] He did so in his *Histoire des minéraux*. Speaking of feldspar, known also as the stone of Labrador, he inserted the following digression:

L'auguste impératrice des Russies a daigné elle-même me le faire savoir, et c'est avec empressement que je saisis cette légère occasion de présenter à cette grande souveraine l'hommage universel que les sciences doivent à son génie, qui les éclaire autant que sa faveur les protège, et l'hommage particulier que je mets à ces pieds pour les hautes bontés dont elle m'honore.[90]

Marmontel and Catherine also exchanged several letters. Of these three letters of Marmontel's were published in his collected works. In 1767 he wrote to Catherine announcing his intention to dedicate his famous *Bélisaire* to her.[91] Catherine's reply was most flattering to the author.[92] She admired greatly Marmontel's work, and herself translated his *Bélisaire* into Russian. Upon learning of this Marmontel wrote her a letter, lyrical in tone, praising her intelligence and *philosophie*.[93] He called her translation of *Bélisaire: un beau monu-*

[87] Bachaumont, *Mémoires*, April 19, 1782, and Buffon, *Correspondance*, II, 392.

[88] Buffon, *Correspondance*, II, 393.

[89] *Ibid.*, II, 142-149, letter of August 18, 1782.

[90] *Ibid.*, II, 465 (notes). Besides the Empress, Buffon corresponded with other Russians (Repnin, Potemkin, etc.). He was a member of the St. Petersburg Academy of Sciences and corresponded with the mathematician Albert Euler; cf. Buffon, *Correspondance*, II, 452-453.

[91] Marmontel, *Œuvres*, Paris, Verdière, 1819, VII, 384-385.

[92] *Ibid.*

[93] *Ibid.*, VII, 386-387.

ment élevé à la gloire des lettres et de la philosophie,[94] and together with Voltaire and Diderot remained to the end a stout champion of the Russian empress. *Que ne fait pas cette étonnante femme*, he wrote to Voltaire, in terms similar to those he employed in letters to other friends, *que vous admirez comme moi, que ne fait-elle pas pour tirer la Russie de l'esclavage et de la barbarie!* [95] Like Voltaire and other Encyclopedists, Marmontel applauded Catherine's victories over the Turks, admired her foreign policy, and even justified her rôle in the divisions of Poland.[96]

This ends the list of the principal exchanges of correspondence between French philosophers and the Russian Empress. A few minor points of contact, however, deserve to be mentioned in this connection.

Eager as Catherine was to enlist the sympathies of the French philosophers and men of letters, there were some among them whom she personally disliked, and with these she made no attempt at a rapprochement. Beaumarchais, for example, was one of these. Although the Empress liked his plays, she seems to have made no attempt to correspond with him. She was, in fact, responsible for causing him a certain degree of embarrassment. According to the unpublished memoirs of Gudin, Catherine suggested to the publisher Panckoucke that he print a collected edition of Voltaire's work in St. Petersburg.[97] Upon learning this Beaumarchais went to the prime minister Maurepas and pointed out to him the disgrace of letting Voltaire's works appear in Russia, whereupon Maurepas proposed that Beaumarchais undertake a French edition and promised his protection.[98] The edition was accordingly undertaken. When it was almost completed,

---

[94] *Ibid.*, VII, 389-390.
[95] *Ibid.*, VII, 493.
[96] *Ibid.*
[97] L. Loménie, *Beaumarchais and His Times*, London, 1856, III, 239.
[98] *Ibid.*, III, 239-240.

Catherine II through her ambassador requested Beaumarchais not to print certain portions of her correspondence with Voltaire.[99] Beaumarchais consented and sent to the Russian court a statement of the expense involved. He sought in vain to be reimbursed. As late as 1790 he wrote to the Prince of Nassau, then in Russia, asking him to intervene in his behalf.[100] He seems never to have received an answer from the Russian court and had himself to stand the expense of the extra cost involved in changing the edition.

A few words may be added about the association of the Duc de Lauzan, of LaFayette, and of Volney with Catherine. In 1775 the Duc de Lauzan wrote to Catherine offering, upon his own initiative, to negotiate a treaty of alliance with France.[101] He then drew up a treaty which Catherine approved. The foreign minister, Choiseul, furious at Lauzan for having started this correspondence without his consent, refused even to consider Lauzan's proposed treaty.[102] Soon after this unsuccessful attempt at a rapprochement, Catherine asked Lauzan to come to Russia as commander-in-chief of all the Cossacks.[103] For a time Lauzan appears to have seriously considered this offer. In the end, however, he changed his mind and went to America instead.[104]

LaFayette wrote one letter to Grimm in 1774 about an officer, Ledyard, whom he wished to be recommended to the Empress. Catherine was referred to in this letter as *celle de l'univers dans tout ce qui tient aux sciences, aux découvertes, aux lettres, à la philosophie, et à la gloire.*[105]

With Volney Catherine's association was very brief. He

99 L. Loménie, *Beaumarchais and His Times*, London, 1856, III, 248.
100 *Ibid.*
101 G. Maugras, *Duc de Lauzan*, London, 1896, ch. vii, pp. 91-93.
102 *Ibid.*, p. 93.
103 Letter of January 10, 1776, MS. Bibliothèque Nationale.
104 L. Lacour, *Mémoires du duc de Lauzan*, Paris, 1858, p. 283.
105 A. Rambaud, "Catherine II et ses correspondants français," *Revue des deux mondes*, 1877.

received a medal from her for his *Voyage en Egypte*. In 1791 when Catherine was beginning a campaign against revolutionary France, Volney, disgusted with her reactionary tendencies, sent the medal back through Grimm.[106]

Among eminent Frenchmen who corresponded with other members of the Russian court were La Harpe and Blin de Sainmore. Rousseau's only letter addressed to a Russian (Count Orlov) might also be mentioned in this connection.[107]

La Harpe's literary correspondence with the Grand Duke Paul and with Shuvalov was arranged by Voltaire. It started in 1774 and continued to the end of 1789.[108] Through this correspondence La Harpe became acquainted with many Russian noblemen and, next to Grimm, was considered in Paris as the best source of information on the happenings at the Russian court.[109] In 1782 he was received on several occasions by the Grand Duke and his wife while they were staying in Paris. On various occasions he was honored by gifts from Catherine II and took every opportunity to express his gratitude for her benevolence.[110]

The content of La Harpe's correspondence was chiefly literary gossip. He frequently stressed the fact that his Russian correspondents were more French than the French and were qualified to appreciate the French *esprit* and literary *badinage*. He wrote to them, in fact, as if they alone could appreciate all the *finesses* of the literary and social life of Paris.[111] He reviewed books and plays, particularly those pertaining to Russia, praised his own *Menzicoff* and condemned

[106] Léon Séché, *Volney*, Paris, 1899, p. 174.

[107] In ch. vi of this study Fénelon's two letters to Peter the Great will be mentioned.

[108] G. Peignot, *Recherches historiques, littéraires, et bibliographiques sur la vie et les ouvrages de M. de la Harpe*, Dijon, 1820, p. 62.

[109] *Ibid.*, pp. 66, 87-89.

[110] *Ibid.*, pp. 70, 97.

[111] La Harpe, *Correspondance littéraire*, Paris, 1826. Cf. especially Vol. I, letters XIII ff.

Dorat's *Pierre-le-Grand*.[112] After the departure of Grand
Duke Paul in 1782, La Harpe spent a good part of his time
writing panegyrics in prose and verse to his Russian correspondents.[113]

Blin de Sainmore (1733-1807), a well-known poet and
playwright of the time, corresponded with Grand Duchess
Marie of Russia from 1778 to 1801.[114] This correspondence
has never been published and was not mentioned by Rambaud and other students of Franco-Russian relations.[115] Blin
de Sainmore was a friend of Voltaire and the Encyclopedists,
and it was through them that he grew interested in Russia.[116]
His *History of Russia* (1798-99) and his epistle on the arrival
of the Grand Duke Paul in Paris were well known at the
time.[117]

Rousseau's contact with Russians was limited to one letter
he wrote to Count Orlov in answer to the latter's invitation
to come to live on his Russian estate.[118] Rousseau declined the
offer and expressed his thanks for the invitation with dignity
and reserve. As reasons for his refusal he instanced the cold
climate, his poor health, and his solitary and unsociable habits.
The latter, he thought, would quickly tire his host.

From the correspondence examined in this chapter one
can see that most of the important representatives of literature and philosophy in eighteenth-century France established
personal relations with the Russian court, and in particular
with Empress Catherine II. They were all attracted by the

112 La Harpe, *Correspondance littéraire*, Vol. II, letter CXVII.
113 *Ibid.*, letter CLXVII.
114 Michaud, *Biographie universelle*, IV, 582-584.
115 This correspondence was not found until the revolution, when it was
discovered in the archives of the Pavlovsk palace. Cf. *ibid.*, and a reference to
Blin de Sainmore in J. Lozinski's article, "Le prince Antioche Cantemir," *Revue
des études slaves*, V, 241.
116 Cf. Michaud, *op. cit.*, IV, 585, and Voltaire's letters to Sainmore of
June 15 and 18, 1764, Voltaire, *Correspondance*.
117 *Ibid.*
118 Bachaumont, *Mémoires*, July 12, 1767, and July 13, 1767.

Empress' many manifestations of political and religious tolerance, her interest in the progress of philosophy and the arts, her wit and lively intelligence. Some, like Diderot, Grimm, and Buffon, were motivated in addition by personal gratitude for the benefits conferred upon them. Diderot was, no doubt, the Empress' most ardent and enthusiastic admirer, and Grimm her closest friend. Voltaire's correspondence would seem to indicate a more "literary" and less personal relationship. The correspondence of D'Alembert, Mme Geoffrin, Falconet, and Meilhan, although friendly at the outset, ended in ruptures, due chiefly to the tactlessness of the Frenchmen. All of these correspondents of the Russian Empress were responsible in varying degrees for the spread of a general vogue for her and for the increase of her personal prestige abroad.

We have now examined all the main points of direct contact between eighteenth-century French and Russian society. There remain to be ascertained—partly as the result of these numerous rapprochements, the nature and extent of France's actual knowledge of Russia during this period.

PART TWO

RUSSIA IN EIGHTEENTH-CENTURY FRENCH LITERATURE

V

THE PRINCIPAL SOURCES OF INFORMATION
ABOUT RUSSIA

THIS chapter deals with the written sources of information about Russia known to eighteenth-century France. It is concerned with the accounts of travelers, the histories of Russia, and the articles on Russia in the periodical literature of the day. The aim is primarily to survey the better-known works (with an attempt to evaluate them) from which the French layman and scholar alike could have derived information.

Until the middle of the sixteenth century there were but few descriptive works on Russia, and those dealt mainly with the Tatar tribes. Among the earliest accounts of travelers pertaining to Russia, those of Benjamin of Tudela and of John di Plano Carpini were probably the best known. Benjamin of Tudela was a learned rabbi who traveled from 1160 to 1173 to Bagdad, and perhaps (on his return) down the Rhine valley and to Paris. The first edition of the account of his travels appeared in Hebrew, Constantinople, 1543, in octavo and ran through several Latin editions in the sixteenth century. Tudela's account appeared in English for the first time in Purchas's *Pilgrims* in 1625, in folio, under the title of *The Peregrinations of Benjamin, the Sonne of Jonas a Jew; Written in Hebrew; Translated into Latin by B. Arias Montanus...* In French this work did not appear until 1735, when it was included in Bergeron's *Collection de voyages,* under the title of *Voyage du célèbre Benjamin, autour du monde, commencé l'an 1173 contenant une exacte et succinte description de ce qu'il a vu de plus remarquable dans presque toutes les parties de la terre* ...

Tudela's account contains only cursory references to Russia. He emphasizes the vastness of the country and the severity of the climate. His geographic knowledge of Russia appears to have been vague. The following description, in which he apparently considers Russia part of Bohemia, is characteristic:

Thence extends the land of Bohemia, called Prague. This is the commencement of the land of Slavonia, and the Jews who dwell there call it Canaan, because the men of that land (the Slavs) sell their sons and their daughters to the other nations. These are the men of Russia, which is a great empire stretching from the gate of Prague to the gates of Kieff, the large city which is at the extremity of that empire. It is a land of mountains and forests, where there are to be found the animals called vair [i.e., a species of marten], ermine, and sable. No one issues forth from his house in winter-time on account of the cold. People are to be found there who have lost the tips of their noses by reason of the frost. Thus far reaches the empire of Russia.[1]

Almost as scant and fragmentary as those of Tudela are the observations on Russia of John di Plano Carpini, an Italian minorite who, together with several other friars, was sent in 1245 by Pope Innocent IV to the khan of the Mongolians. Carpini spent sixteen months in making this journey. He went through Bohemia, Poland, Ukraine (Kiev) and crossed the Don and the Volga. His few scattered remarks about Russia are confined to the climate, and descriptions of the scenery. He apparently failed to differentiate clearly between the Russians and the Bohemians, but seems to have been quite aware of the difference between the Russians and the Tatars. Of Carpini's account there are several Latin texts

[1] Marcus Adler, *The Itinerary of Benjamin of Tudela* ... London, 1907, pp. 80-81.

extant. The oldest text, without date or place of publication, is entitled: *Relacio fratris Joannis de Plano Carpini, ordinis fratrum minorum, de Tartaris . . . anno Domini MCCXLV. . . .* An abridgement of the account was included by Vincent de Beauvais in his *Speculum historiale,* and by Hakluyt in his *Collection of Voyages* of 1598. Fractions of Carpini's narrative appeared in French in Bergeron's *Voyages en Tartarie* in 1634 under the title of *Voyages très curieux faits et écrits par les R.R.P.P. Jean du Plan Carpini, Cordelier, et N. Asclin, Jacobin . . .* and in 1725 in Volume VII of Bernard's *Receuil des voyages du Nord.*

Both Tudela and Carpini serve merely as an introduction to the real "discoverer" of Russia for Europe, the Austrian diplomat, Baron Sigmund von Herberstein (1486-1566). His *Rerum Moscoviticarum commentarii,* published in Vienna in 1549, in folio, is really the first authentic and extensive account of Russia and the Russian people. This work had numerous Latin and German editions in the sixteenth century.[2] An Italian edition appeared at Venice in 1550, in quarto, a year after the publication of the original, under the title of *Commentari della Moscovia et parimente della Russia, et delle altri cose belle e notabili . . .* Herberstein's work was also made known to Europe through its inclusion in the well-known collection, *Rerum Moscoviticarum auctores varii unum in corpus nunc primum congesti,* Frankfort, 1600, folio. Extracts from Herberstein's account appeared in English for the first time in Richard Eden's collection in 1555 under the title

[2] The principal editions were: Basel, 1549, 1551, 1556 and 1571, in folio; Antwerp, 1557, octavo; Venice, 1558, quarto; Frankfort, 1600, folio.

Prior to Herberstein's book one can also mention an intelligent, though short, treatise on Russia by Paolo Giovio (Jovius), *Libellus de legatione Basilii Magnis Principis Moscoviae,* Rome, 1525 *et seq.* This was included in the *Rerum Moscoviticarum* of 1600. It had no French editions. Short chapters on Russia were included also in Joannes Boemus's *Omnium gentium mores,* 1520, *et seq.,* and in Aeneas Sylvius's (Pope Pius II) *Europae Asiaeque descriptio,* written about 1450.

Decades of the Newe Worlde ... There was no French translation made, although most of the French writers on Russia read the book either in Latin or in Italian. His contemporaries were unanimous in praising this account, and throughout the eighteenth century there were few writers on Russia who had not consulted it. "If thou list to know the Russes well," wrote in 1568 Master George Turberville, secretary to Thomas Randolph, the English Ambassador to Russia, "to Sigismundus booke repayre, who all the truth can tell." [3]

Herberstein was sent to Russia by the Emperors Maximilian and Ferdinand to negotiate peace between Russia and Poland and to renew friendly relations with the Grand Duke Vasilii Ivanovich. He spent about a year in Russia, visited many towns and learned the language. In his book he gives brief but judicious sketches of Russia's history, geography, religion, government, peculiarities of warfare, trade and the domestic habits and amusements of her people. He describes in detail the luxury and magnificence of the court; hunting scenes, hawking and harehunt, and the private life of the boyars. Although he observes the predilection for drinking and debauch, he does not seem to be appalled by it. He finds the Grand Duke generous and wise and the nobles hospitable and possessing a certain grace of demeanor. Contrary to so many subsequent writers on Russia, Herberstein maintains throughout the attitude of an impartial observer; he neither condemns nor commends. [4]

After Herberstein, the next account of Russia was that of an Italian Jesuit, Antonius Possevinus (Possevino) (1534-1611), who was sent to Russia by Pope Gregory XIII to nego-

[3] Richard Hakluyt, *Collection of the Early Voyages, Travels, and Discoveries of the English Nation*, London, 1809-1812, 5 vols., I, 432.

[4] See R. H. Major's translation of Herberstein's account, *Notes upon Russia*, London, Hakluyt Society, 1851-1852. Immediately after Herberstein, there was a Russian section in Sebastian Münster, *Cosmographia*, 1550. A map of Russia appeared in Ortelius's atlas, *Theatrum orbis*, 1570 et seq. Russian material is also included in André Thevet's *Cosmographie* of 1575.

tiate a union between the Eastern and Western Churches. His *Moscovia* was published in Vienna in 1586 and had several Latin and Italian editions in the sixteenth and seventeenth centuries.[5] It had, however, no English or French translations. The eighteenth-century French historians such as Levesque and LeClerc used the Latin and Italian editions.

Possevinus's mission was a failure, owing, in part at least, to his narrow-mindedness and lack of tact. Although received very cordially he gives the impression (in his *Moscovia*) of having been maltreated and dismissed without an adequate hearing. He gives a theatrical and exaggerated description of Tsar Ivan the Terrible and his court. Although prejudiced and exaggerated, his account is a fairly informative description of the Russian court at the end of the sixteenth century. His *Moscovia*, however, is narrow in scope, being scarcely more than a travel diary of his sojourn.[6]

Two other contemporaries of Possevinus, an Italian, Alessandro Guagnini of Verona, and a German, Paul Oderborn, visited the court of Tsar Ivan the Terrible and published descriptions of it. Guagnini's account *Saramatiae Europeae descriptio*, appeared in Cracow in 1581, in folio. It appears to have had no translations other than those in Russian and Polish. Guagnini gives a vivid picture of the cruelties of the Tsar, and according to Levesque, is a fairly reliable source for the history of the time. Oderborn's *Joannis Basilidis Magni Moscoviae Ducis vita*, Wittenberg, 1585, 3 volumes, in octavo, is a violent attack on the Tsar and is confused and historically inaccurate. Levesque used it as a source, but judiciously and with full awareness of its shortcomings. Oderborn's work had neither French nor English translations.

The last of the principal sixteenth-century writers on

[5] Antwerp, 1587, octavo; Cologne, 1587 and 1595, folio; Ferrara, 1592, octavo; Montova, 1596 and 1611, quarto.

[6] See Possevinus's biography by Nicholas Dorigny, Paris, 1712, duodecimo, and Mlle L. Karttunen's *Antonio Possevino*, Lausanne, 1908.

Russia who will be mentioned here was Cæsar Baronius (1538-?), Cardinal and scholar, known as the father of ecclesiastical annals. His *Historica relatio de Ruthenorum origine eorumque miraculosa conversione* was published in Cologne in 1598, in octavo. A French translation by Marc Lescarbot, under the title of *Discours de l'origine des Russiens, et de leurs miraculeuse conversion*, appeared in Paris in 1599, in octavo. This work is concerned entirely with the early history of the Russian Church. It was considered reliable by Russian historians but was not used by Levesque and other French historians as a source.

The entire work of Herberstein and many extracts from other sixteenth-century Latin works mentioned here were included in a general compilation of works on Russia entitled *Rerum Moscoviticarum scriptores varii*, which appeared in Frankfort in 1600, in folio. This compilation was known to some of the eighteenth-century French historians of Russia, notably to Levesque and LeClerc.

The early German and Italian works which we have examined, although limited in scope, were in many instances more impartial and historically reliable than many of the works written on Russia in the following two centuries, especially by Frenchmen.

Jean Sauvage (Jehan Savage) was the first and only Frenchman who is known to have gone to Russia in the sixteenth century. He went to Archangel in 1586 with the intention of establishing trade relations with Russia. He wrote a short diary of his trip, which was not, however, published until the nineteenth century.[7] Sauvage's account is merely a guide to future navigators and merchants and contains no general observations on Russia or the Russian people.

---

[7] *Mémoire du voyage en Russie, fait en 1586, suivi de l'expédition de Fr. Drake en Amérique publiés par Louis Lacour*, Paris, 1855, octavo. Cf. also Charles de la Roncière, *Histoire de la marine française*, Paris, 1910, IV, 255-258.

From 1553, when England established regular commercial relations with Russia, until the end of the century there were a number of Englishmen who went to Russia and wrote accounts of their voyages. The majority of these memoirs were not translated into French. Extracts from them appeared in various English compilations of travels. The English voyages to Russia made up, for example, at least one-fourth of Richard Hakluyt's *Principal Voyages* in the first edition (1589); they were reprinted, with additions, in Volume I of the second edition (1598). As some of these voyages were known to the eighteenth-century French writers through the various French collections of travels (such as Bergeron's) the contributions of the early English writers on Russia should also be included in our survey of the French sources.

Richard Chancellor, navigator and commander of one of the ships in Sir Hugh Willoughby's ill-fated expedition to Russia in 1553, and later in charge of a second expedition to that country in 1555, left interesting observations on Russia which are preserved in Hakluyt's collection under the title of *The Booke of the Great and Mighty Emperor of Russia*.[8] Chancellor's account was never translated into French, but was known to some of the eighteenth-century Frenchmen. Extracts from it appeared in Bernard's *Receuil de voyages au Nord*, Amsterdam, 1725-1738 (Vol. I). Although limited to a short description of what he saw in Russia, Chancellor's work is interesting, chiefly because of his observations upon Russia's laws and religion. Similar observations were occasionally made by subsequent English and French writers in their works on Russia. Chancellor was greatly impressed by the leniency and simplicity of the Russian laws. Thus, he tells us, a thief caught for the first time was not hanged as in England, but was subjected to torture; he was hanged only

[8] Hakluyt, *Collection of the Early Voyages, Travels, and Discoveries of the English Nation*, London, 1809-1812, I, 263-283.

after committing his offense for the third time.[9] As to the Russian religion he found it to be full of superstition and absurdities. He reports the following practice as an example: when a Russian died, a scroll of paper was put into his hands on which were written all his religious and civic virtues. The purpose of this was to facilitate the entrance of his soul into Heaven.[10]

Anthony Jenkinson, the next Englishman to write about Russia, was the ambassador of Queen Elizabeth and agent of the Moscovy Company between 1557 and 1572. A short account of his voyage under the title of *The first Voyage by Master Anthonie Jenkinson . . . toward the Land of Russia . . . in the Yeere 1557* is preserved in Hakluyt's collection.[11] A Dutch edition of the account appeared in Leyden in 1707, in octavo.[12] This edition was translated into French and published in Bernard's *Recueil de voyages au Nord*.[13] Jenkinson's account is narrow in scope and strongly prejudiced against Russians. He gives vivid descriptions of the luxury and magnificence of the life at court and condemns the frivolity and licentiousness of the people. Drinking is the greatest vice and the Russian people ". . . are great talkers and lyers, without any faith or truth in their words, flatterers and dissemblers." [14]

An interesting but very unfavorable description of the Russian people was that of Master George Turberville, secretary to Thomas Randolph, ambassador to Russia in 1568. Turberville described his impressions in a series of letters in verse written to his friends in England. These letters are pre-

---

[9] Hakluyt, *Collection of the Early Voyages, Travels, and Discoveries of the English Nation*, London, 1809-1812, I, 280.

[10] *Ibid.*, I, 283.

[11] *Ibid.*, I, 346-351.

[12] *Reys op Ordre van de Engelse, Moscovise Maatschappy, om een Weg door Tartarie naar Catay te ontdekken in het Jaar 1558.*

[13] Jean Bernard, *Recueil de voyages au Nord*, Amsterdam, 1725-1738, IV, 470-505.

[14] Hakluyt, *Collection . . . 1809-1812*, I, 350.

served in Hakluyt's collection but appear never to have been translated into French.[15] The Russian character Turberville finds to be utterly depraved:

> A People passing rude, to vices vile inclinde,
> Folke fit to be of Bacchus traine, so quaffing
> is their kinde.

They are devout but hypocritical:

> Devoutly downe they ducke, with forhead to the ground,
> Was never more deceit in ragges, and greasie garments found.

The Russian women are, according to Turberville, all immoral and their excessive use of cosmetics renders them repulsive. He could, he adds, say many more unpleasant things about the Russians but is afraid to be outspoken for fear of hurting the trade with Moscovy—

> But if no traffique were, then could I boldly pen
> The hardness of the soile, and eke the manners of men.

Another sixteenth-century Englishman, Jerome Horsey, also left a journal of his prolonged stay in Russia. Horsey resided in Russia more or less continually from 1575 until 1591, first as agent of the Russia Company, and subsequently as an envoy from the English court. An abridged account of Horsey's missions to Russia appeared in Hakluyt's collection and in Purchas's *Pilgrims* under the title of *Extracts out of Sir Jerome Horsey's Observations in Seventeene Yeers Travels and Experience in Russia and Other Countries Adjoyning . . .*[16] A complete account of Horsey's travels appeared for the first time in 1856 in Sir Edward Bond's *Russia at the Close of the Sixteenth Century*. There were no French translations of this work until the nineteenth century.

---

[15] Hakluyt, *Collection* . . . 1809-1812, I, 432-435.
[16] Purchas, *Pilgrims*, London, 1625, V, 969.

Horsey's account is an informal narrative, recording incidents in Russian history and describing the principal courtiers at the Russian court. It contains interesting anecdotes of personal adventures in Russia and a great deal of hearsay and gossip. Horsey is, on the whole, friendly to Russia and tolerant of the weaknesses of the Russian people. He evinces a certain interest in the Russian language and gives examples of it.[17] He gives the following interesting description of Tsar Ivan the Terrible:

He was a goodlie man of person and presence, waill favored, high forehead, shrill voice; a right Sithian; full of readie wisdom, cruell, bloudye, merciless; his own experience mannaged by direction both his state and commonwealth affairs.[18]

More important as a source of information on Russia than the preceding is the work of Dr. Giles Fletcher, the last of the sixteenth-century Englishmen to write about Russia. Fletcher, a member of a family illustrious in the history of English literature (his brother, Dr. Richard Fletcher, was the father of John Fletcher, the dramatist) was sent to Russia as an ambassador from Queen Elizabeth to Tsar Feodor Ivanovich in the year 1588. The purpose of this mission was to obtain certain concessions for the Russia Company. Partly because of the Russian government's dissatisfaction with the conduct of this company, partly because of an unfavorable political situation, Fletcher was treated in Russia with studied neglect. After being obliged to submit to many indignities, he finally succeeded in obtaining the necessary concessions and left for England, bearing a deep personal resentment against the Russian government. Upon his return to England, Fletcher wrote a strongly unfavorable study of the government and the conditions prevailing at the time of his visit. The first edition of

[17] Sir Edward Bond, *Russia at the Close of the Sixteenth Century*, London, 1856, p. 235.
[18] *Ibid.*, p. 209.

his *Of the Russe Commonwealth* appeared in London in 1591, in octavo, and was dedicated to Queen Elizabeth. The Russia Company complained that the book might give offense to the Russian government, and it was quickly suppressed. An abridgment of it, in which everything which might prove offensive to the Russian government was carefully deleted, appeared in 1599 in Hakluyt's *Principal Navigations*. A reprint of the first edition, with some suppressions, was included in Purchas's *Pilgrims* in 1625. A second edition of it appeared in London in 1643. A complete text of the first edition was not published until 1856, when it appeared in Sir Edward Bond's *Russia at the Close of the Sixteenth Century*. Although there was no French translation of Fletcher's book until the nineteenth century,[19] it is likely that it was known to some of the eighteenth-century French writers on Russia. However, the principal eighteenth-century French historians of Russia make no reference to it.

Of the Russe Commonwealth gives an extensive geographical description of the country, a detailed description of the major cities and native commodities, an historical sketch of the rulers, and of the political and social conditions of the time. The book abounds in inaccuracies, omissions, and historical and geographical errors. The misspelling of Russian names is much more frequent than in the English works preceding Fletcher's. The point of view is strongly prejudiced against the Russian government. Fletcher views Russia's future with pessimism:

This desperate state of things at home [i. e., oppression, slavery, and inequality of justice] maketh the people for the most part to wishe for some forreine invasion, which they suppose to bee the only meanes to rid them of the heavy yoke of this tyrannous government.[20]

---

[19] *La Russie au XVIe siècle avec une introduction par Ch. du Bouget.* 2 vols. Leipzig and Paris, 1864, octavo.

[20] Edward Bond, *Russia at the Close of the Sixteenth Century,* p. 45.

Besides attacking the government, Fletcher criticises the clergy as ignorant and "godless." The Russian priests, he says, "are very warie to keepe the people likewise in their ignorance and blindnesse, for their living and bellies sake." [21] Oppressed and kept in ignorance by the government and the clergy, the Russian people are merely the result of these conditions; they are cruel, intemperate and depraved: "The whole countrie overfloweth with all sinne of that kinde. And no marveile, as having no lawe to restraine whoredomes, adulteries and like uncleannesse of life." [22] In spite of this rather unrelieved hostility towards Russia, Fletcher has a few favorable observations to make: He praises the grace and solemnity of the Russian Church services, the absence of inquisition and the relative simplicity of the judicial system.

Of the various sixteenth-century accounts of Russia, Herberstein's *Commentarii* stands out as the most impartial, judicial, and authentic. The Italian and German accounts seem, in general, to have been more informative and reliable than the English. They were, moreover, used almost exclusively as sources of information on Russia by the eighteenth-century Frenchmen.

The seventeenth-century writers on Russia did not, as a rule, improve upon their predecessors in scope, range, or reliability of information. The German works are again superior to those of other foreign travelers.

After Herberstein, the next work on Russia to achieve a European reputation was an account of a German traveler, Adam Olearius (1600-1671). The account of his journey, *Offt begehrte Beschreibung der neuen orientalischen Reise . . .*

---

[21] Edward Bond, *Russia at the Close of the Sixteenth Century*, p. 130.

[22] *Ibid.*, pp. 151-152. After Fletcher, one might mention (as a source of information) John Barclay's *Icon animorum*. This survey of national "characters," had a short but informative chapter on Russia. The author gives a very black picture of the Russian character.

appeared in Schleswig, 1647, in folio. It was translated into many European languages and had numerous editions during the seventeenth and eighteenth centuries. Translated into French by Jean Wicquefort as *Voyages très curieux et renommés faits en Moscovie, Tartarie et Perse* ... it had several editions in Paris, Amsterdam, and Leyden.[23]

Olearius was the son of a tailor. He studied philosophy at Leipzig and subsequently entered the service of the Duke of Holstein-Gottorp. In 1633 an embassy headed by Philip Crusius and Otto Brugmann was appointed to negotiate trade relations with the Shah of Persia. The embassy was obliged first to request permission of the Tsar Feodor Mikhaïlovich to pass through Russia. Olearius was made secretary of this embassy. He returned to Holstein in 1639 and was appointed the Duke's court geographer and mathematician.

Olearius had the spirit of a scholar, accurate and careful. He had, moreover, the faculty of presenting his observations and experiences in a vivid and interesting manner. Although occasionally he allowed his imagination to run away with him, his account is, on the whole, accurate and reliable, and in range of information surpasses most of the earlier accounts of travelers. In content, Olearius's account, in addition to a diary of the trip, comprises detailed descriptions of many Russian towns and of the region near the Caspian and Black Seas. His contribution to the geographical knowledge of Russia was, without doubt, considerable. He sketches with fair accuracy the rulers of Russia and the state of the government, and describes in detail the religious ceremonies, customs, and manners of the people. The government he considers a despotic monarchy, oriental in type, under which the people have been born into slavery—*Les Moscovites sont nés pour*

---

[23] Paris, 1656, 1659, 1666, quarto; Leyden, 1719; Amsterdam, 1727 and 1732, folio.
[24] Adam Olearius, *Voyages* ... Leyden, 1719, I, 218.

être esclaves.[24] He characterizes the Russian people as ignorant, brutal, proud, vain, insolent, and discourteous to
foreigners.[25] These observations were frequently repeated by
eighteenth-century Frenchmen, who often saw Russia through
Olearius's eyes. Olearius stresses the fondness of the common
people for drinking and debauch and recounts many anecdotes to illustrate their excesses.[26] These, like his description of
many quaint marriage customs, seem to be based more on
hearsay than fact.[27] So far as the future of Russia is concerned,
Olearius is pessimistic. He records, however, that Western
influences are at work, and he believes these to be salutary.[28]
Although in many respects informative and trustworthy,
Olearius seems to have overstressed the negative side of the
Russian character. This lack of impartiality is unfortunate,
as his work was read by many eighteenth-century Frenchmen.
Voltaire, Levesque, and LeClerc used it for their histories of
Russia; many eighteenth-century travelers to Russia repeated
his observations, and Montesquieu drew information from
Olearius for his *Lettres persanes.*[29]

   Another seventeenth-century account by a German, Baron
Augustin von Mayerberg (1612-1688) enjoyed a considerable reputation. The first edition of his account in Latin,
*Iter in Moscoviam Augustini liberi baronis de Mayerberg . . .
anno MDCLXI ab legatorum cum statutis Moscoviticis ex
russico in latinum idioma ad eadem translatis . . .* appeared in
folio, without date or place of impression. A French translation of this work was published in Leyden in 1688, in duodecimo, under the title, *Voyage en Moscovie d'un ambassadeur
envoyé par l'Empereur Leopold au Czar Alexis Mihaliowicz.*

---

[25] Adam Olearius, *Voyages* . . . I, 210.
[26] *Ibid.*, I, 214-215.
[27] *Ibid.*, see, for example, I, 246 and 248.
[28] *Ibid.*, I, 210.
[29] Cf. Montesquieu, *Lettres persanes,* letter LI; also Voltaire's note to Choiseul
regarding Olearius, Nisard, *Mémoires et correspondances* . . . Paris, 1858, pp.
31-32.

It had also several German editions and one Italian edition in the seventeenth century.

Baron von Mayerberg was sent to Russia in 1661 by the Emperor Leopold I to negotiate peace between Tsar Aleksieï Mikhaïlovich and John-Casimir, King of Poland. The embassy remained in Russia for one year. Their mission was so unpopular that they were made almost prisoners. Although their freedom was curtailed, the envoys were treated with consideration and were finally allowed to return to Austria in 1663. Mayerberg was naturally prejudiced against the Russian government. Nevertheless, his account is a fairly judicious and reliable description of Russia prior to Peter's reforms. His historical and geographical sketches of old Russia are both accurate and informative. He ridicules the Russian religion as bigoted and superstitious and recounts a number of anecdotes to illustrate this. Some of these, such as the story of the public execution of the English ambassador's pet monkey for having entered the Russian Church,[30] were often repeated by subsequent travelers. In spite of Mayerberg's hostility towards the government, he gave a very sympathetic description of the Tsar Aleksieï Mikhaïlovich:

Il est doux et débonnaire, de sorte qu'il n'eût point de crime à punir que de châtier les coupables. Son inclination naturelle le porte à la paix; il est très attaché 'aux dogmes erronés de sa religion, et fort pieux.[31]

The Russian people Mayerberg describes as vain, proud, and very discourteous to foreigners.[32] The reliability of Mayerberg's account is considerably marred by an inconsistent and capricious spelling of Russian names.

Johann Korb, an Austrian diplomat, was the author of a

---

[30] Baron Augustin von Mayerberg, *Relation d'un voyage en Moscovie*, Paris, 1858, 2 vols., I, 68-69 and 83.
[31] *Ibid.*, I, 207.   [32] *Ibid.*, II, 132.

very interesting diary pertaining to the first part of Peter's reign. It was published originally in Latin under the title, *Diarium itineris in Moscoviam*, Vienna, 1700, in folio. This edition was almost entirely destroyed by the order of the court of Vienna, which sought to placate Peter the Great. The Tsar's agents were also ordered to buy up and destroy the remaining stray copies. The *Diarium* remained untranslated until the nineteenth century. A French translation, *Récit de la sanglante révolte des Streletz*, appeared in 1858, in the eighth volume of the *Bibliothèque russe et polonaise*. However, its rarity unquestionably contributed to its vogue. Among the eighteenth-century French writers one frequently encounters observations on Peter the Great which seem to have originated with Korb.

The author was secretary of a legation sent to Russia by the Emperor Leopold and headed by Ignaz-Christoph Herr von Guarient und Rall, in the year 1698. The diary is an account of the early years of Peter's reign and the summary suppression of the Strel'tsy rebellion of which the author was an eyewitness. It comprises descriptions of the Russian court, military power, currency, and revenues, and of Peter's reforms in Church and State. Korb gives a very vivid and minute description of Peter's savage cruelty in punishing the rebels. The Tsar himself, he tells us, was present at their tortures and personally supervised them.[33] The author records dispassionately all the atrocities which he witnessed and appears to justify Peter's actions. He frequently stresses the curious blending in Peter's character of generosity and highmindedness with savage fury and cruelty. Peter's reforms, Korb believes, are most salutary. He describes the people as ignorant, superstitious, and deceitful: "Devoid of honest

---

[33] Johann Georg Korb, *Diary of an Austrian Secretary of Legation at the Court of Czar Peter the Great* ... 2 vols. London, 1863, I, 178-179; 185-187; 190-241.

education, they esteem deceit to be the height of wisdom."[34] The author is also impressed by the oriental character of various Russian customs, particularly those pertaining to the relations between the two sexes.[35] The *Diarium* is, on the whole, a penetrating and impartial account of Russia as seen by a seventeenth-century foreigner.

The seventeenth-century English contribution to French sources on Russia is negligible. It is chiefly confined to the account of the embassy to Russia of Charles Howard, Earl of Carlisle, in the years 1663-1664. The author of this account, Guy Miege, was a Swiss who had lived for many years in England and wrote in two languages. He accompanied the Earl of Carlisle to Russia, though it is uncertain in what capacity. The first edition of his account, entitled *A Relation of Three Embasies from His Sacred Majestie Charles II, to the Great Duke of Muscovie, the King of Sweden, and the King of Danmark. Performed by the Right Honorable the Earle of Carlisle in the Years 1663-1664. Written by an Attendant on the Embasies,* appeared in London, at John Starkey's, in 1669, in octavo. In the same year this account was published in French in Amsterdam under the title of *La Relation de trois ambassades de Monseigneur le comte de Carlisle vers Alexey Michailovitcz, czar et grand duke de Moscovie...* This work ran through at least five editions and seems to have enjoyed considerable popularity in France.[36] It is possible that the original was written in French.

Guy Miege's account contains descriptions of the voyage from Archangel to Moscow, the embassy's reception at the court and the actual conditions in Russia. It is friendly in tone and somewhat naïve. Although limited in range of information, Miege's account touches on several aspects of Russian

[34] *Ibid.,* II, 195 and 197.
[35] *Ibid.,* II, 199 and 208.
[36] The principal editions were: Amsterdam, 1669 and 1670, duodecimo; Rouen, 1670, duodecimo; Amsterdam, 1672 and 1700, duodecimo.

life which had not been observed before. He is, for example, greatly impressed by the magnificence of the Russian court.

A dire le vrai, la cour, du Tzar de Moscovie est si belle, si magnifique et si bien réglée, que je puis dire franchement qu' entre tous les princes Chrétiens c'est lui qui l'emporte en gloire et en magnificence.[37]

He gives a most favorable picture of the Tsar Aleksiei Mikhaïlovich and, what is unusual for the time, praises the benevolent and patriarchal government of Russia.[38] He is, perhaps, the first foreigner to praise the culture and graciousness of some of the Russian nobles (the Orlovs and the Golitsyns, for example).[39] However, he characterizes the nobility as, for the most part, insolent and vain.[40] Miege notices and frequently mentions the great contrasts in Russian climate and in Russian life, the extreme poverty and ignorance of the masses and the refinement and luxury of the aristocracy. He is in agreement with what has been said by most foreign travelers to Russia about the character of the common people. They are, he observes, lazy, servile, dishonest, and addicted to a variety of vices (drinking and sodomy).[41] With other contemporary writers on Russia, Miege considers the Russian religion and the clergy to be largely responsible for the abject condition of the masses:

Comme l'ignorance est la mère de superstition, il s'est glissé parmi eux tant de folies et d'extravagances que l'on peut dire avec raison qu'ils ont presque tout à fait converti leur religion en grimaces.[42]

Another seventeenth-century English work on Russia, of lesser importance as a source for eighteenth-century

---

[37] *La Relation de trois ambassades de M. le comte de Carlisle*, Paris, Jaunet, 1857, p. 345.
[38] *Ibid.*, pp. 120 and 350-352.
[39] *Ibid.*, pp. 303 and 351.   [40] *Ibid.*, p. 310.
[41] *Ibid.*, pp. 308-309.   [42] *Ibid.*, p. 365.

France than the preceding, is that of Samuel Collins, for nine years private physician to the Tsar Aleksïeĭ Mikhaïlovich, father of Peter the Great. His *Present State of Russia, in a Letter to a Friend at London*, London, 1671, in octavo, was translated into French and published in Paris in 1679 in duodecimo, under the title of *Relation curieuse de l'estat présent de la Russie traduite d'un auteur anglais qui a ésté neuf ans à la cour du grand Czar*. Collins's book is a light and entertaining account of his experiences in Russia. It had only one French edition and is not mentioned by the eighteenth-century French writers on Russia.

Finally, John Milton's *A Brief History of Moscovia*, first published in London in 1682, in octavo, had no French translation and appears to have been entirely unknown to eighteenth-century France. Milton's reason for writing this history was his dissatisfaction with the existing accounts of Russia because, as he stated in the preface:

Some too brief and deficient satisfy not; others too voluminous and impertinent cloy and weary out the reader; while they tell long stories of absurd superstitions, ceremonies, quaint habits and other petty circumstances little to the purpose.[43]

He wanted, then, to write a short history of Russia which would give the essentials only, and which would be accessible to the general reader.

Milton's history is admittedly a digest of the memoirs of previous travelers. His principal sources were the sixteenth-century English travelers, Chancellor, Jenkinson, Randolph, Horsey, and others, to whose experiences in Russia he devotes a chapter. As a historian Milton shows little critical judgment; he merely repeats without questioning the stories and anecdotes reported by the earlier travelers.[44] The Russian re-

---

[43] Milton, *Works*, "A Brief History of Moscovia," Preface.
[44] *Ibid.* See, for example, Milton on customs relating to marriage and burial rites, Columbia University edition, 1932, X, 340.

ligion Milton considers superstitious and the clergy corrupt and ignorant; "for Whordom, Drunkenness and Extortion none worse than the clergy." [45] Milton, in depicting the character of the Russian people, merely summarizes the prevalent pessimistic views of the English travelers: "They have no Learning; nor will suffer it to be among them; their greatest friendship is in drinking; they are great Talkers, Lyers, Flatterers and Dissemblers." [46]

An account of a trip to Russia by a Dutchman, John Struys, acquired a considerable European reputation. His *Drie Aanmerkelijke en seer Rampspoedige Keysen . . .* Amsterdam, 1676, in quarto, was translated into French, under the title of *Les Voyages de Jean Struys en Moscovie, en Tartarie, en Perse . . .* in 1681 and ran through several editions in the seventeenth and eighteenth centuries. [47] Struys's account is a lively and informal description of the state of the Russian Empire in 1658. It is a mixture of fact and fiction, with a predominance of the latter. Struys gives a very unflattering description of the Russian people:

Les Moscovites sont inciviles, farouches et ignorans; ils sont traitres, défians, cruels et si brutaux dans leur passions que la Sodomie ne leur semble pas le plus grand des crimes, joint qu'ils n'en font point de secret. [48]

He considers the various Russian customs relating to marriage and divorce brutal and barbaric and emphasizes especially the complete absence of decency and shame among the masses. [49] For the Russian religion he has nothing but contempt. [50] He condemns the severity of the Russian law and

[45] Milton, *Works*, "A Brief History of Moscovia," Preface.
[46] *Ibid.*, p. 341.
[47] Amsterdam, 1681, quarto; Lyon, 1682, duodecimo; 1684, duodecimo; Amsterdam, 1718, duodecimo; 1720, duodecimo; 1724, duodecimo; Rouen, 1724, duodecimo; Amsterdam, 1762, duodecimo.
[48] Jean Struys, *Les Voyages . . .* Amsterdam, 1681, p. 125.
[49] *Ibid.*, pp. 132-135.   [50] *Ibid.*, p. 138.

tells many exaggerated and doubtful stories to illustrate the brutality of the punishment of the "knout" [i.e., *knut*] and the "battoki" [i.e., *batogi*].[51] He is one of the first to describe at length the life of the Cossacks and he gives a complete account of the rebellion of Sten'ka Razin. Struys's narrative is superficial, injudicious, and it is responsible for conveying much information which is not founded on facts.

Among the few seventeenth-century French accounts of Russia, Captain Margeret's *Etat présent de l'empire de Russie* ...was the earliest and probably the best known. This book appeared in 1607 in Paris. It was republished in 1669, but had no eighteenth-century editions. Levesque used it for the epoch of the Pseudo-Dimitrii [52] and considered it reliable. Margeret had a long and adventurous career in Russia. He entered the service of Tsar Boris Godunov and about 1605 Pseudo-Dimitrii made him commander of a regiment of the Guards. After the death of this Tsar, Margeret returned to France, and entered the service of Henri IV. Later he served the King of Poland and in 1612 again offered his services to Russia, but was refused. About 1619 Margeret seems to have gone to Germany and is likely to have entered the service of a Polish nobleman, Prince Radziwill. After 1619 Margeret's career is unknown.[53]

The purpose of his book, as was stated in the Introduction, was to

...lever l'erreur à plusieurs qui croyent que la Chrestienté n'a de bornes que la Hongrie—tandis que la Russie est un des meilleurs boulevards de la Chrestienté et que cet empire et ce pays-là est plus grand, puissant, populeux et abondant que l'on ne cuide.[54]

---

[51] *Ibid.*, pp. 143-145.

[52] In the nineteenth century Margeret's account ran through the following editions: 1821, octavo; 1855, octavo; 1860, duodecimo.

[53] Captain Margeret, *Etat présent de l'empire de Russie*...Paris, Poitier, 1855, Introduction.

[54] *Ibid.*

Although limited in scope, Margeret's book is an intelligent and careful report, with very interesting details of the state of Russia at the end of the sixteenth century. With the exception of a few stories which do not seem plausible, such as the story of the Tsar who deliberately poisoned his subjects and rendered them blind,[55] Margeret tells only what he himself saw and observed. The picture he gives of the Russian people is not flattering—they are lazy, deceitful, and have a great passion for drinking.[56] He describes at some length the richness and fertility of the country but deplores Russia's backwardness and the total ignorance of the Latin tongue. However, he seems to like the easy and leisurely life in Russia and admires greatly her military organization.

La Neuville's *Relation curieuse et nouvelle de Moscovie*, Paris, 1698, and The Hague, 1699, is another French seventeenth-century account which achieved some popularity. The author went to Russia in 1689 and spent some time at the court of the Princess-Regent, Sof'ia, the sister of Peter the Great. More precise and extensive in his work than Margeret, La Neuville is not, however, so keen or intelligent an observer. Nor does he possess Margeret's curiosity and enthusiasm. La Neuville is hostile to Russia and pessimistic about her future. The people he considers little better than savages:

Tous les Moscovites dorment après avoir mangé, quelle que soit leur fortune... Lorsque vient le carnaval, le désordre est si grand que les étrangers qui logent dans les faubourgs n'oseraient quasi sortir et venir à la ville et les Moscovites s'enyvrent et s'assomment comme des bêtes sauvages.[57]

Like Olearius and some other contemporary travelers to Russia, La Neuville is impressed by the shabbiness and the filth of the Russian cities. Here is a description of Moscow:

[55] Captain Margeret, *Etat présent de l'empire de Russie* ... p. 58.
[56] *Ibid.*, pp. 16-20.
[57] Cited in A. Mansuy's *Le Monde slave* ... 1912, p. 468.

Quoique Moscou ait plus d'un demi-million d'habitants, on n'y trouve pas plus de 300 voitures de maître. Chacune des maisons qu'on y trouve ne vaut pas plus qu'une étable à cochon en Allemagne ou en France.[58]

La Neuville gives, besides his observations on Russian people, towns, and government, a detailed account of Russia's trade with foreign countries, particularly with England.

Several French accounts of Russian travels appeared in the second half of the seventeenth century. These accounts were, for the most part, limited to sections of Russia and contained little information about the country as a whole. Among these works one should mention Guillaume de Beauplan's *Description des contrées du royaume de Pologne, contenues depuis les confins de la Moscovie*, Rouen, 1651, in quarto, which is largely a geographic and ethnographic report of the author's prolonged stay in Poland and Ukraine (1631-1649?); [59] also, the Jesuit Gerbillion's account of China with observations on Siberia (1688-1698), and finally La Martinière's naïve story of travels in Finland and central Russia. This last account entitled *Nouveau voyage vers le Septentrion* . . . Paris, 1671, and Amsterdam, 1708, although very limited in scope, superficial, and inaccurate, appears to have enjoyed considerable success and was favorably reviewed in the *Journal des savants* for August, 1708.

These early works on Russia, so far examined, French and

[58] Cited in A. Mansuy's *Le Monde slave* . . . 1912, p. 468.

[59] The second edition of G. de Beauplan's *Description des contrées* . . . appeared under the title of *Description d'Ukraine*, Rouen, 1660, quarto, and Rouen and Paris, 1661, quarto. In addition to the above one might mention a treatise on "political geography" by the French geographer D'Avity. His *Les Estats* . . . *du monde*, 1614, or its enlargement, *Le Monde*, 1643, contained a brief but interesting and informative chapter on Russia. To complete the survey of seventeenth-century works on Russia one might also mention the Elzevir *Moscovia* of 1630. There were two editions: *Respublica Moscoviae et urbes*, Leyden, 1630, and *Russia seu Moscovia itemque Tartaria*, *ibid.*, 1630. Both were known in the eighteenth century but had no French translations and were not important for France as sources of information on Russia.

foreign alike, were, with few exceptions, hostile to Russia and the Russian people. The Germans and the English were less hostile than the French, for occasionally they discovered in Russia something worthy of commendation. Herberstein, for example, praised the hospitality and graciousness of the Russian nobles; Horsey was enthusiastic about the language; Chancellor appreciated the simplicity of the judiciary system; Fletcher praised Russia's religious tolerance. The French, with the exception of Captain Margeret, who admired Russian military organization and Russian hospitality, seemed inclined to view the country with complete lack of sympathy and understanding. All foreigners, regardless of nationality, emphasized the same vices of the Moscovite nation, laziness, debauchery, and absence of honesty. Many of these early travelers also stressed the sharp contrasts: the mixture of immorality and piety, of luxury and poverty, of hospitality and cruelty. All ridiculed the Russian religion and frequently blamed the clergy for the backwardness and ignorance of the common people. The same opinions were repeatedly expressed, as we have seen, by many of the eighteenth-century French travelers to Russia, such as Bernardin de Saint-Pierre, Chappe d'Auteroche, and Rulhière.

Turning now to the eighteenth-century published works on Russia, one can roughly divide them into groups: those addressed primarily to the specialist and the scholar, and those of a more popular nature, addressed to the general reader. The first group was composed, for the most part, of translations from the German. The English contributed considerably to France's knowledge of Russia, chiefly through popular impressionistic memoirs of travels. The French themselves had few works of original observation. We shall first consider the foreign works, since they were often used as sources of information by the French writers of the period.

Among the earliest foreign works on Russia, those of

Herberstein and Olearius which have already been treated
were probably the best known to France in the eighteenth
century. The first eighteenth-century foreign work on Russia to achieve a certain popularity in France was that of a
Dutch painter and traveler, Cornelis de Bruin (or Bruyn).
His account of a trip to Russia in 1701-1703 appeared first
in Dutch: *Reizen over Moskovie, door Persie en Indie*, Amsterdam, 1711, folio. It was translated into French in 1718
under the title of *Voyages par la Moscovie, en Perse et aux
Indes orientales*... 2 vols., Amsterdam, 1718, in folio. In
1725 Abbé Banier published a complete edition of all Bruin's
accounts of travels in five volumes under the title of *Voyage
en Levant*, Rouen, 1725, quarto. Volumes III-V of this edition were on Russia. This work had several eighteenth-
century editions (Paris, 1725, and The Hague, 1732) and
was translated into English in 1737. A long review with many
excerpts appeared in the *Journal des savants* for March, 1719.

Bruin spent about two years in Russia. Although he
appears to have traveled extensively in European and Asiatic
Russia, his contribution to the geographical knowledge of
the country is slight. Bruin's observations on the country
and the people are superficial and seem for the most part
to be those of earlier travelers, rather than the author's
own. In the preface to the 1725 edition of his work, he
freely acknowledges his indebtedness to some of his predecessors, particularly to Herberstein, Olearius and the author
of the account of the Earl of Carlisle's embassy to Russia.
While in Russia, the author painted a portrait of Peter the
Great and made many sketches of Russian scenery. His
sketches, many of which appear in the book, are vivid and
exact and are, perhaps, a more valuable source of information on Russia than the text itself.

An account by an Englishman, Captain John Perry, was
well known throughout the century. His *State of Russia*

under the Present Czar, London, 1716, was translated into French in the following year and went through several editions.[60] A favorable review, with many excerpts from the work, appeared in the *Mémoires de Trévoux* for May, 1717. Bernard's collection of travels also included parts of his account in the 1775 edition (Vol. VII). Montesquieu drew information from it for his *De l'esprit des lois,*[61] Voltaire used it for the preliminary sketch of his history of Peter the Great,[62] and Chevalier de Jaucourt in his article on Russia in the *Encyclopédie* recommended it to the general reader.

Captain Perry was a naval officer and a civil engineer. In April, 1698, Tsar Peter, while on a visit to England, engaged him to come to Russia to superintend the naval and engineering works then in progress. Perry spent fourteen years in Russia. He supervised many important works and received the title of "Comptroller of Russian maritime works." During his entire stay in Russia, Perry claims to have received only one year's salary. Tired of addressing petitions, he finally quarreled with the Tsar and, putting himself under the protection of the English Ambassador Whitworth, left for England. His book on Russia, published in 1716, contains a full account of the personal annoyances he suffered in Russia.

It is difficult to see why Perry's account achieved such popularity with his contemporaries. It is a dull narrative, badly put together, and limited in scope. Moreover, it was largely responsible for perpetuating a number of historical and ethnological errors as well as errors of observation and

---

[60] *Etat présent de la grande Russie* ... Paris, 1717, duodecimo; The Hague, 1717, octavo; Brussels, 1717, octavo; Paris, 1718, duodecimo; Amsterdam, 1718 and 1720, duodecimo.

[61] Montesquieu, *De l'esprit des lois,* éd. Garnier frères, Preface; also Book XII, ch. xxvi, p. 105; book XII, ch. xxviii, pp. 106-107; book XV, ch. vi, p. 183.

[62] Voltaire, *Correspondance,* éd. Garnier, XXXIX, letter to Shuvalov, August 7, 1757.

judgment. Thus, Perry maintained that to join the Russian Church, one had to be rebaptized, since all Christians belonging to other faiths were considered heathens. During the ceremony of baptism, he tells us, the person joining the Greek-Orthodox Church was obliged to spit three times at his former faith.[63] This quite erroneous notion was frequently repeated by other writers on Russia, notably by Voltaire. Another erroneous idea originating with Perry was his statement that there was no word in the Russian language to signify "honor."[64] Ignorance and superstition were largely responsible, in Perry's opinion, for the lack of honor and honesty among the masses.[65] For Peter the Great, Perry shows little personal regard, though he gives lengthy matter-of-fact descriptions of his reforms and marine improvements.[66] In his description of the Russian climate and of the government and the character of the people he lays much stress on the unaccountable blending of diametrically opposed qualities. This, however, as we have noted, had already been observed by a number of Perry's predecessors.

A more informative and reliable work than Captain Perry's was that of a German, Friedrich Christian Weber. His *Das veränderte Russland*, Frankfort, 1721, in quarto, had many editions in several languages. It was translated into French and published anonymously as *Mémoires pour servir à l'histoire de l'empire russien, sous le règne de Pierre le grand, par un ministre étranger résidant en cette cour*, 2 vols., The Hague, 1725, in duodecimo.[67] This edition, with

[63] Captain John Perry, *The State of Russia under the Present Czar*, London, 1716, p. 152.

[64] *Ibid.*, p. 47.

[65] *Ibid.*, pp. 178 and 216.

[66] *Ibid.*, pp. 30 ff.

[67] Another edition appeared under the title of *Nouveaux mémoires sur l'état présent de la grande Russie ou Moscovie* ... 2 vols., Amsterdam, 1725, octavo, and Paris, 1725, duodecimo.

the addition of a biographical sketch of Menshikov, was published under the title of *Mémoires anecdotes d'un ministre étranger, résidant à St. Pétersbourg* ... in The Hague in 1729 and 1737, in duodecimo. Weber's book had long reviews in the *Mémoires de Trévoux* and the *Journal des savants* for September, 1725, which agreed in considering it the most informative and impersonal account of Russia so far published. Levesque used it as a source, especially for the period 1714-1719, and praised it highly.

The author was an envoy from the Hannoverian court to Russia from 1714 to 1717. He had, apparently, opportunity for informing himself with exactness upon the state of Russia and thus wrote a very impartial account of it. He gave valuable information concerning Peter's reforms, the Tsar's relations with the Tsarevich Aleksĭeĭ, and the trade relations of Russia with England. Weber was one of the first foreigners to give a description of St. Petersburg. He was enthusiastic about this newly-built capital and predicted that in time it was likely to become a second Venice for Europeans.[68] Peter's reforms Weber held to be most salutary for the country. He took Peter's side against his son and gave a detailed account based on official records of the trial and proceedings against the Tsarevich.[69] Weber's sketch of Menshikov's life was the first authentic account of the picturesque courtier, and was frequently used by the eighteenth-century French writers on Russia. In Weber's account one notices also a more uniform and correct spelling of Russian names.

A short but intelligent and well-written account of Russia during Peter's reign was that of an Englishman, Lord Charles Whitworth (1675-1725). This work entitled *Ac-*

[68] Friedrich Weber, *The Present State of Russia* ... 2 vols., London, 1723, I, 190.

[69] *Ibid.*, II, 93-206.

count of Russia in the Year 1710 was included in Richard Dodsley's *Fugitive Pieces on Various Subjects*, London, 1758, in octavo. Although it had no French translation, Voltaire used it for his history of Peter the Great. It is likely that Whitworth's work was also known to other Frenchmen at the end of the century.

Whitworth gives a very judicious description of Peter the Great. He considers him a great monarch who merely by the strength of his own genius and contrary to the intention of his people, the Church, and his ministers, has wrought more profound changes in the Empire than any other known ruler in history.[70] At the same time, Whitworth describes Peter as unscrupulous, violent, and extravagant, in spite of an apparent simplicity of manner.[71] The author praises also the "modesty, sense and honor" of some of the Russian nobles he met.[72] Another interesting feature of Whitworth's account is his detailed description of the life of the Russian Cossacks,[73] much of which Voltaire took for his history.

Better known in France than the preceding was an account of Russia by a Swedish officer, Philip Strahlenberg (1676-1747). His *Das nord-und östliche Theil von Europa und Asia* ... Stockholm, 1730, in quarto, was translated into French by Barbeau de la Bruyère as *Description historique de l'empire russien* ... Amsterdam, 1757, in duodecimo. This work was well received and was reviewed in the *Journal de Trévoux* for December, 1758. De Jaucourt recommended it to the general reader as a good source of information on the state of the Russian Empire [74] and Voltaire used it for his

[70] Lord Charles Whitworth, "Account of Russia in the Year 1710," Dodsley's *Fugitive Pieces*, London, 1758, II, 192.

[71] *Ibid.*

[72] *Ibid.*, II, 195-196.

[73] Lord Charles Whitworth, "Account of Russia in the Year 1710," Dodsley's *Fugitive Pieces*, London, 1758, II, 179.

[74] Chevalier de Jaucourt, *Encyclopédie, Neufchatel*, 1751-1756, Vol. XIV.

history. Levesque knew of it also, but considered it unreliable.[75] The author took part in Charles XII's Russian campaigns and was taken prisoner at the battle of Poltava. He spent thirteen years as a prisoner in Russia. The reputation of his work was greater than its merit.

Several German academicians, members of the St. Petersburg Academy of Science, notably Johann Gmelin (1709-1755), a botanist, Professor Gerhard-Friedrich Müller (1705-1783), historian and explorer, and Peter Pallas (1741-1811), naturalist and geographer, gave the most scholarly information about Russia to eighteenth-century France, as well as to the rest of Europe. Gmelin's account of travels in Siberia, *Reise durch Siberien von dem Jahr 1733 bis 1743*, was abridged and translated into French by Keralio as *Voyage en Sibérie, contenant la description des mœurs et usages des peuples de ce pays*, Paris, 1767, 2 vols., in duodecimo. Another abridged version of this work appeared in Vol. XVIII of Prévost's *Histoire générale des voyages*. Gmelin's book is an exact and painstaking account of the country and its inhabitants, very minute and tedious. It had short reviews in *Mémoires de Trévoux*, February, 1768, in Grimm's *Correspondance littéraire*,[76] and in Formey's *Bibliothèque germanique*.[77] The numerous works of Professor Müller in Latin, German, Russian, and French were greatly praised by the principal eighteenth-century writers on Russia. Müller accompanied Gmelin upon his scientfic trip to Siberia and was editor of many learned works of a geographical and historical nature. Although he never wrote a complete history of Russia, he was a mine of information for European geographers and

---

[75] Pierre Levesque, *Histoire de Russie*, 1800, VIII, 341. See also the review of the work in *Mémoires de Trévoux*, December, 1758.

[76] Grimm, *Correspondance littéraire*, éd. Tourneux, VII, 308.

[77] Formey, *Bibliothèque germanique*, VI, 321 and XXV, 364.

historians of the country. Müller's principal work is a compilation of historical material entitled *Sammlung russischer Geschichte,* St. Petersburg, 9 vols., 1732-1764, in octavo. This work was republished in Offenbach, 5 vols., in octavo (1777-1779). It had no French translations, but was known to Voltaire, Levesque, and LeClerc. One might mention also two other works of Müller, both translated into French, one on Siberia, *Voyages et découvertes faites par les Russes le long des côtes de la mer glaciale* . . . Amsterdam, 1766, duodecimo, the other on the history of Novgorod, *Essai abrégé de l'histoire de Novgorod,* Copenhagen, 1771, in octavo.

Pallas furnished the most extensive geographical and ethnographical information on Russia. His best-known work, *Reise durch verschiedene Provinzen des russischen Reichs,* 3 vols., St. Petersburg, 1771-1776, quarto, was translated by Gauthier de la Peyronie as *Voyages en différentes provinces de l'empire de Russie et dans l'Asie septentrionale,* 5 vols., Paris, 1783-1793, folio. Another of Pallas's works was probably the best geographic and ethnographic account of Southern Russia, *Bemerkungen auf einer Reise in die südlichen Statthalterschaften des russischen Reichs in den Jahren 1793 und 1794,* 2 vols., Leipzig, 1799-1801, quarto. This work was translated into French as *Observations faites dans un voyage entrepris dans les gouvernements méridionaux de l'empire de Russie. . .* 2 vols., Leipzig, 1799-1801, quarto, and Paris, 1805. Gmelin's, Müller's, and Pallas's works contributed greatly to France's scientific knowledge of various sections of Russia, of her ethnography and her history. These works were not, however, for the general reader; they were written by specialists and were intended for the scholar. Nevertheless, extracts from these works appeared occasionally in popular French collections of travels, such as Bernard's (Volumes VII and VIII) and La Harpe's *Abrégé de l'histoire générale des voyages.* Many of the

eighteenth-century travelers to Russia had some acquaintance with these learned works.[78]

Among the more popular foreign works on Russia which
achieved recognition in France, the memoirs of Manstein
occupy an important place. They were first published in 1770
in England by David Hume under the title of *Memoirs of
Russia, Historical, Political, and Military from the Year 1727
to 1744*... London, 1770, quarto. The first French translation
under the title of *Mémoires historiques, politiques, et militaires
sur la Russie ... avec la vie de l'auteur par Huber,* appeared
in Amsterdam and Leipzig in 1771, in octavo. Levesque followed Manstein's memoirs closely for the period they covered
(1727-1744) and a favorable review of these memoirs appeared in the *Esprit des journaux* for August, 1772. Of Bo-
hemian origin, Christof Hermann von Manstein was educated in Prussian and Russian military academies. His father
was, for some time, governor of a province under Peter the
Great. Christof served for many years in the Russian army
and took part in many campaigns (1737-1739). During the
reign of the Empress Elizabeth he left Russia, entered the
Prussian service, and became an intimate friend of Frederick
the Great. Manstein's memoirs, not remarkable for their style,
were praised for their candor and impartiality. He gave many
accounts of military campaigns and some lively anecdotes
about the outstanding personalities of the Russian court, particularly those of Menshikov and Marshal Münich. There were
no general observations upon the people or the institutions of
Russia, the memoirs being chiefly a straightforward account
of battles and court intrigues.

The well-known Italian writer, traveler, and friend of

[78] For contemporary estimates of these writers see P. Chantreau, *Voyage
philosophique en Russie,* ch. xix; A. Fortia de Piles, *Voyage de deux Français*...
Preface; C. Masson, *Mémoires secrets*... éd. Barrière, pp. 90-92; W. Took, *View
of the Russian Empire during the Reign of Catherine the Second*... 3 vols.,
London, 1799, II, Introduction.

Voltaire, Count Francesco Algarotti, was the author of a book on Russia in the form of letters, which was well known at the time. His *Saggio di lettere sopra la Russia*, Paris, 1760 and 1763, octavo, was translated into French as *Lettres sur la Russie* in 1769 and ran through several editions.[79] These letters received several complimentary reviews in the periodicals of the time [80] and were read by Voltaire.[81] Count Algarotti spent several months in St. Petersburg in 1739, at the time of the Empress Anna Ivanovna's reign. His letters, addressed to Lord Harvey and Marquis Scipione Maffei, contain brief descriptions of Russia's trade, military forces on land and sea, revenues, and an account of the Russo-Turkish war. His book is rather matter-of-fact and dry. Algarotti is very friendly toward Russia. He praises the discipline, patience, and docility of the Russian soldier and admires Russia's military organization.[82] He found the Russian court sumptuous and gay, and prophesied that with a wise and able prince nothing could prevent Russia from becoming the eventual master of Europe.[83] On the whole, Algarotti seems to exaggerate Russia's military power and commercial potentialities. The account contains no personal observations on religion, manners and customs, or the character of the people—its central subject being military organization and trade.

Two popular works on Russia written by the Germans Stählin and Scherer, may be mentioned here as having been fairly well known in France in the second half of the cen-

---

[79] London, 1769, octavo; Neufchâtel, 1770, octavo; Glasgow, 1770, octavo; Amsterdam, 1785, octavo.

[80] *Mémoires de Trévoux*, June 1769, and *Journal encyclopédique*, January 1 and 15, 1761.

[81] Voltaire, *Correspondance*, letter to Count Algarotti, September, 1760.

[82] Count Francesco Algarotti, *Letters from Count Algarotti to Lord Hervey and the Marquis Scipio Maffei, containing the State of the Trade, Marine, Revenues and Forces of the Russian Empire* ... 2 vols. in one, London, 1769, I, 102, 136-140.

[83] *Ibid.*, I, 140.

tury. The first of these authors, Jacob von Stählin, a native of Dresden, was a resident of Russia for about forty years. He was invited by the Empress Elizabeth to become tutor to the Grand Duke Peter Feodorovich (later Tsar Peter III) and was made a member of the Academy of Sciences in St. Petersburg. His book entitled *Originalanekdoten von Peter dem Grossen*, Leipzig, 1785, octavo, was translated into French as *Anecdotes originales de Pierre le Grand* and published in Strassburg in 1787, in octavo. It had also several English editions. The work contains a short collection of anecdotes dealing with the life of Peter the Great. These anecdotes were based for the most part upon the accounts of eye-witnesses, chiefly persons at court. Some of the anecdotes, such as those of Captain Perry and Weber, were already known in France. Stählin's collection impresses one as rather ponderous and dull. The purpose of the book was, apparently, to demonstrate the greatness of Peter's character—his tolerance, simplicity, and justice.[84]

A more elaborate compilation of anecdotes, observations and historical data on Russia was made by Jean Benoit Scherer. His work, *Anecdotes intéressantes et secrètes de la cour de Russie* ... appeared first in French in six volumes in London and Paris, 1792, in octavo. In the following year it was translated into German under the title: *Sammlung merkwürdiger Anecdoten, das russische Reich* ... The work was re-edited in Paris in 1806. Scherer's book was mistrusted by the more informed writers on Russia. Grimm found it a mass of disconnected material and considered the author unreliable

[84] Another German account by Christoph Schwan, known under the pseudonym of De la Marche, can also be mentioned. His *Anecdotes russes, ou lettres d'un officier allemand à un gentilhomme livonien, écrites de Petersbourg en 1762*, London, 1764, 1766, 1769, octavo; Paris, 1766; Berlin and Dresden, 1765, octavo, were memoirs written in the form of letters and were light and popular in character. Grimm called the author *quelque polisson affamé* and warned the reader against trusting him. See *Correspondance littéraire*, éd. Tourneux, VII, 126-127.

and biased.[85] Fortia de Piles held the same view [86] and Levesque, in the analytical bibliography of his sources, does not mention it. A similar distrustful view was adopted by the reviewer of Scherer's anecdotes in the *Esprit des journaux* for October and November, 1792. Few copies of Scherer's work are extant at present.

The first French sources of information concerning the state of Russian literature were also German works. The first of these was a translation of a lengthy German article by a Russian, Ivan Dmitrievskiï, entitled "Nachricht von einigen russischen Schriftstellern, nebst einem kurzen Berichte vom russischen Theater," which was published in 1768 in a Leipzig magazine, *Neue Bibliothek der schönen Wissenschaften und der freyen Künste*. This work had two French editions in Leghorn in 1771 and 1774, under the title of *Essai sur la littérature russe*. Few French writers appear to have known about the work, though Levesque and LeClerc used the information contained in this essay for their chapters on Russian literature.

The only eighteenth-century bibliographical journal on Russian literature was that of H. L. Bachmeister, a German academician in Russian service. His *Russische Bibliothek*, 11 vols., St. Petersburg, Riga and Leipzig, 1772-1787, octavo, is an analytical bibliography of all the works published in Russia from 1770 to 1786. It had no eighteenth-century French translation and was probably unknown to French writers of that time with the exception of Levesque. In this connection, one might say that most of the principal eighteenth-century Russian works were translated into German by Germans in Russian service. French translations of the foremost Russian writers did not as a rule appear until the beginning of the nineteenth century. It seems safe to conclude that the

[85] Grimm, *Correspondance littéraire*, XVI, 202.
[86] Alphonse Fortia de Piles, *Voyage de deux Français* ... Preface.

knowledge and dissemination of Russian literature was largely confined to Germany and that Germans were the first foreigners to discover it and to further its progress.[87]

In the second half of the eighteenth century there appeared a number of English works on Russia, for the most part accounts of travelers. Some of these enjoyed considerable popularity in France. We shall now examine the more important of these in the order of their publication.

An English traveler, John Williams, was the author of an inferior account of Russia which had only limited success in France. His work, *The Rise, Progress, and Present State of the Northern Governments; viz., the United Provinces, Russia and Poland*, 2 vols., London, 1777, quarto, was translated into French as *Histoire des gouvernements du Nord* ... 4 vols., Amsterdam, 1780, duodecimo, and Yverdon, 1780, duodecimo. A part of the second volume and the whole of the third are devoted to Russia. In scope the work is ambitious; it contains an abridged history of the country and observations on Russian laws, government, religion, customs, and natural resources. In the Preface, the author states that for the Pre-Peter period he used original manuscripts in the Moscow archives and for the later period consulted important

[87] In this connection see A. Shtorkh's and F. Adelung's bibliographical journal of works published in Russia between 1801 and 1806—*Sistematicheskoe obozrĭenĭe literatury v Rossĭi*, 2 vols., St. Petersburg, Schnor, 1810, I, 352. In addition to the eighteenth-century German works on Russia already mentioned, there were a few others which, although of lesser importance as sources for France, were yet translated into French and so deserve to be noted:
a. A. L. Schlözer, *Geschichte von Russland*, Göttingen and Gotha, 1769, 32⁰; translated as *Tableau de l'histoire de Russie*, Göttingen and Gotha, 1769, 32⁰.
b. H. Storch, *Historisch-statistisches Gemälde russischen Reichs am Ende des 18. Jahrhunderts*, 8 vols., Riga and Leipzig, 1797-1803, octavo, translated as *Tableau historique et statistique* ... 2 vols., Basel and Leipzig, 1800 and 1801, octavo.
c. F. Anthing, *Versuch einer Kriegsgeschichte des Grafen Alex. Suwarow-Rymnikski*, 3 vols., Gotha, 1795-1799, octavo, translated as *Essai d'une histoire des campagnes du comte Alex. Suwarow-Rymnikski*, Gotha, 1796, octavo; Paris, 1799, and 1802, octavo.

Russian officials. In the same Preface, he attacks Voltaire's history as partial, incompetent, and full of errors.[88] This criticism, however, can be applied with more justice to his own work. Williams was uniformly hostile to the Russian government, institutions, and people. He considered the government arbitrary, despotic, and corrupt; [89] the people lazy, dishonest and given to all manner of excesses,[90] a veritable nation of slaves. Injudicious and biased, the book contained, moreover, a variety of historical and ethnographical errors. It was severely criticized by Levesque.[91]

William Coxe (1747-1828), historian, traveler, and at one time tutor to the son of the Earl of Pembroke was the author of several works on Russia, some of which achieved considerable European reputation. Coxe had a high reputation among his contemporaries as a scholar and writer on Russia. His first work, *Account of the Russian Discoveries between Asia and America*, 1780, quarto, had several English and German editions. It was translated into French as *Nouvelles découvertes des Russes* ... in 1781 and ran through two editions in Neufchâtel and Paris. This work is a collection of extracts from the works of Russian travelers, Müller, Pallas, and others. It contains, in addition, an historical sketch of the conquest of Siberia, as well as many maps and tables of Russian measures and currency. The spelling of Russian names is more systematic and correct than in most of the preceding accounts of foreign travelers. This work, although painstaking and dull, is reliable and informative, particularly from the geographical point of view.

Coxe's *Travels into Poland, Russia, Sweden and Denmark*, 3 vols., London, 1784, quarto, achieved a greater European

[88] John Williams, *Histoire des gouvernements du Nord* ... 4 vols., Amsterdam, 1780, I, 12 and 33.
[89] *Ibid.*, Vol. III, ch. ii.
[90] *Ibid.*, Vol. III, ch. iii.
[91] Pierre Levesque, *Histoire de Russie*, VIII, 345.

vogue than the preceding. It was translated into many European languages and had a great many editions. The French translation, entitled *Voyage en Pologne, Russie, Suède, Danemark* . . . 4 vols., Geneva, 1785, octavo, was well known at the time. Volumes II and III of this work bearing on Russia appeared in *Nouveau recueil de voyages au Nord*, 1786, quarto. The work had two other editions in 1787 in octavo and in 1805, in duodecimo. Levesque praised it highly; *Esprit des journaux* for November, 1784, gave it a lengthy review, and in his *Mémoires historiques, littéraires* Grimm considered it impartial and reliable.[92]

The range of information in this account is considerable. Aside from an informal diary of his experiences in Russia, Coxe gives detailed descriptions, with many judiciously chosen anecdotes, of the principal Russian cities and of the rulers of Russia after Peter the Great and discusses the state of the arts, commerce, and trade. In several instances, he makes original observations on the life of the peasants, religious ceremonies, and the general progress of the arts and sciences.[93] Coxe's principal source of information was Professor Müller, which source he acknowledges in the Preface to the first English edition of his work. The fifth edition (1802) of the account contains a description of the reign of Catherine the Great, which he appears to have gathered from personal contacts with individuals of her court. Coxe was perhaps the first foreign traveler to point out that the progress effected in Russia by Peter's reforms was exaggerated, that Western influences had been at work before Peter's reign and that in spite of all these influences the bulk of the Russian people remained as yet untouched by European civilization.[94] He granted, however, that some of the Russian nobility were

[92] Grimm, *Mémoires historiques, littéraires* . . . London, 1813, IV, 39-41.

[93] William Coxe, *Travels in Poland, Russia, Sweden* . . . 5 vols., London, 1802, III, 110 ff.

[94] *Ibid.*, III, 134.

highly civilized and cultured, but he thought that there was a wide difference between civilizing a nation and polishing a few individuals.[95] Coxe believed that Peter's reforms had not taken root among the masses. Russia, he thought, although "proceeding towards civilization, is still far removed from that state." [96]

Coxe had apparently spent considerable time in the country. He described at length the simple life of the peasants, their amusements, quaint customs, and superstitions.[97] He has not the contempt for them that his contemporaries had; he merely observes and notes. Coxe had a very high opinion of Catherine the Great, although he criticizes her insincerity and excessive despotism.[98] Coxe's account is impartial and, on the whole, sympathetic with Russia and the Russian people. It suffers from a lack of organization, unnecessary digressions, and a certain dullness of narrative. Besides the two works mentioned, Coxe wrote an account of the prisons and hospitals in Russia. He also described Russian geographical discoveries in Siberia; the latter work was translated into French as *Nouveau voyage en Danemark, Suède, Russie* ... Paris, 1791, octavo. The last mentioned works were, however, of lesser importance than his travels, as their appeal was specialized.

The *Memoirs of Peter Henry Bruce*, Dublin, 1783, deserve also to be mentioned among the English works on Russia. The author of these memoirs was for many years in the service of the Russian government. He died in 1757. The memoirs cover the reigns of Peter the Great and Catherine I. In content they comprise descriptions of Russian campaigns against Turkey and Sweden, the rebellion of the Riflemen (Strel'tsy), the criminal proceeding against the Tsarevich Alexieĭ, descrip-

---

[95] William Coxe, *Travels in Poland, Russia, Sweden* ... 5 vols., London, 1802, III, 134.

[96] *Ibid.*, III, 158.   [97] *Ibid.*, I, 260; 269-276; II, 50-85.

[98] *Ibid.*, III, 110 and 159 ff.

tions of Tatar tribes and a few observations on the religion, customs and manners of the people. This account, although accurate enough historically, is confused and badly put together. It had no French translations.

More important in itself and as a source of information for France was William Richardson's *Anecdotes of the Russian Empire in a Series of Letters Written a few Years ago from St. Petersburg*, London, 1784. This book was translated into French as *Anecdotes de l'empire russe* ... and published in Paris in 1789. William Richardson (1743-1814) was professor of humanities at the University of Glasgow. He acted as tutor to the two sons of Lord Cathcart, and, when the latter in 1768 was appointed ambassador to Russia, he went with him as both tutor and secretary. Upon his return to Glasgow in 1784, he published his *Anecdotes*. Richardson is also the author of several scholarly works, critical essays, and poems. While in Russia, he wrote, with considerable acumen, verve, and judgment, his observations on what seemed to him remarkable and interesting in the country. His letters, the form in which the book is written, have practically no continuity; they make, however, lively and amusing reading. Some of the topics will give an idea of their content: stories and anecdotes of courtiers and historical personages; reports of weather conditions; descriptions of plays given in the court theater, observations on religious ceremonies, on clergy, peasants, and nobles; fables adapted from the German, customs and amusements of the people, and analyses of the national character.

A great many of Richardson's observations, even today, appear fresh and original. Although severe in some of his pronouncements, Richardson yet maintains a certain aloofness and impartiality. His interest in the common people is more pronounced even than Coxe's and is quite unusual for the century. Besides finding the peasants intemperate, abusive, and ignorant, he stresses their servility and brutality, which he attributes to the degrading influences of the despotic government: "Exposed to corporal punishment, and on the footing of irrational animals, how can they possess that spirit and elevation of sentiment which distinguish the natives of a free state?"[99] In their diversions the Russian peasants are, according to the author, infantile and undignified.[100] Moreover, they are inactive and love sensuous pleasures: "The diversions of an Englishman exhibit strength, agility, and the love of exertion. Those of a Russian exhibit sloth, inactivity, and the love of pleasure."[101] Dancing, singing, and the steam bath are their favorite amusements, Richardson tells us. Although the Russian peasants are fickle and not to be relied upon, they are friendly, hospitable, intelligent, and on the whole a merry and likeable people:

They possess a temper and disposition, which, properly improved, and with the encouragements held forth by freedom, might render them as worthy as other, more civilized people. In some cases, they are an amiable and, in many cases, an amusing people.[102]

Their gravest faults are listlessness and lack of perseverance. Regarding the upper classes:

I cannot say much for the taste displayed by persons of high rank in Russia, either in their dress, houses, or retinue. They are pompous and tawdry.[103]

Whatever there is of vice and corruption in the upper circles in Russia is due, in Richardson's opinion, to French influences. He deplores, for example, the presence of menial people as

[99] William Richardson, *Anecdotes of the Russian Empire* ... London, 1784, pp. 197-210.
[100] *Ibid.*, p. 215.
[101] *Ibid.*, p. 212.
[102] *Ibid.*, p. 217.
[103] *Ibid.*, p. 218.

parasites and buffoons in the houses of the nobles. These parasites are generally Frenchmen, "whose lively loquacity seems absolutely necessary for the amusement of those great men, to whose tables they have admission." [104] The education of the sons of the nobles is very inadequate, also owing to the fact that most of the tutors are Frenchmen and usually unfit for the job.[105] He deplores the prevalent skepticism which is also a French fashion, and expresses a hope that "in times of sickness, disgrace and low spirits, they have more faith in St. Nicholas, than in Voltaire." [106] Summarizing his own observations on the Russian national character, Richardson qualifies it as fickle (he often calls Russians "bearded children" and "creatures of the hour"), emotional, sensitive, and musical; its gravest defects are want of firmness, perseverance, and real culture.[107] He feels that despotism and lack of education are the chief obstacles to Russia's progress. The government is largely to blame for this. He considers Russia, however, as definitely not a part of Europe and regards her more as an ancient empire of Persia or Babylonia than as a European state.[108] In spite of Richardson's frequent references to the old Russian customs and manners, his knowledge of pre-Peter Russia seems vague and inaccurate. In addition to having analyzed the Russian character more thoroughly than any preceding traveler to Russia, Richardson was also one of the first to stress the beauty, richness, and flexibility of the Russian language.[109]

Popular and well known in France was another English account of Russian travels, that of Lady Elizabeth Craven. Her *A Journey through Crimea to Constantinople*, London,

[104] William Richardson, *Anecdotes of the Russian Empire* ... London, 1784, p. 220.
[105] *Ibid.*, pp. 222-223.
[106] *Ibid.*, 225.
[107] *Ibid.*, pp. 451-453; also letter XXXIV.
[108] *Ibid.*, p. 375.   [109] *Ibid.*, p. 453.

1789, quarto, was translated into French by Guedon de Ber-
chère as *Voyage en Crimée et à Constantinople en 1786* ...
London, 1789. It ran through several editions in rapid succession (Paris, 1789, 1792, and 1794, in octavo), which would
seem to attest its popularity. The account, written in the
form of letters addressed to the Margrave of Brandenburg,
is a very informative, witty, and amusing journal of travel.
Lady Craven had a short sojourn at the court of St. Petersburg and later traveled through Crimea to Constantinople.
She gives vivid descriptions of St. Petersburg and the magnificence of Catherine's court.[110] She admires greatly the Empress, who, she tells us, "does all she can to invite politeness,
science, and comforts from other countries."[111] However,
Lady Craven, like Richardson, deplores the French influences
at court. She made many friends among the Russians and
praises their gaiety, amiability, and lack of prejudices:

I do not see here the prejudices of the English, the conceit of the
French nor the stiff German pride... Wit and talents will always
be objects of importance to me; I have found them here, and shall
be sorry to quit them.[112]

On the way to Crimea, Lady Craven notes the picturesque
aspects of the country, the beauty of the women and the
"happy simplicity" of the peasants.[113] Friendly and sympathetic to Russia, Lady Craven's memoirs are quite a departure
from the all-too-prevalent hostility of other foreign travelers.
   Andrew Swinton's *Travels into Norway, Denmark and
Russia* ... London, 1792, octavo, is another example of an
informal travel diary, in the form of letters, known in France

[110] Lady Craven, *A Journey through the Crimea to Constantinople* ... London, 1789, pp. 124-129.
[111] *Ibid.*, p. 130.
[112] *Ibid.*, pp. 132-133.
[113] *Ibid.*, pp. 138-142.

at the end of the century. It was translated into French by P. F. Henry as *Voyage en Norwège, en Danemark et en Russie dans les années 1788-1791*...2 vols. in one, Paris, 1798. Swinton's account is a mixture of personal observations of the Russian people and institutions, and of anecdotes and sketches of historical personages. His observations are often judicious and keen; the general tone is friendly and sympathetic with Russia. Swinton's enthusiastic description of the river Neva and of St. Petersburg, his interest in the national songs of Russia, and his exaggerated admiration for Peter the Great are definitely suggestive of the romantic attitude and approach.

Swinton attacks some of the well-known French accounts of Russia, particularly that of Chappe d'Auteroche. He accuses him of having merely repeated what had been said before and of having observed nothing. The Abbé's pronouncement on the imitative and emotional nature of the Russian people, Swinton considers completely false—it is exactly the opposite quality, the imaginative and emotional nature of the Russian, people which impresses him most.[114] He finds the people frequently gay and hospitable, but, he adds, they are not ready for "liberty." [115]

More interesting perhaps than Swinton's own account is a letter by a Frenchman, Richer Sérisy, to the translator of Swinton's book, which is included in the French edition of his work. Sérisy, who had traveled in Russia, pronounces severe judgment on the contemporary French writers on Russia, particularly on Rulhière. He finds them narrow, biased and lacking in knowledge of the country. He praises Swinton's account for its impartiality.[116] Writing in lyrical vein of Catherine's personal character and her reforms, extolling the

---

[114] Andrew Swinton, *Voyage en Norvège, en Danemark, et en Russie...* 2 vols. in one, Paris, 1798, II, 70-75.

[115] *Ibid.*, II, 96-97.   [116] *Ibid.*, II, 329.

beauty of the Russian language, the author of this letter concludes it with the following panegyric on the Russian people:

Actif, industrieux, imitateur, le Russe a bientôt surpassé son modèle: patient, intrépide, pénétré de cette idée commune à tous les peuples du nord, que l'homme ne peut éviter son destin...il souffre sans se plaindre, combat avec audace et meurt sans regret; aussi avons-nous vu de cette nature primitive, informe encore, mais robuste, paraître depuis un siècle, des hommes qui n'ont point de modèle parmi nous, et qui semblent être réservés à ces contrées...[117]

This pronouncement is in direct opposition to the prevalent opinions on Russia expressed by the foreign travelers prior to the nineteenth century.

The last of the eighteenth-century English works on Russia to be dealt with is a history of Catherine the Great's reign by the historian William Tooke. His *View of the Russian Empire during the Reign of Catherine the Second ...* 3 vols., London, 1799, octavo, was translated into French as *Histoire de l'empire de Russie sous le règne de Catherine II...* 6 vols., Paris, 1801, octavo. This French edition was edited by a Russian historian, Smirnov, under the direction of LeClerc, author of the voluminous *Histoire physique, morale, civile et politique de la Russie ancienne et moderne.* Tooke's history was indifferently received in France, as a similar history, covering the same period, by a French historian, J. Castéra, was published in 1797 and had wide-spread success. Scholarly but dull, Tooke's history, although accurate and informative, was not a popular work even in England.

Among the English accounts of Russia which we have examined in this chapter, one of the most prejudiced and one of the least informative, that of Captain Perry, was probably the most widely known. The more informative and unbiased works, those of Richardson, Swinton, and Lady Craven, had

[117] Andrew Swinton, *Voyage en Norwège, en Danemarck, et en Russie...* 2 vols. in one, Paris, 1798, II, 344.

limited success with their contemporaries. They would seem to have been read more in the following century by the French romantic writers, whose views on Russia were more in conformity with those expressed by these late eighteenth-century English travelers to Russia.

Two Russian works of European reputation should be included in the same group of foreign sources of information. The first of these was a translation from the German of a history of Russia by the famous Russian poet and scientist, Lomonosov. Translated by Eidous as *Histoire de la Russie depuis l'origine de la nation russe jusqu'à la mort du grand duc Jaroslaw I* ... Paris and Dijon, 1769, in octavo, it was republished in 1773 and in 1776, in octavo. Lomonosov's history dealt with the origin and the early history of the Russian state—a topic which was not of great interest to eighteenth-century France. Russian history until Peter's reign was generally considered nonexistent. Lomonosov was one of the first to inform France that even prior to Peter, Russia was an organized state and possessed a culture of her own. Diderot, reviewing this work, considered the author grandiloquent and monotonous, his style mediocre, and the subject matter tedious.[118] The review in the *Journal de Trévoux* for December, 1769, was, on the whole, favorable. A long article in the *Journal encyclopédique* for December, 1769, praised this work highly, believing that this history, together with Voltaire's, at last gave a complete picture of Russia to date.

Another Russian work of some importance as a source of information was the *Journal of Peter the Great*. This journal was probably written, not by Peter himself, but certainly under his supervision. It was published, for the first time, in 1770 in St. Petersburg, forty-eight years after Peter's death. At the request of Prince Henry of Prussia, who had a copy of it in Russian, the journal was translated into French by a

[118] Diderot, *Œuvres*, éd. Assézat, XVII, 495-496.

Russian in the Prussian service (Shchepot'ev) and was edited by Formey, secretary of the academy in Berlin. The *Journal de Pierre-le-Grand depuis l'année 1698, jusqu'à la conclusion de la paix de Nystadt . . . traduit sur l'original russe . . .* appeared in two volumes in London and Berlin in 1773. A new edition of it with notes appeared in Stockholm in the following year. The Journal deals entirely with the Russo-Swedish campaigns. It gives especially detailed descriptions of the battles of Narva and Poltava. Being, for the most part, an account of battles, the Journal is of interest chiefly to military men and to historians. It is interesting to note that many facts relating to the Swedish campaigns in this Journal conflict with Voltaire's version of them in his history of Peter the Great. Levesque considered the Journal a reliable source for the period covered, and the *Journal encyclopédique* for October, 1773, reviewed it at length, giving many excerpts from it.[119]

Turning now to the eighteenth-century French works on Russia it will be advantageous to divide them into two general groups, as we did with the foreign works—popular works, i.e., memoirs of travelers (real and imaginary), popular historical and geographical accounts, and so forth, and finally histories of Russia proper, based on more substantial documentation.

One of the earliest popular eighteenth-century accounts of Russia was that of a Frenchman who served as officer in the Russian army, Jean-Nicholas Brasey or (Brasset), comte de Lion (1663-1723). His account, *Mémoires politiques, amusants et satiriques de J.N.D. B.C. de L., colonel du régi-*

---

[119] Two other Russian works by General Betskiï, both on Catherine's system of public education, can also be mentioned here. They were translated from Russian by the historian LeClerc: (1) *Les Plans et les status des différents établissements ordonnés par S. M. I. Catherine II pour l'éducation de la jeunesse* . . . 2 vols., Amsterdam, 1775, quarto, *idem*, 1775, octavo; (2) *Système complet d'éducation publique* . . . 2 vols., Neufchatel, 1777, octavo.

ment de dragons de Cazanski et brigadier des armées de S.M. Czarienne . . . 3 vols., Veritopolie, 1716 and 1735 in octavo, covers the early part of Peter's reign and deals chiefly with the military campaigns in which the author took part. A short notice of this account appeared in the *Choix des journaux* in 1716.[120] Brasey's memoirs seem to have been unknown to the French historians of Russia; they were, however, read by Prévost, who refers to them in his *Aventures et anecdotes.*[121]

The Abbé Pierre-François Buchet (1679-1721), for some time editor of the *Mercure de France,* was the author of a short popular account of the reign of Peter the Great. This book, entitled *Abrégé de l'histoire du Czar Peter Alexiewitz, avec une relation de l'état présent de la Moscovie,* appeared anonymously in Paris in 1717, in duodecimo. It had no other editions, and no references to it by subsequent French or foreign writers on Russia have been found. It had a short notice in the *Mémoires de Trévoux* for May, 1717.

The best-known popular work on Russia in the first quarter of the century was that of Jean Rousset de Missy (1686-1762?), known under the pseudonym of Iwan Nestesuranoy. His *Mémoires du règne de Pierre le Grand* . . . The Hague, 1725, in duodecimo, had several French editions,[122] which were translated into English, German, and Italian. The work was well known throughout the century. Several reviews with many excerpts appeared in the *Journal des savants* for July, 1726, and August, 1727, and in *Mémoires de Trévoux* for September, 1725. Voltaire mentioned these memoirs as

[120] *Choix des journaux,* LXXVI, 51.

[121] Prévost, *Œuvres* . . . "Aventures et anecdotes," Paris, Bouland-Tardieu, 1823, XXXV, 499.

[122] The other editions were: The Hague, 1726, in duodecimo; Amsterdam, 1728 and 1739 (4 volumes in duodecimo); Amsterdam, 1740 (5 volumes in duodecimo). The last editions contained also memoirs of the reign of Catherine I, which were previously printed separately in Amsterdam in 1727 and 1729 in duodecimo.

being popular and apparently used them for his history of Peter's reign, although he stated himself that he considered them untrustworthy and unreliable.[123]

The author of these memoirs was a journalist and a pamphleteer. A Protestant, he lived most of his life in Holland and wrote political pamphlets against France. Although he never went to Russia, he was made a member of the St. Petersburg Academy of Arts and had a special honorary title from the Russian court. Missy's account of Peter's reign is a superficial compilation of historical material taken at second hand from the Swedish and German historians, particularly from Weber's memoirs. After a superficial survey of the early rulers of Russia, Missy gives an elaborate account of Peter the Great's reign. He distinctly gives the impression that Peter is the founder of the Russian state. The purpose of writing the book, Missy states in the Preface to the second edition, was to supply a demand for a complete history of Russia during the reign of Peter the Great, as the existing histories dealt only with isolated aspects of the Russian Empire. Another reason for writing it was to add to the geographical [124] information on the country as *Des terres immenses du côté de la grande Tartarie ne sont encore marquées sur les cartes, que comme de vastes déserts.*[125] His aim, however, was not fulfilled. Neither from the historical nor from the geographical point of view can Missy's book be considered an advance over the works of his predecessors. On the contrary, the memoirs are full of errors in dates, of fantastic misspelling, and of erroneous philological explanations of Russian names.

Missy is a most enthusiastic admirer of Russia's progress and of the creative genius of Peter the Great. He defends the Tsar against possible attacks for his treatment of the heir,

[123] Voltaire, *Correspondance*, Voltaire to Shuvalov, August 7, 1757.
[124] Jean Rousset de Missy, *Mémoires du règne de Pierre-le-Grand*, 4 vols., Amsterdam, 1728, author's Preface.
[125] *Ibid.*

Tsarevich Aleksïeĭ, and compares him to Brutus and Manlius. *Ce sont là*, he tells us regarding Peter's causing the execution of his son, *de ces actions qui caractérisent mieux que je ne pourrais jamais faire, une âme noble et un jugement droit.*[126] In the Preface to the fourth volume of the memoirs, Missy announces his intention of writing a general history of Russia, which work, however, never appeared. In spite of Missy's exaggerations, errors, and inaccuracies, his memoirs are written with considerable enthusiasm and unquestionably met the popular demand for a work of this type.

Not very important as a source of information on Russia, but very popular at the time, was the well-known comic poet Jean François Regnard's account of his journey to Finland. This work entitled *Voyage en Flandre, Hollande, Danemark, Suède, Laponie, Pologne, Allemagne* ... was published in Paris by an anonymous publisher in 1731, fifty years after Regnard's trip, and was re-edited in 1738. This account was a good popularization of a more thorough study of Finland by a German, Johann Scheffer, entitled *Laponia*, Frankfort, 1673, which was translated into French as *Histoire de la Laponie* ... Paris, 1678, quarto.[127] Regnard had the reputation among his contemporaries of having discovered Finland. In 1731 his *Voyage* appeared at the head of his collected works. In that account he shows a complete lack of knowledge of Russia. He seldom mentions her, and in one place calls Russia "Russelande," which apparently is his own adaptation of the German "Russland." Nevertheless, the eighteenth-century ideas of Finland, which was really discovered by Scheffer, were made current through the work of Regnard.

Just as Regnard made Finland known to eighteenth-century France, so a French traveler, Aubry de la Mottraye, was

126 Jean Rousset de Missy, *Mémoires du règne de Pierre-le-Grand*.

127 See Cart's study of John Scheffer's *Laponia* and J. F. Regnard's indebtedness to it, in the *Revue des cours et conférences*, 1900, pp. 321-327. Scheffer's *Laponia* was reviewed in the *Journal des savants* for June 27, 1678.

first to make known the Crimea and the region around the Black Sea. He traveled in Southern Russia in 1707 and in Northern Russia in 1714 and in 1726. His *Voyages en Europe, Asie, et Afrique, où l'on trouve une grande variété de recherches sur l'Italie ... la Tartarie, Crimée ...* 2 vols., The Hague, 1727, folio, was popularly well known and was translated into English in the year of its publication. This account contains a dull but informative description of the Crimea, illustrated by maps and engravings. La Mottraye's second account of travels, *Voyages en diverses provinces et places de la Prussie ducale et royale, de la Russie, de la Pologne ...* The Hague, London, and Dublin, 1732, folio, contains descriptions of Northern Russia; also anecdotes and short biographical sketches of Peter the Great, Catherine I, Le Fort, and Menshikov. La Mottraye was considered by his contemporaries as a trustworthy traveler, but a poor writer and a superficial observer.[128]

Between 1740 and 1750 there appeared several popular French works dealing with the life of Peter the Great. Among these the best known were two anecdotical accounts of Peter's reign, one by D'Allainval, the other by Voltaire.

Soulas d'Allainval, an obscure playwright, was the author of *Anecdotes du règne de Pierre I, dit le Grand, contenant l'histoire d'Eudochia Fedorowna et la disgrace du prince de Mencikow,* 2 vols., Paris, 1745, duodecimo. A review in the *Mémoires de Trévoux* for February, 1750, described this work as amusing, but not reliable from the historical point of view.

[128] See Michaud's *Biographie universelle,* "Supplement." Another popularly descriptive work on Russia, dealing with the reigns of Peter the Great and Catherine I was an account in the form of letters entitled *Lettres Moscovites,* Paris, 1736, octavo, translated into English in the same year by W. Musgrave. The authorship of this work is disputed. Barbier states that of the two copies he has seen, one in a manuscript note gives Count Francesco Locatelli or Count d'Asti as author; the other copy, also in a manuscript note, states that the author was called Bondanelli. Barbier also mentions a criticism of Locatelli by Prince M. A. Obolenskiï.

Dorat's tragedy, *Amilka*, was based on it and Voltaire used it for his history of Peter's reign.[129] Levesque considered the *Anecdotes* an altogether fictitious work. Some of D'Allainval's anecdotes seem to have been taken from Weber's memoirs. The story of Menshikov's disgrace, according to Levesque, was told to the author by Menshikov's granddaughter, Mme Zinov'eva, and had no foundation in fact.

In 1748 there appeared anonymously in Dresden a short collection of anecdotes on various phases of Tsar Peter's life, entitled *Anecdotes sur le Czar Pierre-le-Grand*.[130] The author of it was Voltaire. It was from this modest collection that Voltaire's history of Peter's reign grew. It had several editions and was, like everything else written by Voltaire, well received. The *Anecdotes* do not offer any new material which had not been known in France before their publication. Further mention of them will be made in connection with Voltaire's *Histoire du règne de Pierre-le-Grand*.[131]

Jacques LaCombe, a popular historian, writer on the arts and collaborator in the *Mercure de France*, was the author of two books pertaining to Russia. His *Histoire des révolutions de l'Empire de Russie*, Paris, 1760, duodecimo, was well known at the time. (It was re-edited in 1778 in octavo.) Reviews of it in the *Mémoires de Trévoux* (August, 1760) and in the *Journal encyclopédique* (May and June, 1760) praised it highly. It was considered interesting and well written. *Un style noble, pur, aisé et plein de chaleur; des réflexions solides,*

[129] Voltaire, *Correspondance*, letter to Darget, November 27, 1757.

[130] In Garnier's edition of Voltaire's work these anecdotes are included in the section entitled *Mélanges*, XXIII, 280-293.

[131] Besides D'Allainval's and Voltaire's anecdotes, two other popular works on Peter the Great, published about the same time can be mentioned: (1) Hubert le Blanc, *Le Czar Pierre I en France*, 2 vols., Amsterdam, 1741, octavo, and (2) an anonymous work published in 1742—*Histoire de Pierre I, surnommé le Grand*, 3 vols., Amsterdam, and Leipzig, 1742, in octavo; re-edited in 1742 in quarto. *La France littéraire* of 1769 attributed this work to Eléazar Mauvillon (1712-1779), an obscure translator and grammarian.

philosophiques et amenées heureusement, sans étalage et sans prétention.[132] From the historical point of view, however, the same reviews considered the work unreliable. LaCombe apparently used German historians as sources for the history, and carried it up to the reign of Queen Elizabeth. This work is a very superficial popularization of these writers. It has many errors in dates and misspellings of names, and it gives a distorted picture of Russia's development, through an overemphasis of the barbarism of Russia prior to Peter's reign.

LaCombe's second book, *Abrégé chronologique de l'histoire du Nord . . .* Amsterdam, 1763, is a summary account of the governments of Denmark, Russia, Sweden, Poland, and Prussia. This work, too, was well known. Voltaire is reported to have advised Constant to read this history instead of his own, if he wished to know something about Russia, for La Combe, Voltaire is said to have commented, unlike himself, never received medals and furs from the Russian court.[133] As history, LaCombe's work is unsatisfactory. Although the author states that he used only native historians as sources, the part dealing with Russia shows no evidence of it. It is sketchy and inaccurate and repeats much of the erroneous information of the earlier travelers (Captain Perry, for example). His spelling of Russian names is altogether arbitrary, and his philological explanations of Russian words, such as *Tsar, Velikïĭ kniaz,* and so forth, erroneous.[134] LaCombe's general observations on religion, government, and people are hostile to Russia and show little discrimination or judgment.[135] In spite of these shortcomings, some of which were known to his contemporaries, LaCombe's history was considered a very readable and convenient summary for the general reader.

[132] *Journal encyclopédique,* June 1760.
[133] Prince de Ligne, *Mon séjour chez Voltaire.*
[134] Jacques LaCombe, *Abrégé de l'histoire du Nord . . .* Amsterdam, 1763, I, 586.
[135] *Ibid.,* I, 580-617—"Remarques particulières sur la Russie."

Well known to his contemporaries, chiefly because of the controversy to which it gave rise, was Chappe d'Auteroche's account of his trip to Siberia in 1761 entitled *Voyage en Sibérie fait par ordre du roi en 1761 contenant les mœurs, les usages des Russes et l'état actuel de cette puissance* ... 3 vols., Paris, 1768, in quarto, re-edited in Amsterdam, 1769-1770, 2 vols., in octavo. This superficial and biased work has been dealt with at some length in the first part of our study.[136] The inadequacy of the work was realized by most contemporary German, English, and French writers on Russia.[137] Levesque found it altogether unreliable and considered the author ignorant of the conditions prevalent in Russia at the time of his trip. Nevertheless, reviews, with many excerpts, appeared in the *Journal encyclopédique* (September and October, 1770), and in *Mémoires de Trévoux* (January, 1769). A vigorous attack on the book, generally believed to have been written by Catherine the Great, appeared in the *Journal encyclopédique* for December, 1771, under the title of *Antidote, on examen d'un mauvais livre superbement imprimé*... Levesque used this *Antidote,* instead of the work it attacked, as a source for his history.

Somewhat more informative and impartial than the preceding French accounts was *L'Empire de Russie, son origine et ses accroissements,* Paris, 1772, octavo, by a learned geographer, Jean Baptiste d'Anville. His work is a fairly authoritative account of each successive territorial addition to the Russian empire. It goes back to the earliest time of Russian history and ends with Catherine II's reign. The work was not a popular one and was never republished. A short and rather favorable review of it appeared in the *Journal encyclopédique* for March, 1773.

---

[136] For the controversy regarding the publication of Chappe d'Auteroche's book see Tourneux, *Diderot et Catherine,* pp. 22-23.

[137] See, for example, the Preface to A. Swinton's and A. Fortia de Piles' accounts of travels.

In the last quarter of the century there appeared a large number of popular French accounts of Russia. Some of these were imaginary travels, merely compilations of various material taken usually from German works; some were impressionistic memoirs of travelers; a few were popular historical accounts.

Among the fictitious accounts of travels, the best known was the *Voyage philosophique, politique, et littéraire fait en Russie pendant les années 1788 et 1789 ... traduit du hollandais* ... 2 vols., Hamburg, Paris, 1794, in octavo, by Pierre Nicholas Chantreau (1741-1808). The author was a prolific writer on philology, travel, and history. The account never existed in Dutch, but was a very clever compilation of various materials taken from the works of Pallas, Manstein, Scherer, and Levesque. It was anecdotal in character and was filled with extravagant and erroneous information, much of it being the product of the author's own imagination. The *Voyage* had considerable success and was translated into English and into German. Contemporary reviews were favorable —*Il est difficile de trouver des voyages plus piquants,* wrote the reviewer of the work in the *Esprit des journaux* for October, 1793, *plus instruits, plus agréables à lire que celui que nous annonçons.* The more serious writers on Russia, however, ignored it. *Les erreurs, les fautes y sont très nombreuses,* said the article in Michaud; *quant à sa diction, elle est tour à tour frivole ou emphatique, et habituellement incorrecte.*[138]

Chantreau's *Voyage* covered considerable ground; it gave descriptions of the government, religion, customs, commerce, and literature of the country. The tone of the work is witty and facetious. The author's ideas of the various topics he discusses are, as a rule, vague and inaccurate. Although he attacks Voltaire's history for its contradictions, omissions, and errors in spelling and geography, he adopts, nevertheless, Vol-

---

[138] Michaud, *Biographie universelle,* 1813, VIII, 47.

taire's views on the reforms of Peter the Great.[139] Contrary
to Voltaire, however, he considers progress in Russia since
Peter's time greatly exaggerated and the masses little better
than savages.[140] The peasants, he maintains, have not really
changed; *ils ont peut-être quelques vices de plus et une in-
finité de besoins qu'ils n'avaient pas.*[141] The chief obstacles to
the *lumières* in Russia were, in his opinion, despotic government, religion, and serfdom.[142] He gave a brief and not very
informative account of the state of Russian literature, men-
tioning Lomonosov and Sumarokov.[143] His lengthy discourse
on the Russian language shows a complete lack of knowledge
of the subject.[144] The *Voyage*, as a whole, is a confused mass
of fact and fiction, rather entertainingly put together. It is
representative of the works on Russia which the eighteenth-
century Frenchmen were wont to produce.

Less widely known than the preceding was an account by
Thesby de Belcourt. The author was taken prisoner in Russia
and published an account of his experiences in Siberia entitled *Relation d'un officier pris par les Russes et relégué en
Sibérie* ... Amsterdam, 1776, in octavo. This work, however,
seems to have passed unnoticed.

Fortia de Piles' *Voyage de deux Français en Allemagne,
Danemark, Russie, et Pologne en 1790-1792* ... 5 vols., Paris,
1796, was, as we have already seen, a practical and matter-of-
fact account for travelers. It contained many maps, itiner-
aries, prices, and precise descriptions of Moscow and St.
Petersburg. In the Preface to the third volume, devoted to
Russia, Piles gave a short bibliography of earlier accounts of
Russia. He praised the German works and condemned the
French as for the most part partial and unreliable.

---

[139] Pierre Chantreau, *Voyage philosophique* ... Paris, 2 vols., 1794, I, 99,
110 and 280.

[140] *Ibid.*, I, 280.   [141] *Ibid.*, I, 281.

[142] *Ibid.*, I, 301.   [143] *Ibid.*, I, 322.

[144] *Ibid.*, I, 323 ff.

In 1799 there appeared anonymously in Lausanne a book-
let (208 pp., in octavo) entitled *Coup d'œil sur l'état actuel
de la Russie* ... with a subtitle *L'Antidote; ou, Les Russes tels
qu'ils sont, et non tels qu'on les croit, par un ami de la vérité
et de la liberté* ... The author of this work was a Swiss, Fornerod, who was for some time secretary of the Helvetian
legation in Russia.[145] This pamphlet is of particular interest
because it expresses certain novel views on Russia, unusual
for the century. Thus, for example, the author is one of the
first to point out that Russia was not as barbaric before Peter
the Great as most of the French writers were inclined to believe. Backward as was the country, she had, according to
Fornerod, a civilization of her own.[146] Furthermore, Fornerod
attempted to analyze the national characteristics of the Russian nobility further than had been done heretofore. The
Russian noble is, according to Fornerod, ostentatious, proud,
indolent, pleasure-loving, but at the same time ... *il est doué
de beaucoup de finesse d'esprit et d'un talent pour le persifflage
et pour saisir les moindres ridicules.*[147] The author thus notes
a certain similarity in temperament between the Russian and
French aristocracy. Aside from these rather novel features,
Fornerod gave the usual conventional impression of the country—despotism, indolence of the people, and corruption of
the clergy. *Le paysan russe*, he finds, *est un malheureux animal, qui paraît tenir le milieu entre l'homme et la brute.*[148]

Daniel Lescallier's *Voyage en Angleterre, en Russie et en
Suède* ... Paris, 1800, has been already examined at some
length in Chapter III of this work. Apart from his uncommon enthusiasm for the Russian language,[149] his hostile

---

[145] Quérard, *Supercheries littéraires*, I, 303.
[146] *Coup d'œil* ... Lausanne, 1799, pp. 23-28.
[147] *Ibid.*, p. 31.
[148] *Ibid.*, p. 47.
[149] Daniel Lescallier, *Voyage en Angleterre, en Russie et en Suède* ... Paris, 1800, pp. 261-263.

and biased observations on the people, the religion and government of Russia, contain nothing which had not been said already by previous travelers. Lescallier's *Voyage* was never re-edited and received no notices in the periodicals of the time.

Among the popular accounts of Russia at the end of the century, Charles-François Masson's *Mémoires secrets sur la Russie* . . . 3 vols., Paris, 1800-1802, in octavo, were most successful and ran through many editions in France, England, and Germany.[150] Charles Masson spent ten years in Russia. He was ordered out of the country by Emperor Paul on suspicion of revolutionary sympathies. His memoirs were written in Poland after his deportation and give, in spite of his resentment against the government, a fairly judicious picture of the country at the end of the century. As we have already examined his work in the chapter dealing with Frenchmen in Russia, we shall confine ourselves now to stressing the unusual features of his memoirs. Contrary to most French accounts of travelers published before 1800, Masson's memoirs show many evidences of a genuine fondness for Russia and the Russian people. He praises the flexibility, culture, enlightenment, and hospitality of the Russian nobility and blames their shortcomings on the despotism of the government and the bad example of the West.[151] The peasant, he found, had certain "natural" and "patriarchal" virtues, his vices (servility and lack of honor) being the results of serfdom and of the bad example of the clergy.[152] Masson also evinced a personal interest in the art and literature of the country and left some material for a projected history of the Russian literature.

Among French popular historical accounts dealing with Russia in the second half of the eighteenth century (i.e., the

150 Other contemporary editions were: Amsterdam, 1800-1803, 4 vols., octavo; London, 1802, 2 vols., octavo; Paris, 1804, 4 vols., octavo.
151 Charles Masson, *Mémoires sur la Russie* . . . Paris, 1863, pp. 165, 191 and 194.
152 *Ibid.*, pp. 170-175.

reigns of the Emperor Peter III and Empress Catherine II) Claude Carloman de Rulhière's *Histoire ou anecdotes sur la révolution de Russie en 1762*, Paris, 1797, in octavo, was probably the most widely known.[153] As we have already seen in Chapter III of this work, this account began to circulate in Paris early in 1763. It was only through the intervention of Voltaire, Diderot, and Mme Geoffrin that its publication was postponed until Catherine's death. The *Anecdotes* were hostile to the Empress and pessimistic as to the future of Russia. Historically, the author's direct implication of Catherine in her husband's death is not sufficiently substantiated. The book is superficial in tone and content and lacks personal and original observations on the country and its people. Nevertheless, owing in part to Rulhière's reputation, the *Anecdotes* were widely read and had two editions in the year of their publication. They had also several German and English editions. A long review, complimentary to the author's style, but not to his veracity as an historian, appeared in the *Spectateur du Nord* for March, 1797.[154]

The best-known history of Catherine the Great's life and reign was written by J. H. Castéra. His *Vie de Catherine II, Impératrice de Russie*, 2 vols., Paris, 1797, octavo, ran through numerous French and several German and English

---

[153] Considerable information on Russia's foreign relations can be found in another historical work of Rulhière's, *Œuvres posthumes*, "Tableau esquissé de la fermentation qui agite actuellement l'empire Ottoman, la Russie et la Pologne," Paris, 1792, in duodecimo; also, to a lesser extent, in his *Histoire de l'anarchie de Pologne* . . . 4 vols., Paris, Nicolle et Desenne, 1807, in duodecimo.

[154] Several popular histories, less widely known than Rulhière's and dealing specifically with the reign of the Emperor Peter III, deserve to be mentioned:
(1) De Goudar, *Mémoires pour servir à l'histoire de Pierre III* . . . Frankfort and Leipzig, 1763; octavo; (De Goudar was also the author of a short account of Russia's military power entitled *Considération sur les causes de l'ancienne faiblesse de l'empire de Russie et de sa nouvelle puissance*, Amsterdam, 1772, octavo).
(2) De Beauclair, *Histoire de Pierre III*, London, 1774, octavo.
(3) Jean C. Laveau, *Histoire de Pierre III, empereur de Russie* . . . suivi de l'histoire secrète de Catherine II . . . 3 vols., Paris, 1799, octavo.

editions.[155] The author was an editor of the *Mercure de France* and appears to have done some traveling in *le Nord*. There is no evidence, however, that he had ever visited Russia. It is likely that he got some material for his history from various foreign diplomats whom he probably met in Poland. In the Preface to the first edition of his history, Castéra mentions a close friend of Gregory Orlov (one of Catherine's favorites) as one of his sources of information. Volume I of the first edition begins with letters addressed to William Pitt from Russia, containing anecdotes of Peter the Great, descriptions of St. Petersburg, court intrigues, and the diplomatic background prior to Catherine's accession to the throne. The second volume deals with Catherine's life. It gives the major political, military, and social events of her reign, details of the Empress's private life and of her trip to the South of Russia, sketches of court life, and descriptions of the émigrés. The first part of Castéra's work has several interesting features. In the first place, he gives an interesting and penetrating description of Peter the Great, emphasizing the singular mixture of creative genius and savage cruelty in the Tsar's character.[156] He also gives interesting sidelights on Catherine's character through an imaginary conversation between the Empress and her friend Countess Potocka.[157] Finally, Castéra describes most enthusiastically the picturesqueness of St. Petersburg and its principal river, the Neva, which description indicates, however, that the author could not possibly have seen the city himself.[158]

The second volume, dealing with Catherine's life, seems to

[155] The principal French editions were as follows: *Vie de Catherine II*, 2 vols., 1797 in octavo (twice); *ibid.*, Warsaw, 1798, octavo; *Histoire de Catherine II*, 4 vols., Paris, 1800; duodecimo; *ibid.*, 3 vols., 1800, octavo; *ibid.*, 4 vols., 1809, duodecimo.

[156] J. H. Castéra, *Vie de Catherine II* ... 2 vols., Paris, 1797, I, 15-20.

[157] *Ibid.*, I, 49-52.

[158] *Ibid.*, I, 8.

have been based to some extent upon Rulhière's *Anecdotes*. Although frequently praising Catherine's intelligence and charm, Castéra's attitude toward the Empress is hostile. He reproaches her chiefly for her lack of sincerity and pictures her as a very clever dissimulator. Castéra's work presents, on the whole, a rather disconnected mixture of anecdotal, fictitious, and factual information. It is not satisfactory as a biography, chiefly because the author fails to give a living picture of the Empress. However, as a popular account of Catherine's reign, it was adequate enough for the time.

Perhaps the best illustration of France's interest in Russia at the end of the century was Blin de Sainmore's illustrated history of Russia. The *Histoire de Russie depuis l'an 862 jusqu'au règne de Paul Ier, representée par figures gravées par F. David, accompagnées de discours par Blin de Sainmore*, appeared in 2 volumes, Paris, 1797, in quarto, and 1798-1799, in 2 volumes, in quarto. In his prefatory discourse on Russia, Blin de Sainmore marvels at Russia's extraordinary rapid progress, which during a period of fifty years had brought her from complete obscurity to the fore rank of European powers. *C'est donc un grand spectacle*, he observes, *à offrir au monde, que l'histoire d'une nation, qui naguères comptait presque pour rien, et qui joue maintenant un rôle si important dans l'univers.*[159] He ascribes this progress entirely to the genius of Peter the Great. The aim of bringing out this history, he states in the Preface, was not instruction, since Levesque had already published a most complete, authentic, and reliable historical survey of the country, but entertainment.

It is interesting to note that the first two volumes of Sainmore's work deal with the early history of Russia, the

---

[159] Adrien Blin de Sainmore, *Histoire de Russie*...2 vols., Paris, Boiste, 1797, I, 2.

second volume ending with the reign of Tsar Feodor Alek-
sieevich (1682). This was unusual, as throughout the century
the early period of Russian history was completely ignored.
The illustrations done by David usually portray fierce battle
scenes, with the warriors looking like savages and clad in
picturesque and quite fantastic costumes.

In this connection one may also mention a collection of
engravings by the painter Jean Baptiste Le Prince (1733-
1781) who spent several years in Russia. This collection
contains seventy plates illustrating Russian landscapes and
the life of people in town and country. It was entitled *Divers
ajustements et usages de Russie... dessinés en Russie d'après
nature et gravés à l'eau forte par J. B. le Prince,* Paris, 1775,
and earned, it appears, considerable success.

The above were some of the better-known French works
on Russia of popular character and addressed chiefly to the
general reader. We may turn now to the more serious studies
wherein the methods were more critical and the documentation more solid. Among these Voltaire's history of the reign
of Peter the Great, chronologically at least, should occupy the
first place.

As we saw in the preceding pages, works on Peter the
Great were not lacking in France before Voltaire. A large
number of popular accounts dealing with the Tsar's reign,
French and foreign alike (Abbé Buchet, D'Allainval, Rousset de Missy, Stählin, and others) supplied the demand. There
were even works dealing exclusively with Peter's reign. What
chiefly distinguished Voltaire's history, however, from the
preceding ones (aside from the author's renown) was that,
for the first time (so far as French historical accounts of
Russia went), a great deal of Russian source material was
used. In a general way, Voltaire's sources can be divided into
three groups: popular French and foreign writers; historical
data and State papers from the Russian government and the

St. Petersburg Academy; and information from various individuals, chiefly Russian friends of Voltaire.

From Voltaire's correspondence one can determine what
works he used for the history. He himself acknowledges
having employed the following: Strahlenberg's and Perry's accounts; [160] an English account by Whitworth; [161] Algarotti's
letters on Russia; [162] D'Allainval's collection of anecdotes; [163]
Olearius; [164] and, for the second volume of his history,
Rousset de Missy's memoirs.[165] Most of these, as we have seen,
were popular writers and not very reliable. By using them
Voltaire rendered himself at once vulnerable to criticism.
He received most of the Russian material, including the
unpublished memoirs of Peter's favorite, Le Fort, and the
journal of Peter himself, directly from the Russian court,
through Count Ivan Shuvalov.[166] He himself felt that this
official material was one-sided, and he saw the necessity of
supplementing it by memoirs, and by whatever information
he could obtain from various individuals. He seems, accordingly, to have had occasional recourse to the Russian ambassadors in Paris (Kantemir, Saltykov, and Panin) and to his
friends, such as the two Shuvalovs, Countess Bassevich, Algarotti, and others.[167]

Voltaire's interest in Peter the Great goes back to the days
of his youth when he saw the Tsar during the latter's visit
to Paris.[168] When he wrote the history of Charles XII, it
was inevitable that a similar history of the Russian Tsar should

[160] Voltaire, *Correspondance*, letter to Shuvalov, August 7, 1757.
[161] *Ibid.*, October 6, 1759.
[162] *Ibid.*, letter to Algarotti, September ?, 1760.
[163] *Ibid.*, letter to Darget, November 27, 1757.
[164] Charles Nizard, *Mémoires et correspondances historiques, littéraires inédites*, Paris, 1858, pp. 31-32.
[165] Voltaire, *Correspondance*, letter to Shuvalov, November 9, 1761.
[166] *Ibid.*, see Voltaire's correspondence with Shuvalov, 1760-1761.
[167] Voltaire, *Correspondance*, letter to Shuvalov; see general correspondence for the years 1757-1760, *passim*.
[168] *Ibid.*, letter to Thieriot, June 11, 1759.

follow. In 1748 he published anonymously his *Anecdotes sur le Czar Pierre-le-Grand.*[169] About nine years later Shuvalov persuaded Voltaire to expand this work and write a complete history of Peter's reign.[170]

The assertion is sometimes made that Voltaire's sole motive in writing the history was the expectation of favors from the Russian court. Such assertions seem manifestly unfair. His correspondence with Shuvalov, examined in the preceding chapter, appears to indicate sufficiently that it was not venality but excess of zeal for the Tsar which may be charged against Voltaire. It seems more probable that, whatever favors he may have expected, his primary object in writing the history was to show to all Europe the greatness of Peter's character and reforms.

The first volume of *Histoire de l'empire de Russie sous Pierre-le-Grand, par l'auteur de l'histoire de Charles XII,* appeared in 1759; the second, in 1763. The first volume was especially successful. Both friends and enemies of Voltaire were pleased with it and were eagerly awaiting the continuation.

Le roi est content de l'histoire de Pierre-le-Grand [Voltaire wrote to Thieriot]; Mme de Pompadour pense de même. M. le duc de Choiseul, en digne ministre des affaires étrangères, en fait plus de cas que de celle de Charles XII.[171]

During 1760, Voltaire sent copies of the history to all his friends, warning the ladies that the reading would not be interesting: ... *rien de plus ennuyeux, pour une Parisienne, que des détails de Russie,* he wrote to Mme de Fontaine;[172] the book is not written for amusement, he wrote to Mme du Deffand, it is a study;[173] *Que ferez-vous de la grande Permie*

---

[169] First published in Dresden at Walther's.
[170] Voltaire, éd. Garnier, XVI, 373-376.
[171] Voltaire, *Correspondance,* letter to Thieriot, November 19, 1760.
[172] *Ibid.,* letter to Mme de Fontaine, September 29, 1760.
[173] *Ibid.,* letter to Mme du Deffand, October 10, 1760.

et des Samoyèdes? he asked the Countess D'Argental.[174] The history had a great many editions in the second half of the century, though not quite as many as that of Charles XII.[175]

In spite of the relative success of the history, even in Voltaire's own time its shortcomings became obvious. Diderot, as is well known, thought it brilliant, but, as a whole, apt to leave no lasting impression on the reader.[176] In Grimm's *Correspondance littéraire,* the criticism was more serious; the history was found to be full of omissions, suppressions, and falsification of facts; it left, moreover, no permanent impression—

Elle plaît jusqu'à la fin; mais quand on y est arrivé, si l'on se demandait quel grand tableau on a vu, quelle réflexion profonde on a retenue, de quel endroit sublime on a été frappé, quel est le morceau qu'on voudrait relire, où est la ligne de génie, on ne saurait que se répondre.[177]

In Grimm's opinion, Voltaire's history of Peter the Great was to remain among his inferior works. Levesque, too, was skeptical as to the value of the history. He considered the material furnished to Voltaire prejudiced and unreliable and thought that the history made interesting reading, but was inadequate as a study.[178] Chantreau, on the other hand, criticized Voltaire for not using more exhaustively the documents sent to him by the Russian court,[179] and Masson considered the history partial, incomplete, and unreliable.[180] The periodicals

[174] *Ibid.,* letter to Countess D'Argental, October 13, 1760.
[175] The principal eighteenth-century editions were as follows: Vol. I, Geneva, 1759, in octavo; Vol. II, Geneva, 1763, in octavo; Lyons, 1761, 1763, 2 vols., in duodecimo; Amsterdam, 1761, in octavo; Leipzig, 1761, 1764, 2 vols., in octavo; Geneva, 1765, 2 vols., in octavo; Amsterdam, 1765, 2 vols., in duodecimo; Lausanne, 1771, in octavo; Geneva, 1773, 2 vols., in octavo; Amsterdam, 1780, in duodecimo; Paris, 1803, 2 vols., in 18º.
[176] Diderot, *Œuvres,* letter to Mlle Volland, October 18, 1760.
[177] *Correspondance littéraire,* éd. Tourneux, IV, 308-313; November 1 and 15, 1760.
[178] Charles Levesque, *Histoire de Russie,* 1800, VIII, 341-342.
[179] Pierre Chantreau, *Voyage philosophique,* I, 99-101.
[180] Charles Masson, *Mémoires secrets ... Paris,* 1863, Introduction.

of the time, were, nevertheless, most flattering to Voltaire, proclaiming his history the most interesting and authoritative work on Russia to date.[181]

The most serious contemporary criticism of Voltaire's history was that of a German academician, Müller. This was printed in the *Journal encyclopédique* for December, 1762. The criticism stressed in general the insufficiency of Voltaire's documentation, his excessive reliance on legends and popular French writers. Voltaire's specific faults were faulty orthography with respect to Russian names and numerous geographical and historical errors. *Il semble,* said the reviewer, *que M. Voltaire n'ait écrit son histoire que pour nier les faits les plus connus.*

The editors of the *Journal encyclopédique* thought it necessary to defend Voltaire's integrity as an historian and on May 1 and May 15, 1763, published a counter attack on the German scholar's critique, accusing him of unfairness and pedantry. Nevertheless, Müller's criticism was, in the main, substantiated by subsequent French and Russian critics.[182] Today, viewing Voltaire's work in the perspective of time, it certainly appears to be inadequate as a history, even for its own time. Perhaps the gravest fault of the history was not so much its want of scholarship as the distorted picture it gave of the social and political development of Russia, through an excessive glorification of Peter the Great and an overemphasis of his reforms. But even considered as a popular account, it was not worthy of Voltaire's pen. For when all is said, Voltaire failed in the end to give a convincing and living picture of his hero. As propaganda for Russia, however, the history's rôle was important.

[181] *Journal encyclopédique,* September and October, 1760; *Journal littéraire de la Haye,* XIX, 427.
[182] See, for example, Lomonosov's article in the *Bulletin du Nord,* for July, 1828. For a complete list of Voltaire's critics, see E. Shmurlo, *Voltaire et son œuvre "Histoire de l'empire de Russie sous Pierre le Grand,"* Prague, 1929.

The first extensive and authoritative French studies of Russian history and culture in the eighteenth century were those of Levesque and Le Clerc.

Pierre Levesque, as we have seen, spent seven years in Russia. He acquired there a good knowledge of the language, modern Russian and old Slavonic, and so was enabled to use Russian sources for the early history of the country. The author's *Histoire de Russie* in five volumes in octavo appeared in Paris in 1782. It ran through several editions and was praised highly by all French and Russian contemporaries.[183] In the Preface to the 1800 edition, Levesque emphasized his complete disinterestedness in writing the history, indicated his general point of view towards Russia, which was the characteristically optimistic, Voltairean view, and declared that the only way to write a scholarly history of Russia was to go there and—

S'y livrer pendant plusieurs années à une étude sèche et opiniâtre, apprendre non seulement le russe moderne, mais encore l'ancien dialecte slavon-russe, dans lequel sont écrits toutes les chroniques.

All this he had done himself.

In the same Preface Levesque pointed out the fact that in spite of a general interest in Russia no complete history of the country had as yet appeared; only brief and unreliable accounts of single reigns had been written which contained *quelques vérités et un grand nombre de mensonges, tirés de voyageurs peu instruits ou prévenus*... Of all the foreign accounts of Russia, the most authoritative were written, in his opinion, by Germans and the least authoritative by Frenchmen.

In the eighth volume of the 1800 edition of his history Levesque gave a complete analytical bibliography of his

---

[183] The other editions of the history were: in 6 vols., Iverdon, 1783, duodecimo; in 8 vols. (carried to the end of Catherine the Great's reign), Hamburg and Brunswick, 1800, octavo; and *ibid.*, Paris, 1800 and 1812.

sources.[184] He used chroniclers such as Nestor and Nikon, early church fathers, and many of the most important French and foreign works which we have examined in the preceding pages.[185]

In the 1800 edition Levesque's history covered the period from 826 to 1796. The edition of 1812, published by Malte-Brun in Depping, carried the history to 1802. It was the first French study of the general culture, and the historical and ethnographical evolution of the Russian Empire.

Even today the work can be considered as a fairly authoritative account of Russia for the period it covered. It is clear and well arranged. Its fault, if it is a fault, lies chiefly in the characteristic eighteenth-century overemphasis upon the reforms of Peter the Great and of the "liberalism" of Catherine the Great. The chaotic spelling of Russian names in most of the preceding works on Russia is in Levesque's history greatly improved, and a guide for a uniform spelling and pronouncing of Russian names is supplied.[186] The chapter on literature, although brief,[187] gives judicious selections from the principal contemporary writers. As outstanding figures in Russian literature Levesque gives Lomonosov, *le prince de poètes russes,* Sumarokov, founder of the Russian theater (but inferior to the French classics, whom he imitated; his strength being mainly, in Levesque's opinion, in fables, in which he came next only to La Fontaine), Kheraskov, the epic poet (also imitative of the French, but possessing a certain originality of his own). Even these few examples, the author stated, are sufficient to show that Russians are *bien éloignés de cet état de barbarie qu'on se plaît à leur reprocher.* With

---

[184] Pierre Levesque, *Histoire de Russie,* 1800, VIII, 330-346.

[185] Herberstein, Possevinus, Olearius, Oderborn, Margeret, Korb, Weber, Strahlenberg, Voltaire, Manstein, Williams, Müller, Coxe, Stählin, Rulhière, and Castéra.

[186] Pierre Levesque, *op. cit.,* I, pp. xvii-xix.

[187] *Ibid.,* VIII, 146-162.

the natural beauty and richness of the Russian language and with more encouragement of the national genius, Russian literature, Levesque thinks, will have a great future. The chief evidences for the country's capacity to produce original literature are the poems and songs of ancient Russia, which in directness, simplicity, and imaginative qualities can be compared with the best that Europe had produced. In these observations Levesque had opened a new field of interest in Russia for eighteenth-century France.

La composition de cette histoire [wrote a contemporary critic, Dacier] est sage et savante; le style en est facile et naturel; les faits y sont bien enchaînés et racontés avec tant d'exactitude, que l'ouvrage est resté classique en Russie.[188]

The long review of the history in Grimm's *Correspondance littéraire* was most flattering. *Personne avant M. Levesque n'avait rassemblé autant de matériaux essentiels à l'exécution d'un travail si difficile* . . .[189] In spite of its excellence, said the reviewer, the popular success of the history was mediocre because, he continued, *On comprend aisément que l'histoire ancienne de Russie ne pouvait pas être susceptible d'un grand intérêt; ces premiers temps n'offrent ques des monuments de guerre et de mœurs sauvages.*[190] La Harpe found Levesque's history well written, clear, and authoritative, but lacking in vivid characterization—in the case, for example, of Peter the Great.[191] Blin de Sainmore, Fortia de Piles, and Masson all praised Levesque's history in the prefaces to their books. Until the works of Rambaud, Léger, and Leroy-Beaulieu in the second half of the nineteenth century, Levesque's history remained the most important French study of Russia.

Le Clerc's *Histoire physique, morale, civile, et politique de*

[188] Michaud, *Biographie universelle*, 1819, XXIV, 374.
[189] *Correspondance littéraire*, XIII, 70-78.
[190] *Ibid.*
[191] La Harpe, *Correspondance littéraire*, letter CLVII.

la Russie ancienne et moderne ... 1783-1794, 6 vols., in quarto, although even more extensive than the history of Levesque, is inferior to the latter in style, method of presentation, and reliability of data. As we have seen, Le Clerc, like Levesque, spent many years in Russia and knew the language. The last three volumes of his history were written in collaboration with his son.

In the Preface to his history Le Clerc assured the reader that he had done everything he could to get the necessary material for his work— ... *j'ai fait tout ce que j'ai dû, sans cesser d'être bon Français.*[192] He owed, he asserted, much of his material to many eminent Russian friends, particularly Prince Shcherbatov.[193] He did not, however, specify his sources, and there is no evidence that he used the Russian chroniclers. Much of his material comes, in fact, from Levesque, and this fact, it appears, was known to contemporaries.[194] Le Clerc retaliated against accusations of plagiarism, however, by attacking Levesque's vanity, his unnecessary display of erudition, and his serious omissions.[195] Thus, for example, Levesque devoted only twenty pages to Russian literature, while Le Clerc had one hundred.[196] *A quoi bon apprendre,* Levesque had replied to this accusation, *aux Français les noms d'une centaine d'auteurs, que les Russes ne nomment jamais eux mêmes?* [97] Such an attitude, Le Clerc believed, was altogether unjustifiable. A detailed account of Russian literature was, no doubt, Le Clerc's strong point, although the great majority of the authors he examined were little known and did not survive their own time. Like

[192] N. G. Le Clerc, *Histoire phisique* ... 1783-1785, I, Preface, x.
[193] *Ibid.,* I, xii.
[194] *Ibid.,* second Preface, II, x.
[195] *Ibid.,* II, x-xv.
[196] *Ibid.,* II, xxi.
[197] *Ibid.*

Levesque, Le Clerc considered Russian literature to a large extent imitative but capable of development along purely national lines.[198]

In the Preface to the sixth volume of the first edition (the third volume of modern history) the publishers asserted that the works of Pallas and Le Clerc were the only authoritative works on Russia. They gave excerpts from many testimonials of contemporary writers (anonymous) who praised Le Clerc's erudition and impartiality. The history was, no doubt, used by some of the more popular writers on Russia. Chantreau's *Voyage*, for example, is largely based on it.[199] In Russia it was severely criticized, both for its manner of presentation and for its content. A long critique appeared in St. Petersburg in 1787 under the title of *Remarques sur l'histoire de la Russie ancienne et moderne*, written by General Boltin at the request of Catherine, who did not approve of the history.

Nevertheless, besides a more extensive survey of Russian culture and literature, Le Clerc's history was superior to that of Levesque in that it contained a considerable number of maps and illustrations. In this respect, his work may be said to have had a wider and more popular appeal than Levesque's. On the other hand, when one examines Le Clerc's history today, the general impression is one of bewildering confusion. Its lack of system and its extreme prolixity and diffuseness must have seriously detracted from its value as a reference work or a source of information for the general reader.

In addition to the French and foreign works surveyed in this chapter, other sources of information about Russia were the contemporary periodicals and journals. A bibliography of

[198] *Ibid.*, IV, 170.
[199] Pierre Chantreau, *Voyage philosophique* ... I, ch. xviii.

articles pertaining to Russia which appeared during the century in some of the best known periodicals of the time is appended at the end of this study.

The earliest literary periodicals, the *Journal des savants* and the *Mémoires de Trévoux*,[200] printed a number of articles on Russian topics. These articles, some of which were of considerable length, were, for the most part, reviews of the most important foreign and French books on Russia, usually accounts of travelers. The topics most widely discussed in these reviews were the personality, the reforms, and the wars of Peter the Great. With short interruptions the articles on Russia in these periodicals run almost continually from the end of the seventeenth century to the middle of the eighteenth. About 1730, however, the number of articles fell off considerably, especially in the *Journal des savants*. The reason for this may in part be that other, more cosmopolitan periodicals began, at about that time, to identify themselves more closely with the Northern countries in general and Russia in particular.

In the second half of the century the best-known literary journals interested in foreign countries were Fréron's *L'Année littéraire* (1754-1790), the *Journal étranger* (1754-1762) (edited successively by Suard, Grimm, Prévost, Fréron, and Arnaud), and Pierre Rousseau's *Journal encyclopédique* (1756-1780). The first two were the most widely read, and were chiefly instrumental in the diffusion of foreign literatures.[201] The books most discussed in these periodicals were English and German. The first of these journals, *L'Année littéraire*, had, throughout its existence, only two articles on Russia. This number, when compared to the 317 articles on

---

[200] The first of these appeared on January 5, 1655, and continued, always in front rank, for the next 200 years; the second, a Jesuit publication, was published from 1701 to 1775.

[201] Joseph Texte; *J. J. Rousseau et les origines du cosmopolitisme littéraire*, 1895, pp. 266-267; and van Tieghem, *L'Année littéraire*, 1917.

England, seems to show a definite lack of interest in the Moscovites.[202] The *Journal étranger*, next in importance as a cosmopolitan publication, manifested an equal indifference. Its lack of interest in Russia is difficult to account for, considering especially that at least two of its editors, Grimm and Arnaud, were definitely interested in Russia and in close contact with everything Russian. This journal also printed only two articles on Russian topics. As in the case of *L'Année littéraire*, England again furnished most material, especially under the editorship of Suard. After 1756 the *Journal étranger* had regular correspondents in most European capitals and in the East, with the conspicuous exception of Russia. The *Journal encyclopédique*, on the other hand, furnished considerable information about Russia. It had long reviews with many excerpts from the more important foreign and French books on Russia; it printed Catherine's *Antidote*, and her letter to D'Alembert; it reviewed current plays on Russian subjects, and, in general, apparently registered all the important literary and historical events pertaining to Russia.

In the last decade of the century the *Esprit des journaux* and the *Spectateur du Nord* purveyed some information about Russia. Both of these showed interest in the state of Russian culture. The former introduced the first work on Russian mythology and reviewed at length the works of Chantreau and Pallas. The latter published a long article on Karamzin's novel, *Julie*, and printed a lengthy study, in the form of a letter, of the state of contemporary Russian literature.

Other periodicals of the time, less important in their content, did not differ materially from those mentioned above, although a few had special characteristics. Formey's *Nouvelle bibliothèque germanique*, for example, specialized in review-

202 During its existence *L'Année littéraire* contained 317 articles on English topics, 94 on German, 105 on Italian; the rest of the European countries were far behind the above. Russia merited only two articles, cf. van Tieghem, *op. cit.*, Introduction.

ing Russian books of a scientific nature and published all the important reports of the Imperial Academy of Sciences at St. Petersburg. The *Mercure de France* as early as 1750 began to print news from the Russian court. This information became, toward the end of the century, more detailed and extensive in scope. Letters from the Russian court were also regularly published in Linguet's *Journal de politique et de la littérature* (1774-1776). All of the above-mentioned periodicals reviewed the more important foreign works pertaining to Russia.

It will be interesting to note here the changes in the course of the century that took place in the prevalent views on Russia and the Russian people in the periodicals we have examined. In the *Journal des savants* for May 19, 1698, for example, we find the following general observations on the people and the state of the country's civilization:

Les Moscovites sont ordinairement de moyenne taille, robustes, farouches, cruels, haïssant les Polonais, les Suedois, les Tartares et tous leurs autres voisins... Le peuple quoique robuste, vit dans l'oisivité, ne s'occupant qu'à tromper, ce qui bien loin d'être condamné comme un vice, passe pour une marque d'habilité et d'adresse. ... Ils [i.e., the Moscovites] n'ont ni collèges, ni universités, n'apprennent qu'à lire et à écrire, et quiconque voudrait savoir davantage se rendrait suspect, et se mettrait en danger d'être puni.

The same review mentions the absence of money and the practice of barter, the absence of medical knowledge and the superstitious character of the Russian Church. In a review in the same journal for August, 1710, the reviewer gives the following curious description of the people:

Ils sont soupçonneux et défians, cruels, sodomites, gourmands, avares, gueux et poltrons, tous esclaves, excepté le prince Sirkache [?], ci-devant Seigneur du pays du même nom, et qui a des richesses immenses, Gallitzchen [i.e., Prince Golitsyn], Hartemonovitz [?]... Ils sont encore par-dessus tout cela fort grossiers et même brutaux,

Such views were quite prevalent in the literary reviews at the beginning of the century. From about 1717 (the year of Tsar Peter's visit to France) these exaggerated and hostile descriptions of the country are seldom found. Most reviews dealing with Russia begin to give enthusiastic accounts of Peter's reforms and praise their salutary effects on the country.[203] Towards the end of the century the picture is almost diametrically opposite to what it was at the beginning. The "enlightenment" and progress in Russia now became the principal topics. The Russian people begin to be described as gay, imaginative and not unlike Frenchmen themselves.[204] Russia's culture, we are told, now is to be taken seriously into account. Works like those of Karamzin, for example, said a reviewer in the *Spectateur du Nord* for February, 1797, will suffice to show that "... *dans un pays, qu'en France on ne se déshabitue pas encore de regarder comme un peu barbare, il se trouve des écrivains qui peuvent rivaliser avec les Marmontel et les Florian.* Such observations, by no means uncommon, were perhaps just as exaggerated estimates of the Russian enlightenment as the descriptions of Russia at the beginning of the century were exaggerated statements of the country's backwardness.

Besides the reviews and articles in the literary journals we have surveyed, there were also frequent references to Russian topics in the *Correspondances littéraires* of the century. The more important of these—Grimm's, Métra's, La Harpe's, and Bachaumont's—have been referred to frequently throughout this study.

The works reviewed in this chapter show how information about Russia had gradually filtered into France. One might say that in the eighteenth century, France's principal

[203] See, for example, *Journal des savants*, April, 1734, and *Mémoires de Trévoux*, August, 1760.

[204] Cf. *Esprit des journaux*, April and November, 1784; June, October, and November, 1792.

foreign sources of information about Russia were of three types: the early sixteenth- and seventeenth-century German and Italian accounts, contemporary (eighteenth century) German historical and ethnographical works, and eighteenth-century accounts of English travelers. In range and reliability of information the German works were superior to all others. Most of the earliest English works, by Chancellor, Horsey, Fletcher, and others, were not translated into French until the nineteenth century and were known only through brief résumés published in French collections of travels. As sources of information they were comparatively unimportant.

On the other hand, a number of eighteenth-century English works achieved considerable popularity; some of these, like Captain Perry's, undeservedly so, as they were biased and unreliable; others, like Coxe's work, enjoyed a well-deserved recognition. Many of the prevalent eighteenth-century French views on the government, people, and customs of Russia seem to have originated in the accounts of Herberstein, Olearius, Baron Mayerberg and other early travelers to Russia. Prior to the eighteenth century France had no important descriptive works on Russia. During the century, however, there were published a large number of French works consisting of travelers' memoirs, collections of anecdotes, and popular histories.[205] As a rule these works were superficial, biased, and unoriginal, being based in many instances on earlier German and English accounts. Levesque's history, however, represents the first serious attempt on the part of the French to study Russia from a more scholarly, more general, and all-inclusive point of view. The large number of French popular accounts published during the eighteenth-century and the many editions

[205] The works of well-known Frenchmen who were in close contact with Russia, such as Grimm, Ségur, and De Ligne, were not published until the nineteenth century. Some of these, however, were circulated in manuscript form long before their publication.

through which some of them ran,[206] would indicate a marked popular interest in Russia. The same interest is also attested by the articles and reviews on Russian topics in some of the periodicals of the time.[207] Generally speaking, most of the eighteenth-century French writers on Russia were interested in the country from an historical, geographical, and ethnographical point of view. It is only in the last quarter of the century that a certain interest in the cultural state of Russia began to manifest itself. To judge from the French memoirs, articles, and historical accounts we have examined in this chapter, a remarkable change had taken place in the course of the century in France's general attitude toward Russia; from complete indifference and hostility at the beginning of the century to an interested and friendly curiosity towards its end.

[206] For example, such works as those of Rousset de Missy, Chappe d'Auteroche, Chantreau, Voltaire, and Masson.

[207] *Journal des savants, Mémoires de Trévoux, Journal encyclopédique,* and in the last decade of the century, the *Spectateur du Nord.*

VI

THE SOCIAL AND POLITICAL VIEWS ON
RUSSIA HELD BY EIGHTEENTH-CENTURY
FRENCH MEN OF LETTERS

IT HAS often been observed that the function of eighteenth-century philosophy was not to search for abstract truth but to study man in his relation to society. The chief pre-occupation was, in other words, the analysis of social, political, and economic problems, the solution of which engaged the attention of many of the important writers of the century, especially those of France. Russia was one such problem, though no doubt a minor one. Here was a vast country, for centuries altogether uncivilized, but suddenly, thanks to the enlightenment of its rulers, assuming an important place among the older nations of Europe. Was this progress to continue, or was it only temporary and ephemeral? What was the nature of Peter the Great's reforms, and how did they affect the country? Were the Russians capable of assimilating Western culture, or was their country to be ruined by it? These were some of the questions which presented themselves to eighteenth-century French philosophers and men of letters. All had something to say, but the answers they propounded to these questions remained, then as now, inconclusive, showing merely the personal bias of each writer.

Fontenelle was one of the first to speak about Russia. His interest in the country was aroused by Peter the Great's visit to France in 1717. As secretary of the Academy of Sciences he wrote two letters to the Tsar; one complimenting him on his reforms and the success of his wars, the other thanking him for the honor of consenting to become a member of the Academy.[1]

In the Preface to his *Eloge du Czar Pierre I*, he eulogized the monarch as his fellow academician ... *mais Académicien roi et empereur, qui a établi les sciences et les arts dans les vastes états de sa domination.*[2] Before Peter the country was in a state of complete barbarism. *Ce n'est pas*, he observed, *que l'on ne découvrit dans les Moscovites de la vivacité, de la pénétration, du génie, et de l'adresse à imiter ce qu'ils auraient vu: mais toute industrie était étouffée.*[3] It was the liberal reforms of the Tsar which first brought the country into the sphere of civilization. After giving a detailed account of the major social, religious, administrative, and educational reforms of Peter the Great, Fontenelle pronounced them most salutary and promising for the country. The religious reforms (i.e., the separation of Church and State) especially met with his approval. For, before Peter, the Russian religion *à peine méritait le nom de religion Chrétienne.*[4]

The creative genius of Peter the Great had, for Fontenelle, no parallel in history, and he considered the Tsar greater than the Roman Augustus, for if the latter, he observed, *se vantait d'avoir trouvé Rome de brique et de la laisser de marbre, on voit assez combien, à cet égard, l'empereur romain est inférieur à celui de la Russie.*[5]

The Marquis d'Argenson, friend of the Encyclopedists, and author of the famous memoirs, held views on Russia substantially the same as those of Fontenelle. Before Peter the Great, Russia for him did not exist—*L'empire de Russie ou*

[1] Letters of December 27, 1719, and December 15, 1721; cf. *Œuvres de Fontenelle*, Paris, 1825, II, 409-412.
[2] Fontenelle, *Œuvres*, "Eloge du Czar Pierre I," II, 102.
[3] *Ibid.*
[4] *Ibid.*, II, 125.
[5] *Ibid.*, II, 127.

Moscovie, he said in his *Considérations,*[6] *n'était compté, il y a cinquante ans, que parmi les nations barbares; on confondait les Russes avec les Tartares et les Cosaques.*[7] The progress made by Russia in such a short time was due entirely to Peter the Great who was all at once ... *législateur et conquérant, ce qui constitue un des plus grands hommes que le monde ait vus.*[8] He approved all the reforms and believed that the progress Peter had begun would continue. The imitation of Western Europe and the attraction of foreigners to the country was, in D'Argenson's opinion, the only possible course for Russia to take.

Contrary to Fontenelle's and D'Argenson's views on Russia are those of Montesquieu. He derived most of his information, as we have seen in the preceding chapter, from Olearius and from the Englishman Perry.

Russia, he considered, was worthy of Europe's interest because of the rapid progress she had made since the reign of Peter the Great.[9] There were, to be sure, two almost insuperable obstacles to the process of Russia's Europeanization. The first was the cruelty and barbarism of the people; *il faut écorcher un Moscovite pour lui donner du sentiment.*[10] The second was the despotism of the government and the institution of serfdom—*M. Perry dit que les Moscovites se rendent très aisément. J'en sais bien la raison: c'est que leur liberté ne vaut rien.*[11] The growth of serfdom and the absence of political liberty he ascribed to the influences of the climate—*Que la noblesse moscovite ait été réduite au servitude par un de*

---

[6] The *Considerations* ... was published first posthumously by D'Argenson's son in Amsterdam in 1764.

[7] *Ibid.,* Amsterdam, 1784, p. 91.

[8] *Ibid.,* pp. 93-94.

[9] Montesquieu, *Œuvres,* "De l'esprit des lois," éd. Garnier frères, Vol. III, Book IX, ch. ix, 351.

[10] *Ibid.,* Vol. IV, Book XII, ch. xxviii, 106-107.

[11] *Ibid.,* Vol. IV, Book XV, ch. vi, 185.

ses princes, on y vera toujours des traits d'impatience que les climats du midi ne donnent point.[12]

Regarding the reforms of Peter the Great, Montesquieu condemned them as a whole on the ground that a sudden and violent change of the laws and institutions of a country leads to the country's ruin. A change can be accomplished only gradually and by example from above—never by arbitrary laws.[13] Nevertheless, he approved some minor reforms, such as those concerning the taxation of the peasants by the landlords instead of by the government.[14]

In spite of the many obstacles, Montesquieu believed that Peter's reforms were partially successful. He ascribed this partly to the climate, partly to the variety of different nationalities comprising Russia. Peter's reforms took root more easily because Russia's old customs and institutions—

... étaient étrangères au climat, et y avaient été apportées par le mélange des nations et par les conquêtes. Pierre I, donnant les mœurs et les manières de l'Europe à une nation d'Europe, trouva des facilités qu'il n'attendait pas lui-même.[15]

It appears then that Montesquieu recognized the inevitability of Russia's adopting Western culture and civilization, but that he disapproved of Peter's accomplishing this through sudden and arbitrary legislation.

Il n'avait donc pas besoin de lois pour changer les mœurs et les manières de sa nation: il lui eût suffi d'inspirer d'autres mœurs et d'autres manières.[16]

Just as many another political and social problem of the century found two diametrically opposed exponents in Vol-

[12] *Ibid.*, Vol. IV, Book XVII, ch. iii, 240-243.
[13] *Ibid.*, Vol. IV, Book XIX, ch. xiv, 321-323.
[14] *Ibid.*, Vol. IV, Book XII, ch. vi, 119.
[15] *Ibid.*, Vol. IV, Book XIII, ch. vi, 322.
[16] *Ibid.*, Vol. III, Book IX, ch. ix, 351.

taire and Rousseau, so also did the problem of Russia's progress and Peter the Great's reforms.

Voltaire's interest in Russia was of long standing. Even more than his predecessors, Voltaire completely disregarded the social and political development of Russia before the reign of Peter the Great. His enthusiasm for the Tsar-reformer was reiterated in his correspondence, and expressed repeatedly in his history of Peter's reign.[17]

Rousseau, on the other hand, was more interested in Poland than in Russia. He maintained no relations with the Russian court as did so many of his contemporaries. His attitude towards the Russian government and people was consistently hostile.

Malgré l'expérience assez frappante que les Russes viennent de faire en Pologne [he wrote in his *Considérations sur la Pologne*], rien ne les fera changer d'opinion. Ils regardent toujours les hommes libres comme il faut les regarder eux-mêmes, c'est à dire comme des hommes nuls, sur lesquels deux seuls instruments ont prise, savoir, l'argent et le knout.[18]

His views on Russia were as pessimistic as his predictions about the depopulation of Europe. A revolution, and a complete subjugation of Russia by the Tatars was, he believed, inevitable and not far off. These views he set forth in the *Contrat social*. He said:

Les Russes ne seront jamais policés, parce qu'ils l'ont été trop tôt. Pierre avait le génie imitatif, il n'avait pas le vrai génie, celui qui crée et fait tout de rien. Quelques unes des choses qu'il fit étaient bien, la plupart étaient déplacées. Il a vu que son peuple était barbare, il n'a point vu qu'il n'était pas mûr pour la police et l'a voulu civiliser quand il ne fallait que l'aguerrir. Il a d'abord voulu faire des Allemands, des Anglais, quand il fallait commencer par faire des Russes. L'empire de Russie voudra subjuguer l'Europe et sera

---

[17] See also *Essai sur les mœurs*, éd. Garnier frères, XI, 43 ff.
[18] Rousseau, *Œuvres complètes*, Paris, 1823, V, 361.

subjugué lui-même. Les Tartares, ses sujets ou ses voisins, deviendront ses maîtres et les nôtres. Cettes résolution me parait infaillible.[19]

These sentences provoked a very spirited reply from Voltaire which was published in his *Dictionnaire philosophique*.[20] Regarding Rousseau's remarks about Peter the Great's lack of creative genius, he said:

Il faut avouer que le Russe qui en 1700 devina l'influence des lumières sur l'état politique des empires, et sut apercevoir que le plus grand bien qu'on puisse faire aux hommes est de substituer des idées justes aux préjugés qui les gouvernent, a eu plus de génie que le Genevois qui en 1750 a voulu nous prouver les grands avantages de l'ignorance.[21]

The progress of Russia was due entirely to Peter's creative genius and *lumières*.

Les Russes ont fait en 85 ans, que les vues de Pierre ont été suivies, plus de progrès que nous n'en avons fait en quatre siècles: n'est-ce pas une preuve que ces vues n'étaient pas celles d'un homme ordinaire?[22]

To Rousseau's assertion that the Russians would never become civilized, Voltaire replied:

J'en ai vu du moins de très-polis, et qui avaient l'esprit juste, fin, agréable, cultivé, et même conséquent, ce que Jean-Jacques trouvera fort extraordinaire.[23]

Regarding the assertion that it was impossible for the Russians to develop their national character because of Peter's introduction of foreigners, Voltaire remarked:

Cependent ces mêmes Russes sont devenus les vainqueurs des Turcs et des Tartares, les conquérants et les législateurs de la Crimée et de vingt peuples différents; leur souveraine a donné des lois à des na-

[19] *Ibid.*, ed. of 1827, V, Book II, ch. viii, 83-84.
[20] Voltaire, *Nouveau mélanges*, éd. Garnier, XX, 218-220.
[21] *Ibid.*
[22] *Ibid.*
[23] *Ibid.*

tions dont le nom même était ignoré en Europe. . . . Je voudrais en général que lorsqu'on juge les nations du haut de son grenier on fût plus honnête et plus circonspect. . .[24]

According to Rousseau, then, Peter the Great was wrong in imposing foreign institutions upon Russia; Voltaire thought he was right. One prophesied Russia's ruin; the other, a glorious future. The controversy here set forth crystallized the general views on Russia. About 1760 most political writers and men of letters, including those who went to Russia, took, in a general way, either the side of Voltaire or that of Rousseau.

The group of the Encyclopedists was, naturally, following in the wake of Voltaire. Diderot's views on Russia, as pointed out earlier in this work, are difficult to define. For although it may be true that he uttered his pessimistic sentence reported by Ségur—*La Russie, c'est un collosse aux pieds d'argile,*[25] his theoretical works on Russia imply a complete acceptance of the optimistic views of Voltaire. D'Alembert was somewhat more reserved and less enthusiastic about the progress of the *lumières* in Russia; yet he too seemed to share Voltaire's views on the past and future of the country.[26] La Harpe was an enthusiastic admirer of the Russian enlightenment, and at times in his praise seemed to exceed even Voltaire himself.[27] Marmontel used Voltaire's history of Tsar Peter's reign as a source, and seemed to be in complete accord with its general ideas regarding the personality of the Tsar, and the ultimate outcome of his reforms.[28]

[24] Voltaire, *Nouveau mélanges,* éd. Garnier, XX, 218-220.

[25] L. P. de Ségur, *Mémoires,* III, 214.

[26] See his correspondence with Voltaire in 1762-1763; especially his letter to Voltaire of February 12, 1763; Voltaire, *Correspondance,* éd. Garnier, Vol. XLII.

[27] See especially his poem read in the French Academy on May 27, 1782, and his "éloge" of Catherine II in his *Poème sur les femmes,* read in the Academy on June 5, 1784.

[28] Marmontel, *Œuvres complètes,* Vol. XVIII; *Régence du duc d'Orléans,* ch. viii, "Voyage du Czar Pierre à Paris."

Chevalier de Jaucourt's article about Russia in the *Grande encyclopédie* is also partly based upon Voltaire's history.[29] Peter the Great is described in this article as a very great ruler whose reforms were, on the whole, salutary for the country. *Avant le Czar Pierre, les usages, les vêtements, les mœurs en Russie, avaient toujours plus tenu de l'Asie que de l'Europe Chrétienne.*[30] He praised, however, a few of the old Russian customs, adding that *presque tous les autres usages étaient grossiers.*[31] As for the Russian religion, he considered it largely a superstitious and ignorant Christian sect. The pagan element of the population was, in his opinion, which was based on the accounts of travelers, better than the Christian. *L'ingénieur Perri et le baron de Strahlenberg, qui ont été si longtemps en Russie, disent qu'ils ont trouvé plus de probité dans les payens que dans les autres.*[32] This he explained, rather inconsistently, was because the pagan element of the population was nearer to nature and so less corrupted.

Among the eighteenth-century Frenchmen who visited Russia the chief exponents of Voltaire's social and political views on the country were Ségur, Falconet, Levesque, and the Belgian De Ligne.

Turning now to the views of the partisans of Rousseau, we find among them a greater variety of opinions, though Rousseau's ideas expressed in the *Contrat social* are at the base of them all.

Abbé Mably comes perhaps closest to Rousseau in his hostile and pessimistic attitude towards Russia. Like Rousseau he was asked by the Polish government to draw up a constitution and spent a year in Poland studying local condi-

[29] Chevalier de Jaucourt, *Encyclopédie*, XIV, 442-445. Jaucourt was, however, skeptical of some of Voltaire's estimates, that of population, for example: *il faut se défier*, he said in this article, *de tous les dénombrements d'un pays que démontrent par besoin les souverains, parce que pour leur plaire on a grand soin de multiplier, d'exagérer, de doubler le nombre de leurs sujets.*

[30] Chevalier de Jaucourt, *Encyclopédie*, XIV, 442-445.

[31] *Ibid.*   [32] *Ibid.*

tions. His reflections on Russia are scattered in the twelfth
volume of his collected works.[33]

Mably attacked the despotism of the Russian government
and denied the country all enlightenment and progress. Here
is his comparison between France and Russia:

> La nation française cultive les arts et les sciences; vaine, frivole,
> dissipée, spirituelle, glorieuse, légère, inconstante, elle s'est fait un
> goût fin et delicat sur les bienséances et les procédés qu'il serait
> dangereux d'offenser. Rien de tout cela n'est en Russie. A force
> d'ignorance, d'injustice, et de barbarie, les hommes, distribués d'ail-
> leurs en différentes classes, y sont tous mis dans la dernière.[34]

Mably completely disapproved of Peter the Great's reforms. In the first place, Mably believed that the Tsar relied
too much on Le Fort's suggestions and that Le Fort was not
fit to give advice.[35] Peter failed, also, to train his subjects to
become good citizens and was wrong in transplanting French
elegance and culture to Russia.[36] *Peut-être*, Malby observed,
*avez-vous fait trop d'honneur à l'Europe en la prenant pour
votre modèle.*[37]

The actual power and importance of Russia, Mably believed, would soon disappear, as Peter failed to provide for
the permanence of his reforms. Having made the people bel-
ligerent and having at the same time failed to make them
happy, his reforms would vanish soon after him, and the
nation would revert to its original state of barbarism. Mably
saw, in fact, no hope whatever for the Russian empire and
was more pessimistic about its future than Rousseau himself.[38]

Condillac, friend of Rousseau and Diderot, was also pes-

[33] Abbé de Mably, *Œuvres*, Desbrière, 1794-1795; XII, cf. especially, Pt. II,
ch. i; Pt. III, chs. i, ii, and iii.
[34] *Ibid.*, XII, 137.
[35] *Ibid.*, XII, 298-299.
[36] *Ibid.*, XII, 307.
[37] *Ibid.*, XII, 305.
[38] *Ibid.*, XII, 310-314.

simistic regarding the future of Russia, though his attitude was less hopeless and hostile than that of Rousseau.[39] He held that before the seventeenth century Russia, as a nation, *en méritait à peine le nom.* The people lived *dans une ignorance profonde, remplis de préjugés absurdes, livrés à des superstitions grossières, sans arts, sans police, sans mœurs* . . .[40] Thus, Condillac concluded, it was not necessary to know anything about this country before the reign of Peter the Great. He admired the vitality and creative genius of the Tsar reformer but disapproved of Peter's reforms. The latter tried to do too much, and the changes he inaugurated were too violent to be salutary. Like Montesquieu, Condillac believed that the customs and folkways of a nation can be changed only gradually, not by arbitrary legislation. Peter was wrong too in introducing foreigners into the country and in mixing too much in European affairs. He should have tried instead to improve the agriculture and to inspire his subjects with *l'amour des lois, de l'ordre, et du bien public.*[41] Instead of a peaceful and "enlightened" internal policy, Peter was concerned too much with conquest and with strengthening his absolutism; as a result—*Je vois partout la vigilance, la fermeté, le courage, les talents de Pierre le Grand, mais je ne vois point encore un bon gouvernement.*[42] Such government of liberty and order could be achieved, thought Condillac (like Montesquieu), only through a balanced distribution of power, a principle of which Peter knew nothing whatsoever. Moreover, the Tsar was altogether wrong in imposing European institutions upon Russia. *Les nations de l'Europe mal gouvernées of corrompues ne pouvaient que le jeter dans l'erreur. Leur politesse et leurs*

---

[39] See his *Cours d'études pour l'instruction du prince de Parme,* "L'étude de l'histoire," Pt. III, chs. ii and iii.

[40] *Ibid.,* ch. ii.

[41] *Ibid.*

[42] *Ibid.,* ch. iii.

arts n'étaient pas ce qu'il fallait aux Russes.[43] Influenced by Europe, Russia would become, in Condillac's opinion, more and more corrupt socially and politically, and, since there would be no Peter to rule over this vast empire, it would eventually fall to ruin. *Tout est perdu si vos sujets ont besoin de czars qui vous ressemblent.*[44]

Abbé Raynal's general views on Russia seem likewise influenced by Rousseau's.[45] Unlike Rousseau, however, he praised Peter's enlightenment and reforms, at the same time doubting the possibility of a lasting and continuous progress in Russia. The chief obstacles to further progress were, in Raynal's opinion, the despotism of the government, the climate, the absence of a middle class, and certain national traits, such as pride.[46] Peter, though a great ruler, had not found, the Abbé believed, the principles necessary for the formation of a well-constituted state. The Tsar was wrong in relying too much on foreigners, and in introducing indiscriminately foreign customs and ideas of government into Russia.[47]

Raynal praised also the constructive genius of Catherine II, distrusting, however, her *philosophie* and liberality of thought. She was at bottom a despot, he believed, and her befriending the philosophers was nothing but a gesture.

Catherine a très bien senti que la liberté était l'unique source du bonheur public. Cependant a-t-elle véritablement abdiqué l'autorité despotique? En lisant avec attention ses instructions aux députés de l'empire, chargés en apparence de la confection des lois, y reconnaît-on quelque chose de plus que le désir de changer les dénominations, d'être appelée monarque au lieu d'autocratrice, d'appeler ses peuples sujets au lieu d'esclaves? Les Russes, tout aveugles qu'ils sont, pren-

---

[43] *Cours d'études pour l'instruction du prince de Parme,* "L'étude de l'histoire," Pt. III, ch. ii.

[44] *Ibid.,* ch. iii.

[45] Raynal, *Histoire philosophique et politique des établissements et de la commerce des Européens dans les deux Indes,* Book V, ch. ii, and Book XIX, ch. ii.

[46] *Ibid.*   [47] *Ibid.*

dront-ils longtemps le nom pour la chose, et leur caractère sera-t-il assez élevé par cette comédie à cette grande énergie qu'on s'était proposé de lui donner? [48]

The last of the eighteenth-century political thinkers to be dealt with here, Mirabeau, held opinions on Russia largely based upon Rousseau's ideas.[49] Mirabeau denied a creative genius to Peter the Great, arraigned his introduction of foreigners into Russia, condemned his interest in conquest rather than in creating a sound and civilized nation.

Qu'a-t-il fait pour la nation qu'il a laissé esclave, malheureuse, abérrée? Les Russes avaient un caractère national; ils n'en ont plus.[50]

Moreover, Peter did nothing for the political liberty of his subjects, for agriculture, for strengthening and developing the national character.[51] Mirabeau exclaims apologetically:

O Russes, je n'ai pas voulu vous calomnier, ou vous insulter; c'est de la pitié, non du mépris que vous méritez; vous pouviez, vous pouvez être heureux, vous avez droit de l'être; ceux qui vous gouvernent ont seuls perpétué vos malheurs.[52]

In Mirabeau's opinion, Peter was responsible for starting Russia's development in the wrong direction. The Russian empire should have cultivated the land, instead of building fleets and expanding armies; it should have liberated serfs before developing commerce.[53] Unfortunately, Peter was only too human and

... voulait des victoires et des conquêtes, parce que la mode éternelle des hommes est de célébrer avant tout les héros.[54]

[48] Ibid., Book XIX, ch. ii.
[49] Mirabeau, Doutes sur la liberté de l'Escaut, London, Faden, 1784. Mirabeau's chief sources of information on Russia were Manstein, Perry, and Voltaire. Cf. ibid., Appendix.
[50] Mirabeau, Doutes sur la liberté de l'Escaut, p. 72.
[51] Ibid.   [52] Ibid., p. 73.
[53] Ibid., Appendix, p. xv.   [54] Ibid., p. xvii.

It was said:

Le but de la politique encyclopédiste est de poursuivre l'établissement de la liberté individuelle; le moyen est de faire régner la philosophie, de l'installer sur le trône, afin qu'un gouvernement juste, éclairé, paternel, en s'efforçant de répandre les lumières, prépare l'adoucissement des mœurs, et l'affranchissement des esprits.[55]

Voltaire and the Encyclopedists regarded Russia from this point of view. Peter the Great and Catherine the Great were for them perfect examples of enlightened monarchs. They tended to exaggerate the importance of Peter's reforms, disregarding entirely Russia's development before the latter's reign. They approved wholeheartedly of the reforms and prophesied for the country continuous national progress and development. The opposite views were held by Montesquieu and by the followers of the democratic theory of government, headed by Rousseau. These, although granting the progress made by Russia and often admiring Tsar Peter's vitality and creative power, were not convinced that the process of Europeanization started by the Tsar was salutary for the country. The absence of political liberty, the climate, and certain negative national traits would eventually lead, they believed, to the country's downfall. Both sides, the encyclopedists and the democrats, showed little interest in the national culture of Russia and condemned the Russian clergy and religion as chief causes of the country's backwardness and chief obstacles to its further progress.

[55] Albert Bayet and François Albert, *Les Ecrivains politiques du XVIII*e siècle, Paris, 1917, Introduction, p. xxxii.

VII

TRACES OF RUSSIA IN EIGHTEENTH-CENTURY FRENCH BELLES LETTRES

THE eighteenth-century's taste for world-wide travel and its interest in the most diverse peoples were naturally reflected in the works of a great number of its writers. As Mornet has observed, *le Nord* was for the seventeenth century only a vague figure of speech. For the eighteenth, it definitely represented England, Germany, the Scandinavian countries, and Russia.[1] This cosmopolitan tendency became especially marked in French literature after 1750.[2] From then on there followed a succession of novels, tales, plays, and comic operas, the settings and characters of which often belonged to distant countries. At the same time English literature provided material for numerous translations.[3] Having examined in the preceding chapter the historical and political literature pertaining to Russia, we shall now attempt to measure the extent of Russia's rôle in the imaginative literature of France.

We shall begin with the drama. In comedy and tragedy alike, Voltaire was probably one of the first to turn to foreign countries rather than to antiquity for settings, characters,

---

[1] Daniel Mornet, *French Thought in the Eighteenth Century*, New York, 1929, p. 111.

[2] See, for example, Grimm's introductory Preface to the *Journal étranger* in 1754, about the advantages of cosmopolitanism.

[3] Gustave Lanson's *Manuel bibliographique*, for example, gives 254 translations from English, 76 from German, 52 from Italian, 20 from Spanish, and 20 from other languages.

and subjects. This practice became general about the middle of the century. Being primarily a polemist, Voltaire paid little attention to local color and historical accuracy in his plays. This was true of eighteenth-century drama in general. Everything was metamorphosed to suit French taste. Plays with foreign settings or characters had little, if any, national flavor. So far as the costumes and stage decorations went, Favart had already used Chinese costumes as early as 1756. No serious attempt to evoke the historical milieu was made, however, until the production of De Belloy's plays about 1770. Mlle Clairon and Talma were the two names most closely associated with this more realistic tendency on the stage.[4]

Eighteenth-century comedy and comic opera offer several instances of Russian subjects, characters, or settings. One of the earliest comedies concerned with Russia was Le Sage's *Zémine et Almanzor* (1730). The action of this play is laid in Astrakhan, on the Caspian Sea, and apparently harks back to the period before 1554, when the Kingdom of Astrakhan was incorporated into the Russian empire. The play has a Russian character, Prince Alinguer, the villain, who woos the adopted daughter of the king of Astrakhan. He tries to poison the king's mind against his rival, the king's son, who is brought up, away from the court, by a shepherd. The suit of the Russian prince fails, and he is dismissed from the court. It is difficult to say exactly why Le Sage chose to lay the action of this play in Russia, as there is nothing besides the name to suggest its locality. What the author wanted, apparently, was to give the play an Oriental character and the introduction of the king of Astrakhan and the Russian prince was deemed sufficient to produce the desired Oriental effect.

A more or less similar plot, that of a king who tests his son's character by sending him away to be brought up by

[4] G. Lanson, *Esquisse d'une histoire de la tragédie française,* 1920, p. 136.

shepherds, is found in Boissy's *La Vie est un songe* (1732).
Here the scene is laid in Poland. One of the characters, a
grand duc de Moscovie, goes incognito to the court of Poland
to win the hand of the king's daughter. He is represented as
a fearless warrior and lover, but rather rude in manner and
speech. He fails as a suitor and is dismissed by the king, who
considers the grand duke *trop barbare*. Like the preceding,
this play is suggestive of an Arabian Nights extravaganza in
spite of the scene being laid in Poland.

Chronologically, the next play to be mentioned in this
group is Bernardin de Saint-Pierre's *Empsail et Zoraïde*. This
drama, written about 1775, was never produced and was not
published in the eighteenth century.[5] The theme of the play
is vengeance conquered by love. It also purports to be an
indictment of civilization. Petrovna, one of the characters in
the play, is a Russian. She is a passionate but kindly woman,
and is called by the heroine, whom she is helping in charity
work, *la bonne Russe*. This rather vague character and the
Observations sur la Russie are the only echoes in Saint-Pierre's
works of his stay in Russia.

Two references to Russia in Mme de Genlis' *Voyageur*
(1781) and in Boissy's *La Frivolité* (1753) are indicative
of contemporary interest in Russia. In the *Voyageur* a young
traveler just back from a trip to England, Spain, Italy, and
Holland expresses a desire to go next to Russia:

Oui, je compte faire le voyage du Nord. J'irai d'abord en Russie,
parce que je médite un ouvrage très piquant sur les progrès rapides
des Russes dans les arts et dans la politique...[6]

In *La Frivolité* a character noting the various transformations

[5] Maurice Sourieau, *Empsail et Zoraïde*, Caen, 1905, Introduction, pp. xxvii
and xxx.
[6] Act II, scene iii.

accomplished by the civilizing influence of France, observes as follows:

> L'Europe maintenant et que plus est l'Asie,
> Présentent à nos yeux un différent tableau.
> Le beau sexe n'est plus esclave en Italie,
> Et l'on boit du vin en Turquie.
> En France l'on s'est mis à l'eau,
> Et l'on fait des vers en Russie.[7]

There was produced for the first time on January 13, 1790, at the Opéra Comique, a musical comedy entitled *Pierre-le-Grand* (four acts, in prose) by Jean Bouilly—music by Grétry. The object of the play was, according to the author, to glorify Peter the Great who had formed *d'une multitude de barbares sans mœurs, sans principes et sans talents, une société d'hommes instruits et policés.*[8] Moreover, such a play had, Bouilly thought, a timely interest as the Russian monarch with his friend and counselor, Le Fort, bore in his opinion a striking resemblance to Louis XVI and his minister, Necker. Both Louis and Peter were examples of enlightened and benevolent monarchs who had made many sacrifices for the "happiness" of their people.

The scene of the play is laid in a Russian seaside village. The principal characters, Peter and Le Fort, are both in disguise and are working as carpenters. Peter meets Catherine, a young peasant woman, who is all virtue and charity, and they fall in love. Menshikov appears and announces the news of a conspiracy against the Tsar, and Peter is obliged to go to St. Petersburg. Menshikov then discloses to the villagers Peter's identity. In the last act Peter himself appears in all his splendor and, amidst general acclaim, announces his intention of making Catherine empress of Russia. The play ends with the chorus of villagers:

---

[7] Act I, scene ii.
[8] Jean Bouilly, *Pierre le Grand*, Tours and Paris, 1790, p. 1.

Béni soit à jamais
Notre prince dont la tendresse
S'occupe sans cesse
Du bonheur de ses sujets.[9]

The opera is full of arias in praise of democracy, such as these:

Grands rois, superbes potentats,
Quittez vos cours, vos diadêmes;
Ainsi que lui [i.e., Peter], sortez de vos états
Voyagez, travaillez vous mêmes;
Et vous verrez que la grandeur
Ne fait pas toujours le bonheur.[10]

To these Peter answers as follows:

Pour moi quelle jouissance!
Sous l'habit de l'indigence
Je trouve le vrai bonheur.[11]

The characters in Bouilly's opera are symbols rather than living people: Peter is the personification of an enlightened monarch who sacrifices everything for the happiness of his subjects; Le Fort is the wise guide and teacher of the monarch; Catherine is the loving and virtuous peasant-queen. The play is swift in action and light and amusing in tone. The author's main intention was, evidently, to pay a tribute to the King and Queen of France who were so soon to pay with their lives for the "happiness" of their people.

Bouilly's production apparently earned a certain measure of success, and it was said that Marie Antoinette liked it and presented the author with a snuff box and her portrait.[12] Grimm found it too long, diffuse and *sans vraiseblance*.[13]

[9] *Ibid.*, p. 105.
[10] *Ibid.*, p. 65.
[11] *Ibid.*, p. 73.
[12] *Dictionnaire universel de Larousse*, "Bouilly."
[13] Grimm, *Correspondance littéraire*, XV, 585.

The play was published, however, and, to judge from the number of editions it ran through, must have enjoyed considerable popularity.[14]

Another comic opera, Russian in subject, was written by the well-known playwright of the time, Alexandre Duval. *Beniowski ou les exilés du Kamchatka* was a comic opera in three acts, music by Boïeldieu, produced for the first time June 8, 1800. Although the author does not mention specifically the source of this play he undoubtedly adapted the theme from A. F. Kotzebue's play, *Graf Benjowski oder die Verschwoerung auf Kamtschatka*, produced in Berlin in 1795 and translated into English in 1798.

The action of Duval's opera takes place in a camp for exiles in Siberia. The principal characters are Millow, governor of the province, his niece, Aphanasie, who is in love with Beniowski, a Polish officer taken prisoner by the Russians and exiled to Siberia, and a Russian officer, Stephanow, also in exile. Beniowski is the leader of a plot, the object of which is to gain the freedom of the exiles. Both he and Stephanow are in love with the governor's niece and are also rivals for the leadership of the exiles. The governor has complete confidence in Beniowski and finally consents to his marrying his niece. Beniowski is torn between his gratitude to the governor and his duty as a conspirator. On the day of his wedding Stephanow betrays him to the governor and Beniowski is at once condemned to die. In a fit of remorse Stephanow confesses to the exiles that he has betrayed their leader. A battle then ensues between the governor's troops and the exiles. After several changes in the fortune of the combatants, the exiles finally win. Beniowski is in the arms of Aphanasie; he sets free the governor, who is now a prisoner, and magnanimously pardons Stephanow's treachery. The exiles acclaim

---

[14] Tours and Paris, 1790, in octavo; Paris and Brussels, 1792, in octavo; Amsterdam, 1792, in octavo; Paris, 1801 and 1814, in octavo.

Beniowski as their leader and march off to their newly-won freedom.

The libretto of the opera is exceedingly poor. It is full of melodrama, sentimentality, and false pathos. The characters are scarcely more than shadows. A certain attempt to portray the locality was made through the staging of the forest, the bear hunting and the appearance of the Cossacks. Furthermore, in the character of Stephanow the author evidently intended to express the complexities and the contradictions of the Russian nature. *Il a allié*, one of the characters of the play says of him, *la grandeur d'âme à la perfidie*.

The play was at first a success. The *Journal des débats* for June 10, 1800, gives the following description of its first production:

Sa seule réputation [i.e., of this play] avait attiré une prodigieuse affluence de spectateurs. La surprise et l'étonnement n'ont pas permis au public d'apercevoir les défauts: étourdi par le bruit de la musique et de la pantomime théâtrale, il s'est abandonné par un mouvement aveugle à ce que la pièce a d'imposant, sans faire attention au plan et aux caractères.

The opera was apparently considerably talked of and called forth two parodies: one, *Jenesaiky; ou, Les exaltés de Charenton*, the other, *Bentowski dans l'île des cygnes*, both of which were produced shortly after Duval's première.[15] In spite of the initial success of Duval's opera, however, it soon died a well-deserved death.

Besides *Beniowski*, Duval was the author of another play, Russian in subject. This was a comedy in prose entitled *Le Menuisier de Livonie ou les illustres voyageurs*. Although this play was not produced until March 9, 1805, it was completed sometime during the summer of 1802, a short time before Duval's departure for Russia.[16] The historical sources of the

[15] *Journal des débats*, June 24, 1800 (4 messidor an VIII).
[16] Alexandre Duval, *Œuvres complètes*, V, 395.

play were, according to the author, an anonymous collection of anecdotes as well as Voltaire's history of Peter's reign.[17] Duval showed some concern regarding the local color and took the play with him to Russia in order to find, as he stated in the Preface to the play, *si j'avais bien fait parler mes personnages, conformement aux mœurs et aux usages du pays.*[18]

Le Menuisier de Livonie was the first of a series of Duval's historical comedies (the others were on Henry V and Charles II of England). The action takes place in a Livonian village and its principal characters, besides Peter and Catherine, are two young orphans, Charles Scavronski, a village carpenter who is later found to be the brother of the Empress Catherine, and Eudoxie Mazeppa, daughter of the traitor Hetman. The orphans are in love with each other. Peter and Catherine arrive in disguise and stop at the inn where the orphans are living. The Tsar, anxious to discover Charles's origin, questions him, but the latter is impertinent and refuses to tell who his parents are. At the command of Peter he is then taken into custody by a stupid and corrupt village magistrate who is the principal comic character of the play. In the meantime Catherine recognizes Charles as her brother. In the last scene of the play Peter discloses his identity and becomes the *deus ex machina* who sets everything aright. He punishes the magistrate for his corrupt administration, bestows on Charles the title of Count, and announces the latter's engagement to Eudoxie, to whom he restores all the possessions which were confiscated by the government as a result of her father's treachery.

The play has little to commend it. It is full of surprises of all sorts, incognitos, disguises, and sudden transformations of character—devices typical of Duval's plays. History is almost nonexistent. The two orphans are totally fictitious

---

[17] Alexandre Duval, *Œuvres complètes*, V, p. 391.   [18] *Ibid.*, p. 395.

characters. Peter symbolizes the ideal benevolent monarch. Catherine is depicted as a *bonne bourgeoise* whose principal function is to calm Peter's violent outbursts of temper. The magistrate and another minor character, a Jewish usurer, represent an attempt at local color. The violent and impetuous but generous Charles evidently also represents a typical Russian noble. In spite of its many weaknesses *Le Menuisier de Livonie* is superior, as a play, to *Beniowski*. It shows, at least, a fairly good sense of the stage.

The play was enormously successful and, according to the author, was produced about three hundred times.[19] Nevertheless it was severely criticized by the critic Geoffroy as weak, melodramatic, and possessing too many *stratagèmes de la médiocrité intrigante*.[20]

The fashion of going to Russia at the beginning of the nineteenth century was satirized in a short vaudeville entitled *Allons en Russie, vaudeville épisodique, en un acte et en prose, par M.M.M....et Henrion, auteurs des Amours de la Halle...* Paris, 1802. The author of this play was C. F. Moreau de Commagny (1783-1832) well known at the time as a writer of light operas and dramas and later collaborator with Eugène Scribe. This vaudeville was produced successfully in Paris, December 21 or 22, 1802. The scene is laid in Paris. The characters are Flibourg, agent of the St. Petersburg Theater; Cloris, a French actress; Berville, her lover; a dancer; a hairdresser; an author; a painter; and a prompter. The Russian agent is besieged by a mob of artists of all types and descriptions, all anxious to go to Russia. *Tu sais bien que c'est la mode aujourd'hui d'aller en Russie,* says one of the characters. *Dis plutôt que c'est la fureur,* remarks another. All this

---

[19] Duval, *Œuvres complètes*, V, 392 and 394. Cf. also a review of the play in the *Journal de Paris*, March 10, 1805.

[20] Geoffroy, *Cours de la littérature dramatique*, Vol. V, "Menuisier de Livonie."

"native talent" is unrecognized in Paris. Everybody wants to go to Russia and become famous and rich—

> Allons en Russie,
> On y prise le talent,
> Tout nous y convie,
> On y paye argent
> comptant.[21]

Some, like the dancer Pirouette, declare that they are not going for gain but to improve their art. The majority confess that their object is venal; some begin at once to borrow money from the agent. A complication arises when the actress, Cloris, discloses the fact that she has signed two contracts at the same time, one for going to Russia, the other to England. At the end she is persuaded to give up her English engagement, and agrees to leave for Russia with her lover the following day. This amusing little farce ends with an air sung by Cloris and addressed to the public:

> Nous voyons partir chaque jour
> Maint auteur qui se décourage;
> Et sans désirer leur retour
> On les voit se mettre en voyage.
> Si l'on chassait avec rigueur
> Un auteur dès qu'il vous ennuie,
> Ah! les nôtres auraient bien peur
> D'aller faire un tour en Russie.[22]

In the more serious dramatic genre—the melodrama and the tragedy—we likewise find instances of dramatic relationship with or interest in Russia, particularly in the last quarter of the eighteenth and the beginning of the nineteenth century. There were, in fact, a number of French tragedies written during the century entirely on Russian subjects. Most of these tragedies and melodramas dealt with Peter the Great

---

[21] C. F. Moreau, *Allons en Russie*, Act I, scene iv.
[22] *Ibid.*, Act I, scene xii.

and his picturesque favorite, Menshikov, who seems to have held considerable fascination for eighteenth-century playwrights.[23] Pierre Morand's *Menzikoff* was the earliest tragedy of this type.[24] It was first produced on December 12, 1738, under the title of *Phanazar*, by the Italian actors of the King.[25] Later Morand altered the play itself, changed the title to *Menzikoff*, and dedicated it in 1740 to the empress Anna Ivanovna.[26] The plot of this one-act play is as follows: Menshikov falls in love with the daughter of Amilka, a prince of the blood, and leader of a conspiracy against Tsar Peter (a prototype, most probably, of the Tsarevitch Alexis). Amilka promises his daughter in marriage to Menshikov on condition that Menshikov join the conspiracy against the Tsar. Menshikov declines. The play ends with a panegyric to Peter delivered by Menshikov.

The aim of *Menzikoff* was, as the author announced in the dedicatory Preface, to glorify Peter the Great. The plot was largely fictitious and, aside from its two principal characters, had no foundation in fact. The general tone was highly declamatory, and the characters suggest seventeenth-century

[23] Among the chief contemporary sources of information on Menshikov were Duclos' memoirs, Abbé d'Allainval's anecdotes, Rulhière's history, Weber's memoirs and Levesque. Prince Aleksandr Danilovich Menshikov (1663?-1729) was, it is generally thought, a son of an ostler or a bargee. At the age of twenty he was a fruit vendor on the streets of Moscow. Found by Le Fort, he soon became the chief favorite of the Tsar, and in the course of time became prince, field marshal, and wealthiest man in Russia. After Peter's death it was through Menshikov's efforts that the Tsar's widow, Catherine I, and later the son of the Tsarevitch Alexis, Peter II, were raised to the throne. During these reigns (1725-1727) Menshikov was practically the absolute dictator of Russia. A plot formed against him by the old nobility finally succeeded in overthrowing him. He was deprived of his wealth and titles, and was banished with his family to Siberia, where he died on the 12th of November, 1729.

[24] Pierre Morand (1701-1757), playwright, member of the court of the Duchess of Maine, and one of the founders of the *Journal encyclopédique*.

[25] It formed a part of a four-act drama, *Les Muses*.

[26] Pierre Morand, *Menzikoff*, Introduction.

French rather than Russian courtiers. The success of the play was, it appears, mediocre, and there is no evidence that it was acted more than once. Grimm did not mention it in his literary correspondence, and La Harpe considered it beneath contempt.[27]

Dorat's tragedy *Amilka; ou, Pierre-le-Grand*, published by Sebastian Jorry in 1767, had a similar theme.[28] It was acted for the first time under the title of *Zuleika* on January 7, 1760. Later Dorat changed the title and made other alterations with the help of Crébillon. In this revised form the play was produced again on December 1, 1780. Dorat explained the reason for rewriting the play in the Preface to the final version:

C'est un tableau vraiment digne de notre scène que celui d'un héros législateur qui à travers le choc des esprits, l'âpreté du climat, l'opposition même de la nature, élève sur des glaçons ensanglantés l'édifice des mœurs et des lois, change une horde sauvage en peuple policé, s'instruit par ses revers, se dévoue, pour atteindre son but, à tous les poignards de la trahison, et prouve à l'univers surpris qu'un Roi peut être cruel pour l'intérêt même de l'humanité.[29]

In the same preface Dorat gave a résumé of an unpublished story entitled *Czarewitch* by Chevalier de Votan, which he used, in part, for his play. Furthermore, he said, the subject of his drama should be of great general interest because

Il présente un local neuf, des mœurs singulières, des contrastes frappants; il prouve, surtout, jusqu'où peut aller l'influence d'un homme sur des millions d'autres.[30]

The plot of this play was very similar to that of Morand's.

[27] La Harpe, *Œuvres*, Paris, 1821, I, 250. Next to Morand's, chronologically, should be mentioned a tragedy of L. J. Fallot, *L'Innocence opprimée; ou, La mort d'Iwan, Empereur de Russie* . . . without place of impression, 1765, octavo.

[28] For a biographical sketch of Dorat see Desnoiresterres, *Le Chevalier Dorat et les poètes légers au XVIIIᵉ siècle*, Preface; also, Petitot, *Répertoire*, XXV, 1-20.

[29] C. J. Dorat, *Amilka* . . . Paris, 1767, "Discours préliminaire," p. 155.

[30] *Ibid.*, p. 176.

The main characters are the same—Menshikov, Peter the Great, Amilka, the rebel prince, and his daughter, Ametis. The scene is laid in St. Petersburg. Menshikov is forced to join the conspiracy against Peter in order to win Amilka's daughter. *Si ce soir*, Amilka threatens Menshikov, *tu n'égorges pas l'empereur, je tuerai ma fille.* At the beginning of the play Peter appears as a savage and bloody tyrant, but in the course of the action he becomes magnanimous and kind. He discovers the plot and pardons the rebels. Amilka, profiting by this magnanimity, attacks the palace. The end is perhaps the most extravagant of all the play's features: surrounded by his enemies, Peter challenges Amilka to stab him. The latter hesitates, but suddenly overwhelmed by the courage and magnanimity of the Tsar, kills himself instead. Menshikov is then pardoned and marries Amilka's daughter.

The première of this tragedy failed completely.

Toutes ces extravagances puériles [wrote La Harpe] ont été hués à la première représentation de la pièce, comme elles devaient l'être.

Regarding the local color which Dorat had promised in his introduction, La Harpe observed—

à l'égard des mœurs, elles ne sont pas plus vraies que les caractères, et l'on n'est plus en Russie qu'au Japon.[31]

Grimm was of the same opinion. The play was a failure, and was called jokingly "Pierre-le-Long."[32] Dorat himself described his anticipation of success and the fiasco of his tragedy as follows:

Je voyais déjà ma pièce aux nues; J'entendais les applaudissements retentir à mon oreille; je n'aspirais à rien moins qu'à l'immortalité....

The day of the performance, however:

[31] La Harpe, *Correspondance littéraire*, II, letter CXVII.
[32] Grimm, *Correspondance littéraire*, XII, 349. A review in the *Journal encyclopédique* for August, 1767, praised Dorat's "Discours préliminaire," but was less enthusiastic about the tragedy itself.

...le charme, hélas, disparut et le temple de la postérité se ferma pour moi. Mes quatre premiers actes furent cependant reçues avec transport; mais le cinquième, sur lequel je comptais le plus, échoua...[33]

Dorat's tragedy was acted, however, six or seven times at the Comédie Française, but with mediocre success.[34]

The reception accorded to Dorat's play by contemporaries seems today more than justified. Its highly declamatory tone and the rapid succession of impossible catastrophes make the play appear altogether ridiculous. Throughout the play there is a mixture of authentic fact and philosophical declamation which was pleasing to contemporary audiences but seems unbearably dull today. The locality of the drama was evidently intended to be conveyed through an emphasis on the crudeness and savagery of the people and the irreconcilable contrasts in the characters of the protagonists. Yet, when all is said, Dorat's Pierre le Grand was not inferior to the average mid-eighteenth-century melodrama.

In 1772 appeared L'Histoire du Prince Mentzikoff, a volume of prose narrative which contained a three-act tragedy entitled Mentzikoff, written by Jean Marchand and Pierre Nougaret. These two authors, perpetrators of numerous satires, parodies, and poems, were forgotten even in their own day. Marchand was known as un plaisant de société. The tragedy was never produced and the whole volume, it seems, passed unnoticed. It appears to have received no reviews in the periodicals of the time, and no notices in the correspondances littéraires. La Harpe, whose tragedy on the same subject appeared a few years later, was silent on the subject of this predecessor.

That he had been the most severe critic of the plays on Peter the Great so far examined did not deter La Harpe

---

[33] Michaud, Biographie universelle, 1814, XI, 572-573.

[34] La Harpe, Correspondance littéraire, letters CXX and CXXII; also J. Desnoiresterres, Le Chevalier Dorat...p. 16 n.

from adopting the theme for his own purpose. His five-act drama, *Menzicoff*, was, perhaps, not only the best known contemporary play on a Russian subject, but also the most severely criticized. It was produced unsuccessfully in Fontainebleau on November 10, 1775. The Russian ambassador found parts of the play prejudicial to the Russian government and requested La Harpe to suppress them.[35] Perhaps partly because of this protest the play was never produced in Paris. It aroused considerable interest, however, in various literary and social circles. Voltaire was curious about the play, and wrote to Thibouville:

Vous ne me dites point si vous avez vu *Menzicoff* à Fontainebleau, et si ce garçon patissier, devenu prince et maître d'un grand empire, et pauvre esclave en Sibérie, a réussi à la cour autant que je le souhaite.[36]

Later, when Voltaire read the play, which had been sent to him by the author, he was quite enthusiastic about it.[37] Moreover, this drama seems to have been known in Paris before its production, for La Harpe read it to the queen and to groups at various salons, probably including those of Mme Geoffrin, Mme du Deffand, and Mlle Lespinasse, where he was wont to read many of his works.[38]

Menzicoff was written, it appears, partly to please Grand Duke Paul of Russia, La Harpe's correspondent, and partly in emulation of the playwright's predecessors. Historically the play had no more solid foundation than those written earlier on the same theme, in spite of La Harpe's assertion to the contrary.[39]

---

[35] G. Peignot, *Recherches historiques, littéraires* . . . p. 66.

[36] Voltaire, *Correspondance*, Voltaire to Thibouville, November 19, 1775.

[37] G. Peignot, *Recherches historiques, littéraires* . . . pp. 67 and 80.

[38] *Ibid.*, pp. 66 and 87-88.

[39] La Harpe gives some of the sources for his play in the "Précis sur Menzicoff"; they were: (1) *Mémoires du général Manstein;* (2) *Journal de Pierre le Grand;* (3) "Histoire de Menzicoff" in the *Anecdotes du Nord*, 1770.

Les caractères des principaux personnages [he says in his Preface to the tragedy] et les faits de l'avant-scène qui fondent l'action, sont conformes à la vérité historique, les mœurs sont fidèlement peintes; tout le reste est d'invention.[40]

Besides Voltaire, there were other admirers of the play, and the author himself considered it a success. He wrote to the Grand Duke Paul:

L'histoire de Russie m'a fourni un sujet de tragédie que l'on regarde ici comme ce que j'ai fait de plus passable... Ce qu'il y a de plus heureux dans mon ouvrage, c'est que j'ai trouvé le moyen de mettre le projet dans la bouche de Menzicoff tout ce que l'Auguste mère de Votre Altesse Impériale a réellement exécuté.[41]

The action of *Menzicoff* is laid in Tobolsk, Siberia. The principal characters are Menshikov, his son, Alexan, his wife, Arsénie, and his enemy Wademar, also in exile. The main theme is love and vengeance. Menshikov and his son, exiled to Siberia, encounter there Wademar (whom Menshikov was responsible for sending to Siberia). Wademar now plans revenge. Arsénie, the wife whom Menshikov had formerly abandoned, and who has since forgiven him, arrives to join her former husband and son. Wademar, in the meantime, is pardoned and appointed governor of the province. He is now in a position to take his revenge. In a very melodramatic scene he tells Arsénie that unless she marries him, her son will perish. After fruitless pleadings she finally consents. During the wedding, as she walks up to the altar, her eyes fall upon the body of her son. In despair she stabs Wademar. She and Menshikov are pardoned.

According to La Harpe himself, the production of his play at Fontainebleau was successful.

[40] La Harpe, *Œuvres*, 1821, I, "Précis sur Menzicoff."
[41] La Harpe, *Correspondance littéraire*, I, letter XIII.

On a trouvé ma fable intéressante [he wrote to Shuvalov] si je juge surtout par les larmes qu'elle a fait répandre... Tous les Russes de ce pays m'ont entendu et applaudi.[42]

Opinions differed, however. Bachaumont records the tragedy's complete failure. It seemed, he said,

Mauvaise aux gens les plus difficiles, médiocre aux spectateurs indulgents, et d'un noir épouvantable à tout le monde.[43]
On a trouvé [wrote Grimm] de grandes beautés dans le premier acte et dans le troisième, peu d'intérêt dans le quatrième, et le dénouement, qui d'ailleurs ressemble à tout, a paru odieux sans être dramatique.[44]

Aside from its dramatic defects, the play was also criticized for incorrect history and faulty presentation of national character and customs.

On se plaint qu'ayant choisi un évènement dont la mémoire est encore si récente et si connue, le poète n'ait pas été plus fidèle à l'histoire, et n'ait respecté ni le caractère de son héros, ni les mœurs du siècle, ni le costume du pays.[45]

Métra wrote a long review of the play and considered its production a complete failure.

On a fait [he observed in conclusion] cette mauvaise épigramme sur la pièce encore plus mauvaise du Sr. de la Harpe:

> La Harpe au défaut du génie,
> A su transporter rarement,
> Dans son pitoyable roman
> Toutes les glaces de Russie.[46]

Finally, the playwright Ducis admired the acting of Kain in

---

[42] *La Harpe, Correspondance littéraire,* I, letter XIII.
[43] Bachaumont, *Mémoires,* November 14, 1775.
[44] Grimm, *Correspondance littéraire,* XI, 142-143.
[45] *Ibid.*
[46] Métra, *Correspondance secrète, politique, et littéraire,* November 25, 1775.

Menzicoff, but condemned the play itself as weak and life-less.[47]

La Harpe's highly melodramatic and fantastic composition is unsatisfactory even when judged by the dramatic standard of the time. The action of the play has no unity or continuity and the characters are lifeless. Menshikov, admittedly the mouthpiece of the philosophy of enlightenment, is a typical French courtier. Aside from the names of the characters and the numerous references to the icy climate, it would be difficult to find any other indication that the action takes place in Russia. In this respect La Harpe's tragedy is less effective even than Dorat's.

In 1786 the playwright Desforges, wishing to profit by his experience in Russia, wrote a play based, according to him, upon an old Russian tale. His *Féodor et Lisinka; ou, Novgorod sauvée*, a prose drama in three acts, was produced for the first time at the Italian theater on October 3, 1786, and was published the following year in Paris.[48]

The play is concerned with two young lovers of Novgorod whose families are engaged in a feud with each other. In spite of the danger involved, the lovers contrive to see each other secretly. The heroine, Lisinka, takes into her confidence a wicked debauched slave, who uses her confidence to achieve his own wicked ends. One night he decides to satisfy his own desires and then give the girl to his drunken companions. Summoning her courage, the girl sets fire to the wooden house where her tormentor and his companions are feasting, and they all, with the exception of the heroine, perish in the flames. She then goes to the Empress Catherine, receives forgiveness, and ends her life in a convent.

The action of this play might as well have been laid in

[47] Ducis, *Œuvres*, Paris, 1826, letter to Lemierre, November 15, 1775; pp. 262-263.

[48] Paris, 1787 and 1788 in octavo; Avignon, 1791, in octavo. Cf. Petitot, *Répertoire*... Paris, 1817, XV, 135-161.

the Antipodes as in Russia. To give some local color Desforges makes his characters say "thou" to each other, and sometimes explains that this or that was done or said *à la manière russe*. As in some of the preceding plays, the author tries to give an impression of *exotisme* through emphasis on the passionate, almost savage nature of his characters. This, however, is exaggerated to a point of absurdity. Weak dramatically and lacking even a semblance of psychology, the drama deserves the criticism it received.

Bachaumont, reviewing the play shortly before its production, described it as follows:

... ce sujet étant bizarre, noir, atroce, le costume et les accessoires en étant tout à fait extraordinaires et invraisemblables, Desforges a cru devoir prévenir le public par une annonce insérée aujourd' hui dans le *Journal de Paris*... Il prétend qu'indépendant du mérite du fond, sur lequel c'est aux spectateurs à prononcer, on acquerra du moins par son ouvrage, surtout lorsqu'il sera imprimé, beaucoup de notions nouvelles sur les Russes, peuple qui mérite plus que jamais l'attention de l'Europe et le regard de l'observateur.[49]

Grimm, after seeing the performance, observed,

Cette pièce, grace à la nature même du sujet ou au talent de l'auteur, a paru plus froide encore qu'elle n'est atroce, et ce n'est peu dire sans doute; on n'y a pas trouvé très heureusement une seule situation qui produise son effet.[50]

Petitot was even more severe:

En 1787 Desforges voulut mettre à profit les connaissances qu'il avait acquises en Russie. Il résulta de cette entreprise le drame le plus monstrueux qui eût jamais paru sur notre scène.[51]

In spite of these severe criticisms, the play seems, at the beginning at least, to have enjoyed a certain amount of popu-

[49] Bachaumont, *Mémoires*, September 25, 1786.
[50] Grimm, *Mémoires historiques, littéraires et critiques*, London, 1813, III, 467-468.
[51] Petitot, *Répertoire*... XV, 150.

lar success. It was produced several times in Paris and also in the provinces.[52] Its relative success may be explained perhaps by the fact that here, for the first time, Russian decorations and costumes were used on the stage.[53] This new *exotisme* may well have appealed to the audience. But even this novelty did not hold playgoers after the third presentation of the drama in Paris.[54] In 1793, however, the play was revived for a short time, although after this it was never produced again.[55]

Jean François Ducis (1733-1816), the well-known imitator and adapter of Shakespeare, had also tried his hand at a Russian play. *Feodor et Wladamir; ou, La famille de Sibérie*, a drama in five acts, was given for the first time at the Théâtre Français on April 24, 1801. The scene of this play was laid in Siberia, and the theme was strongly reminiscent of the "Menshikov" plays. Two courtiers, Romanov and Clodoskir, are exiled with their families to Siberia. The twin sons of the Romanovs, Wladamir and Feodor, are both in love with Ozéphine, daughter of Clodoskir. She, however, loves only Wladamir. Feodor saves her from drowning in an icy stream, and her family promise her to him out of gratitude. Feodor, suspecting Ozéphine's real feelings, however, generously gives her up to Wladamir.

This play has already a certain flavor of the romantic melodrama. Not only is the locality expressed with greater precision, but the dreariness of the Siberian landscape plays a certain rôle in the action itself. The characters are not very convincing; at times their long monologues are mawkishly sentimental, while at other times they become too abstract and declamatory. The play seems to have been a failure. There were several attmpts by Chenier, Arnault, and Legouvé to

[52] Petitot, *Répertoire* ... XV, 152.
[53] Grimm, *Correspondance littéraire*, XIV, 472.
[54] *Ibid.*
[55] Petitot, *Répertoire* ... XV, 152.

improve it, but it never was able to hold the stage.[56] Petitot considered it Ducis' weakest play and believed that it should never have been published.[57]

We can conclude this examination of plays on Russian subjects with the *Pierre-le-Grand* of Carrion Nizas.[58] This tragedy was not produced until 1804, but in treatment of subject, in spirit, and in reception it belongs more to the eighteenth than to the nineteenth century.

The play is concerned with the conspiracy against Peter and the rebellion of the Riflemen ("Strel'tsy"). The principal characters are the Tsar, Menshikov, and Le Fort. The plot seems to have followed the main events of Peter's reign with more historical accuracy than the preceding plays on the same subject. Dramatically, the play is weak. It has little continuity in action, is melodramatic and declamatory. The characters are wooden. Although the depiction of manners is slight, there is a definite effort to convey the national type through an emphasis on the vehement, passionate, and contradictory character of the protagonists.

Geoffroy, a contemporary critic, thus described the play's failure on the stage: ... *l'acteur ne disait pas quatre vers sans être interrompu par des huées, des sifflets, et des éclats de rire*...[59] Despite a good cast, including the great Talma in the part of Peter the Great, the audience seems to have been set against the author. The performance had to be stopped in the middle of the fifth act amidst general clamor and jeering.[60] Geoffroy himself believed that the play deserved a better reception. The theme of the play was, he observed, of the greatest general interest:

[56] O. Leroy, *Etudes morales et littéraires sur la personne et les écrits de J. F. Ducis*, Paris, 1832, p. 178.

[57] Petitot, *Répertoire* ... VI, 61-62.

[58] For a sketch of Nizas' life and dramatic career see Michaud, *Biographie universelle*, 1823, XXXIV, 360.

[59] Geoffroy, *Cours de littérature dramatique* ... Paris, 1819, IV, 79.

[60] *Ibid.*, p. 81.

La Russie sera-t-elle replongée dans l'ignorance et dans la barbarie dont elle commence à sortir? Continuera-t-elle sa marche vers la civilisation, ou sera-t-elle forcée de rétrograder... Arrêté dans le cours de ses utiles projets, Pierre périra-t-il victime de son amour pour la grandeur de son pays? [61]

In spite of this reception, Nizas' drama does not by any means mark an end of dramatic concern with the personality and career of the Russian Tsar. On the contrary, this continued far into the next century. We have already mentioned Duval's hybrid tragi-comedy dealing with Peter and his spouse which, produced for the first time in 1805, had a long and continuous success on the stage. One can mention also two plays on Peter the Great by a fairly popular playwright of the time, A. A. Pillon. One of these, a tragedy entitled *Un Petit mot sur Pierre-le-Grand,* was produced and published in Paris in 1804; the other, a comedy, *Pierre et Paul; ou, Une journée de Pierre le Grand,* was produced and published at the Odéon in 1814. A comedy by J. J. Cuvelier, *L'Officier cosaque,* was produced successfully in 1803. J. J. Duperche's melodrama, *Les Strelitz,* was produced and published in Paris in 1808. Plays on the Menshikov theme also continued to appear. J. H. Lamartellière's opera, for example, *Menzikof et Feodor; ou, Le fou de Bérézof,* had a certain success on the stage in 1808. More successful was a short parody, in music, on the Menshikov theme by François Moreau and Désaugiers, produced for the first time in Paris at the Théâtre de Vaudeville in March, 1808. This amusing and sparkling extravaganza was a successful take-off on the sentimental melodramas having as subject Menshikov's exile to Siberia.

The plays we have examined in this chapter have at least one definite feature in common—they are all weak dramatically and not one of them deserved a better reception than

[61] Geoffroy, *Cours de littérature dramatique*...Paris, 1819, IV, p. 81.

that accorded by their author's contemporaries. Some of the lighter plays and operas like Bouilly's *Pierre le Grand*, Duval's *Le Menuisier de Livonie* and Moreau's *Allons en Russie* possessed, perhaps, certain artistic merit, but the tragedies were uniformly poor. It is worth noting, however, that in spite of adverse criticism and unfavorable public reception, plays on Russian subjects continued to appear. It seems as if the Russian material, the careers of Peter and Menshikov especially, had a certain fascination for the contemporary playwrights. La Harpe, Ducis, Desforges, Dorat, and Duval, to mention the better known names, had all tried at least once to publish and produce a play on a Russian subject. Several of these plays, in spite of their intrinsic mediocrity, succeeded in holding the stage for some time and were, apparently, appreciated by the people. In the majority of the plays we have examined, history provided the names of the principal characters. The locale and some of the episodes of the plots remained, however, largely fictitious. In the early eighteenth-century plays, like those of Le Sage and Boissy, the introduction of Russian scenery and characters indicates merely a striving for a general exotic effect. The Russian character is depicted in these early plays as primitive, brutal, and warlike, but at the same time magnanimous and kind. In the late eighteenth-century and early nineteenth-century plays more definite indications of the national character, manners, and scene can be observed. Peter the Great, for example, besides being symbolized as the eighteenth-century ideal of an enlightented monarch, is also depicted as a primitive, elemental hero, with sharply contrasting characteristics: he is violent, savage, and bloodthirsty but, at the same time, a great, wise, magnanimous ruler. Something of the same irreconcilable contradictions of nature are found in other Russian characters (Duval's Charles Scavronski and Stephanow.) The women are usually portayed as passionate, active, and energetic in their pursuits, also as compassionate and kind (Lisinka, Menshikov's wife, Ozéphine, Petrovna). The ways of suggesting the locality were naïve and crude. Thus, frequent references to the icy climate were made, certain Russian words like *Kozacs* (i.e., "Cossacks") and *Knout* (i.e., "Knut") were introduced whenever possible, and the characters said "thou" to each other. Perhaps the only realistic attempt at local color was that of Duval's in his *Le Menuisier de Livonie* where the dialogue between the Jewish village usurer and the young noble conveyed something of the provincial Russian atmosphere.

Turning now to the poetry of the period we likewise find instances of interest in Russia. This interest manifested itself chiefly among a number of well-known contemporary men of letters in the second half of the century when a number of poems appeared, for the most part addressed to or inspired by the two great eighteenth-century rulers of Russia, Peter I and Catherine II.

Among the chief panegyrists in verse were Voltaire and La Harpe. Voltaire wrote numerous *épîtres* and occasional verses in glorification of Catherine II. In 1769 he composed, for example, a stanza addressed to the Empress on the occasion of the Russian victories over the Turks. The stanza ended as follows:

> O Minerve du Nord! O toi, sœur d' Apollon!
> Tu vengeras la Grèce en chassant ces infâmes,
> Ces ennemis des arts, et ces geôliers des femmes.
> Je pars: je vais t'attendre aux champs de Marathon.[62]

Besides frequently applauding Catherine's victories over the Turks, Voltaire's other themes were: Catherine's superiority over Peter the Great,[63] her wisdom, tolerance, and her *philosophie*.

[62] Voltaire, *Œuvres*, Garnier, VIII, 533.
[63] *Ibid.*, X, 435.

Tu cherches sur la terre un vrai héros, un sage,
Qui méprise les sots et leur fasse du bien,
Qui parle avec esprit, qui pense avec courage,
Va trouver Catherine, et ne cherche plus rien.[64]

Since, however, all the short poems of Voltaire addressed to the Empress are of the same pattern, there will be no profit in examining them further.[65]

In this connection Voltaire's satire in verse on false patriotism, hypocrisy, and ignorance should also be mentioned. *Le Russe à Paris* was published in 1760 under the pseudonym "Ivan Ilethof." [66] It deals indirectly with the progress of Russia. The poem is a dialogue between a Parisian patriot and a visiting Russian. The Russian came to France to learn— *voir un peuple fameux, l'observer, et l'entendre.* The Parisian accuses the Russian of ignorance and is appalled at his not having heard of the *Journal de Trévoux* and the *Journal du Chrétien. Les barbares!* he exclaims, *Hélas! en leur faveur mon esprit abusé avait cru que le Nord était civilisé.* The Russian then learns of the sad state of affairs in France. Molière is now forgotten, and Rousseau is taking his place. But this, says the Frenchman hopefully, can't go on—things are bound to change. Whereupon the Russian bids him farewell and says: *Adieu, je reviendrai quand ils seront changés.* This is the extent of Voltaire's contribution to the subject in verse.

La Harpe's poetry is more elaborate than Voltaire's and even more laudatory of the Russian sovereigns and the progress of the country. In his *Poème sur les femmes* he included a long *éloge* of Catherine II, which remained, however, unfinished. It was read in the French Academy on June 5, 1784, in the presence of the King of Sweden, and was con-

---

[64] *Ibid.,* X, 588.

[65] Voltaire expressed his profound admiration for the Russian Empress also in the epistles he exchanged with Count Shuvalov. These were published in the *Journal encyclopédique,* October, 1765; LXXIX, 121-123.

[66] Voltaire, *Œuvres,* Garnier, X, 119-131.

sidered tactless in view of the praises addressed to the rival of the sovereign present.[67] It ended with the following line referring to Catherine II—*Tout le Nord est soumis ou tremble sous sa loi.*

In 1779 La Harpe published a long descriptive poem entitled *Epître au Comte de Schouvaloff sur les effets de la nature champêtre et sur la poésie descriptive,* and upon the arrival in Paris of the Grand Duke Paul in 1782, the poet delivered a long, laudatory poem in his honor in the French Academy. This composition dealt extensively with the general progress and enlightenment of the Russian empire.[68] Aside from Voltaire and La Harpe other men of letters had written occasional verse addressed to Russian sovereigns or important personages at court. Contant d'Orville, for example, was the author of a laudatory epistle in verse addressed to Catherine II. This poem, entitled *Les Fastes du Nord moderne,* was published in Geneva in 1773. Mme de Stassart published a collection of poems in praise of Catherine II and of Count Alexis Orlov, *Poèmes à Sa Majesté l'Impératrice de toutes les Russies et à S. E. le comte Alexis d'Orlov,* which appeared in Florence in 1775. The author of the tragedy *Pierre le Grand,* C. J. Dorat, also wrote short panegyrics in verse to the Russian Empress. His *Epître à Catherine II* was published in Paris in 1765. Perhaps the best known occasional poem addressed to a Russian was the playwright A. Duval's elegy on the death of Praskov'ia, Count Sheremetev's wife. Sheremetev, a brilliant courtier and a man of fabulous wealth, had asked Duval, during the latter's sojourn in Russia, to become his private secretary and tutor to his children.[69] Unable to accept the offer, Duval wished to show his gratitude for the Count's benevolence and composed two hundred

[67] J. Peignot, *Recherches historiques* . . . p. 97.
[68] *Ibid.,* p. 80; cf. ch. ii, of this work.
[69] Alexandre Duval, *Œuvres,* VII, 14.

elegiac verses addressed to the Count's deceased wife. At the insistence of the Count, this poem, entitled *A l'ombre de Parascovia*, was first privately printed by Didot. To the dismay of the author, who was aware of the poem's shortcomings and was ashamed to publish it, it had considerable circulation in the St. Petersburg and Paris salons.[70] Later, Duval included the poem in the collected edition of his works,[71] principally, as he stated in the Preface to the poem, to show his personal regard for the Count and his gratitude for the Count's generous gifts:

Puissent mes méchants vers [he stated] faire connaître au moins en France cet estimable étranger! et puissent tous les auteurs, mes confrères, en composer de meilleurs pour quiconque lui ressemble, et qui soient surtout aussi bien récompensés.[72]

Duval's poem, mechanical and uninspired, dealt at length with the many virtues of the Count's wife, Praskov'ia, as well as the Count's own achievements as a patron of the arts, a statesman and a philanthropist.

A more ambitious undertaking than the occasional verse of Voltaire, La Harpe or Duval was the epic *Pétréide* of the academician Thomas. Thomas was a well-known writer in his day but, like so many other second-rate writers of the eighteenth century, is today completely forgotten. He cultivated a variety of genres and obtained a certain success in each. One can hardly find a representative more typical of the encyclopedic spirit than Thomas.

Il s'est préoccuppé [said his recent biographer, Micard] surtout de fournir une carrière bien orthodoxe dans les voies indiquées par les habitudes de son temps [and] son caractère assez complexe nous révèle certains dessous du tempérament littéraire à la mode entre 1760 et 1780.[73]

---

[70] *Ibid.*, VII, 21. [71] *Ibid.*, VII, 24-29. [72] *Ibid.*, VII, 23.
[73] Etienne Micard, *Un Ecrivain académique au XVIIIe siècle: Antoine-Léonard Thomas* (1732-1785), Paris, pp. 13-14.

Thomas was a member of the French Academy, wrote many *éloges*, frequented the salons, composed treatises on scientific subjects, and, above all, dreamed of giving the century a great epic poem on Peter the Great.[74] As Micard has adequately shown, the *Pétréide* unquestionably occupied the first place in Thomas's life. It was destined, however, to remain unfinished. At his death there were only six cantos completed out of the twelve originally planned.[75] From about 1767 Thomas's correspondence is full of references to the many difficulties of his subject. He seems to have read fragments of the poem to many of his friends, anxious, no doubt, to get criticism and approbation.

Before embarking on his Russian epic, Thomas first attempted a smaller poem, entitled *Jumonville*, on an English subject, which he had published in 1759.[76] The reception of this poem was, on the whole, favorable, and, feeling encouraged, Thomas embarked on his more ambitious undertaking—the epic of Peter the Great. Thomas seems to have conceived this epic about 1759. The progress he made is clearly seen in his correspondence. Marmontel, one of his friends, at first encouraged him, but later attempted to dissuade him from the undertaking. Another friend, Barthe, was most enthusiastic about the poem from the beginning to the end.[77] Several reasons can be advanced for Thomas's choice of this subject for his epic. In the first place, he seems always to have been interested in Russia, and on one occasion was on the point of going there. In the second place, most of his friends were enthusiastic admirers of Catherine II (including Voltaire, Marmontel, Ducis, and La Harpe). He was caught by the vogue for the Russian Empress prevalent among the literary men of his time. *Il se trouve pris,*

---

[74] *Ibid.*   [75] *Ibid.*, p. 38.
[76] *Ibid.*, pp. 78 and 80-82.
[77] *Ibid.*, p. 88.

said Micard, *inconsciemment dans les filets d'une propagande habile.*[78]

In 1759 Thomas, apparently already contemplating the poem, was eagerly awaiting the publication of Voltaire's history of the Tsar. *J'ose dire*, he wrote to Barthe, *qu'il n'y aura pas de Russe qui le lise avec plus d'intérêt que moi.*[79] At the same time he admired Catherine II and, after the publication of her letter to D'Alembert, wrote as follows:

Jamais lettre n'honora plus le trône ... Quel style, mon cher ami, pour le pays des anciens Tartares et des Saramates! Il faut avouer que les gens du Nord nous donnent de belles leçons sur plusieurs articles.[80]

Thomas's material for the epic came partly from individuals. Some of it he obtained from Count André Shuvalov; some, chiefly on the private life of Peter the Great, from Comte de Staël.[81] He also read scrupulously all the contemporary works on Russia.[82] Voltaire seems to have supplied considerable material, but above all he provided enthusiastic encouragement. He wrote to Thomas on September 22, 1765:

On m'a dit, que vous faites un poème épique sur le Czar Pierre. Vous êtes fait pour célébrer des grands hommes; c'est à vous à peindre vos confrères. Je m'imagine qu'il y aura une philosophie sublime dans votre poème. Le siècle est monté à ce ton-là et vous n'y avez pas peu contribué.[83]

Thomas's views on Russia were the standard views of the

---

[78] *Ibid.*, p. 94.

[79] "Correspondance inédite entre Thomas et Barthe," edited by Henriet, *Revue d'histoire littéraire*, 1917, p. 123.

[80] Letter to Barthe, September 27, 1763. *Ibid.*, 1918, p. 149.

[81] *Bulletin de bibliophile*, 1917, pp. 304-306.

[82] Cf. "Correspondance..." *Revue d'histoire littéraire*, letters of April 8, 1760, and July 22, 1760.

[83] At the same time Voltaire seems to have doubted Thomas's power to handle the subject adequately, and he wrote to Walpole condemning his *Jumonville*: *J'ai toujours douté de l'assassinat de M. Jumonville, qui a produit en France plus de mauvais vers que de représailles.*—Voltaire, *Œuvres*, XLVI, 57.

encyclopedic group. He admired the swift progress of the country which was initiated, he believed, by Peter the Great. This new enlightenment of Russia he believed was evidenced in her new men of letters. Thomas was especially enthusiastic about Lomonosov, whose works he appears to have carefully read.[84] He predicted a great future for Russia, and praised highly the liberality of Catherine II.

Les Russes ont un esprit facile et souple; leur langue est après l'italien la langue la plus douce de l'Europe ... les arts même de l'imagination, transportés dans ces climats, pourront peut-être y prendre racine, et être un jour cultivés avec succès.[85]

Thomas's *Pétréide* was to be composed on the plan of Virgil's *Æneid*. Most of the Frenchman's friends gave their approval to this general plan. Thomas wrote to Barthe regarding Marmontel's estimate of it,

La grandeur du plan, intérêt, variété, pathétique, épisodes, caractères, situations, peintures neuves, il [i.e., Marmontel] y trouve tout. Je commence à me sentir le courage de l'exécution.[86]

Barthe was in raptures over this original draft of the poem and called it *un des prodiges de l'imagination.*[87] Mme Geoffrin also gave her encouragement and referred to Thomas as *le sublime poète du Czar.* Diderot, on the other hand, while approving the subject and plan of the poem, doubted its success and so wrote to Falconet.[88] There were many readings of the poem as it progressed. Its first public rendering took place at the French Academy on December 28, 1766,[89] and

---

[84] Probably in German translations; cf. Thomas, *Œuvres,* "Essai sur les éloges," Amsterdam, 1773, II, 370-376.

[85] *Ibid.,* II, 376.

[86] "Correspondance..." *Revue d'histoire littéraire,* 1917, p. 123.

[87] *Ibid.,* p. 491.

[88] "Correspondance..." *Revue d'histoire littéraire,* 1919, pp. 625-626, note; letter to Falconet, February, 1766.

[89] Only one canto on Peter's visit to France was read. Cf. "Correspondance...," *Revue d'histoire littéraire,* 1918, p. 477.

a second followed on February 1, 1767, on the occasion of Thomas's election to the Academy.[90] Thomas had many disappointments and discouragements. About 1760 Fréron wrote to him that he had a rival, the poet Baculard d'Arnaud, who was also writing an epic poem on Peter the Great.[91] Another minor poet besides, Robert Lesuire, was known to have started to work on the same subject.[92] The progress on the poem was slow, and Thomas frequently expressed doubts as to ever finishing it. Nevertheless, he persisted and even as late as 1777 was full of hope and enthusiasm for his work.

Laissons mûrir [he wrote to Barthe about that time] en silence ce grand ouvrage pour lequel je me sens plus encouragé que jamais... je ne regretterai ni mon temps ni l'espèce d'obscurité où s'écoulent les plus belles années de ma vie.[93]

The six cantos of the *Pétréide* which Thomas had completed were first published in 1802, fifteen years after his death.[94]

Today the seven thousand verses of the *Pétréide* appear as altogether dull, painstaking, and lifeless versifying. The poem is, in fact, an endless encyclopedia of Peter's travels, in correct but uninspired verse.

[90] Grimm, *Correspondance littéraire*, VII, 218.

[91] "Correspondance...," *Revue d'histoire littéraire*, 1917, p. 131. Letter of Thomas to Barthe, April 8, 1760. That D'Arnaud was also writing an epic on Peter the Great was, apparently, well known in the literary circles of the time. Bachaumont, speaking of D'Arnaud's epic, said that he was *dans une fâcheuse concurrence avec Thomas*. Cf. Bachaumont, *Mémoires*, I, 283. Marmontel, too, was alarmed about Thomas, but did not consider D'Arnaud's competition serious. Cf. "Correspondance..." *Revue d'histoire littéraire*, 1917, p. 493. Letter of Thomas to Barthe, July 22, 1760. D'Arnaud's poem was, it appears, never published.

[92] Etienne Micard, *op. cit.*, p. 93; Thomas's letter to Ducis, (?), 1785; cf. also about Lesuire, Michaud, *Biographie universelle*, 1819, XXIV, 333-335. It seems that his poem also remained unpublished.

[93] "Correspondance..." *Revue d'histoire littéraire*, 1929, p. 419; letter to Barthe, July or August, 1777.

[94] A. L. Thomas, *Œuvres*, 2 vols., Paris, 1802. Fragments of the *Pétréide* appeared also in the *Mercure de France*, February 20, 1802.

Le Czar [observes Micard] ne fait que s'étonner ou poser quelques questions devant le défilé incessant de villes, d'œuvres d'art, d'exploitations industrielles ou commerciales qui passent sous ses yeux.[95]

The main theme of the cantos is the economic and political development of the countries visited by Peter the Great (Holland, England, and France). Peter's character is lifeless and full of traits that cannot be regarded as national. He becomes quite monotonous and wearisome with his constant remarks to Le Fort (who accompanied him in his travels and serves as a kind of chorus) about the progress of industries in Holland and Germany. The Tsar is, in fact, a mouthpiece of the encyclopedic philosophy and represents the ideal of an enlightened monarch. He is also reminiscent of Virgil's Æneas and Voltaire's Télémaque.

Aside from the inherent difficulty of the subject, the chief reason for the *Pétréide*'s failure is that cited by Thomas's early biographer, Saint-Surin: *Son génie*, he observed, *n'était pas inspiré par la muse de l'épopée.* This was, in general, the verdict of his contemporaries. Grimm found Thomas unequal to the task and deplored his dealing so much with various European countries instead of Russia.[96] Collé found the poem uninspired—*Sans imagination et sans invention.*[97] Diderot and Marmontel condemned it also on more or less similar grounds.[98]

Thomas, as we saw, was not the only writer to attempt an epic on Peter the Great. There were other equally sterile attempts. Baculard d'Arnaud, for example, a friend of Voltaire and a well-known writer of the time, was writing at the same time as was Thomas, an epic similar to the latter's. This

[95] E. Micard, *op. cit.*, p. 106.

[96] Grimm, *Correspondance littéraire*, VII, 218 ff.

[97] Collé, *Journal*, January 1767; E. Micard, *op. cit.*, p. 102.

[98] Diderot, *Œuvres*, éd. *Assézat*, XVIII, 103; Marmontel, *Œuvres*, Vol. I, Book XI, Pt. 2.

poem aroused considerable interest in contemporary literary circles. It was not finished, however, and never appeared in print.[99] Another minor poet, Robert Lesuire, is also known to have started an epic with Peter as hero. This poem likewise remained unfinished and was not published.[100] Another epic poet of the Russian Tsar was an adventurer and an obscure writer, G. S. de Mainvilliers (?-1776). He was known chiefly through a collection of satires, *Le Petit maître philosophe* and an epic poem, *La Petréade; ou, Pierre le créateur.* This poem was published in Amsterdam in 1763. It was republished the following year but appears to have failed to attract attention and had no reviews in the principal periodicals of the time.

So far as the eighteenth-century fiction is concerned, only a few instances of Russian topics can be found. These corroborate the evidence of the drama and poetry for a contemporary interest in certain personages of Russian history. Langlet du Fresnoy, who made an elaborate survey of the principal novels of the world, up to 1734, did not include Russia in his chapter on "Le Nord." He mentioned, however, a good number of German, Hungarian, Polish, and Swedish novels and stories.[101] The only French novel on a Russian subject in the first quarter of the centu.y was de la Rochelle's *Czar Demetrius; ou, Histoire moscovite.* This was published in Paris, 1715, was republished the same year in Paris, and in The Hague, 1716. It was mentioned by Langlet du Fresnoy,[102] and it received a short review in the *Journal littéraire de la Haye.*[103] This historical novel seems to have been based on

[99] Thomas, "Correspondance . . ." *Revue d'histoire littéraire,* 1917, p. 131; cf. also L. Bachaumont, *Mémoires,* I, 283.
[100] Michaud, *Biographie universelle,* XXIV, 333-335.
[101] Langlet du Fresnoy, *Bibliothèque des romans,* 2 vols., Amsterdam, 1734, I, 324-326, and II, 120-121.
[102] *Ibid.,* II, 121.
[103] *Journal littéraire de la Haye,* VII, 443.

a work of Bisaccioni, a seventeenth-century Italian historical writer.[104]

Mention should also be made of a fictitious tale based on the life of Menshikov, entitled *Kovchimen* (anagram of "Menchikov") by Le Prince. It was published in Paris and Amsterdam in 1710 and was re-edited with another tale, from Spanish history, under the title *Histoire de l'origine du Prince Menzikov et Dom Alvar del Sol*, Paris, 1728.

In 1721 there appeared at Cologne and at Metz a tale of semifictitious nature dealing with Peter the Great and the experiences of a Frenchman in the services of the Tsar. The title of this book was *L'Heureux Esclave; ou, Histoire d'un gentil-homme lorrain ci-devant capitaine des Grenadiers à cheval du Czar*. Its author was a certain Rochonville whose identity it was impossible to establish. This work was translated into German in 1758.[105] Neither of the two last-mentioned works appears to have been reviewed in the periodicals of the time, and they seem to have passed unnoticed by the writers interested in Russia. In 1735 there appeared anonymously in Paris a book entitled *Le Militaire en solitude; ou, Le philosophe Chrétien... entretiens militaires, édifians et instructifs...* This work contained a lengthy discourse on the perplexities of Peter the Great's nature. It was briefly reviewed in the *Journal des savants* for May, 1736.

In addition to the preceding works, mention may also be made of two prose works on a Russian subject and seemingly of fictitious nature. The first of these was listed in the *Catalogue de la section des Russica* under the author's name, La Bergère. It was published at Liège in 1737, in duodecimo. The second, by Du Hautchamp, *Histoire de Ruspia; ou, La*

---

[104] *Demetrio Moscovita, historia tragica del Bisaccioni*, Rome, 1643, in duodecimo.

[105] Cf. *Catalogue russica*, "Rochonville." A. F. Prévost's sketches of imaginary travels in the South of Russia can also be mentioned. A. Prévost, *Œuvres*, "Le Monde moral," Book XVI.

belle Circassienne, 1754, was mentioned by Mornet in his critical edition of *La Nouvelle Héloïse.* No references to these tales in works of contemporary writers or reviews could be found. Contant d'Orville was the author of an historical novel on a Russian subject which achieved considerable success in the second part of the century. *Mémoires d'Azéma, contenant diverses anecdotes des règnes de Pierre le Grand, empereur de Russie et de l'impératrice Catherine son épouse, traduits du russe par M. Contant d'Orville* appeared in Amsterdam and Paris in 1764. It was translated into German in 1766 and had several editions under the title *Die Schöne Russinn; oder, Wunderbare Geschichte der Azema.* A long and flattering review of the book appeared in the *Journal encyclopédique* for February, 1764, in which it was stated that the *Mémoires d'Azéma* was an outstanding book of the year. Although D'Orville published the memoirs as a translation from Russian, the work was entirely his own. The story is largely fictitious and centers around the famous Cossack chief, Mazepa.[106] Metima, a Circassian captive, is in love with Mazepa, who is indifferent to her because of his love for Azéma, daughter of Osakoi, a courtier of Peter the Great. Mazepa elopes with Azéma and in an encounter with her father, wounds him. Osakoi and the Circassian belle plot against Mazepa and accuse him of betraying Peter the Great. After the defeat of Charles XII at Poltava, Mazepa flees with him and later dies in exile. The Circassian captive, in despair, kills herself. Azéma lives on, becomes lady in waiting to

---

[106] Ivan Mazepa (1644-1702), as the legend has it, was tied to a wild horse by a jealous husband. In this fashion he was brought among the Cossacks who soon acclaimed him as their chief. He fought for Russia until 1706 when, through ambition, he betrayed Peter the Great and entered the service of Charles XII. After the latter's defeat at Poltava, Mazepa followed him into exile in Turkey. Fearing to be given up by his new master and returned to Russia, Mazepa poisoned himself. Among the artistic works on the subject the best known are Byron's poem and Vernet's painting.

Catherine I, and has many impossible adventures. She travels in France and in Turkey, is captured by pirates, and finally returns to Russia where Menshikov falls in love with her. She does not, however, return his love, as in the meantime she had fallen in love with an Englishman whom she had met during her travels. According to D'Orville, it was Azéma herself who wrote these memoirs which he had discovered and had translated into French. With the exception of a bare outline of Mazepa's history, the rest of the plot is purely fictitious and is a fantastic medley of impossible adventures and melodramatic surprises. It seems as though the author were determined to work into his story all the important Russian historical figures of the time, Peter, Catherine I, Mazepa, and Menshikov. The relationship which he depicted between these characters was, however, largely fictitious. The principal character, Azéma, seems to be an echo of Princess Dulska, a Polish lady, who is generally supposed to have been Mazepa's paramour. The frequent shifting of scene from Russia to Turkey, the pirates, and the character of the Circassian captive all lend D'Orville's work an oriental aspect suggestive of the Arabian Nights. The success of his work would seem to indicate that these features were highly appreciated by contemporary readers.

In the same group of imaginative prose works should be included various anecdotes of a semifictitious nature, such as those of Voltaire, Rousset de Missy, Soulas d'Allainval, and Rulhière, which have already been treated in the chapter dealing with the sources of information on Russia. We can also mention here Fontenelle's *Eloge du Czar Pierre I*, Sénac de Meilhan's bizarre *Comparaison de St. Pierre de Rome avec Catherine II* (1791), both of which have been discussed in previous chapters, and an anonymous *L'Ombre de Catherine II aux Champs Elysées* (1797). The last-mentioned pamphlet is a short imaginary dialogue between Catherine II and Louis

XVI and between Peter the Great and Frederick of Prussia. The various reminiscences and sketches of Russian court life by eminent Frenchmen who visited Russia, such as Bernardin de St. Pierre, Grimm, Ségur, De Ligne and Mme Vigée Le Brun, were not published until the first quarter of the nineteenth century. These works have already been examined at some length in the first part of this study.

In ending this discussion of Russian subjects in the prose of the century, we may add that there appeared during the Empire a number of novels based entirely on Russian subjects and often on themes taken from Russian history. We can mention here Mme Arman de Roland's *Alexandra; ou, La chaumière russe* (1808), Victor Perceval's *Un Amour du Czar* (Peter the Great), and Mme Cottin's *Elizabeth; ou, Les exilés de Sibérie* (1806). The last mentioned work ran through a great many editions and was translated into German, English, and Italian. Two melodramas were based on this novel, one by M. Dorvo, *Elizabeth; ou, Les exilés de Sybérie*, produced for the first time October 28, 1806, and one by Guilbert de Pixérecourt, *La Fille de l'exilé*, produced at the Théâtre de la Gaîté, March 13, 1819. The latter had a long and continuous success on the stage.[107]

The number of translations from Russian imaginative works published during the century is naturally small. During the period under discussion Russian literature was still in its infancy. Even the outstanding men of the time, Sumarokov, Derzhavin, Lomonosov, Fonvizin, and Karamzin were largely imitators of the Western writers, chiefly the French. These men, as well as minor literary figures of the century, are important, however, as being first to direct the development of Russian literature along national lines.

Abbé Guasco's translation of Prince Kantemir's satires

---

[107] Willie Hartog, *Guilbert de Pixérecourt* . . . Paris, 1913, p. 141. *La Fille de l'exilé* had 445 productions.

was one of the first translations of the century. His *Satires du Prince Kantemir avec l'histoire de sa vie* was published in London in 1749. It was republished the following year but attracted little attention.

A tragedy of the foremost Russian playwright of the time, Alexis Sumarokov (1718-1777), was translated into French in 1751 under the title *Sinave et Trouvore* by a Russian, Prince Dolgorukïï. Detailed and laudatory accounts of this tragedy appeared in several periodicals of the time.[108] This work is a typical eighteenth-century French pseudo-classic tragedy. The protagonists, in spite of their ancient Slav or Varangian names, are mere abstractions and are in essence the Frenchmen of Corneille, Racine, and Voltaire. Several other tragedies of Sumarokov, all following the same pattern as *Sinave et Trouvore*, were translated and published by Léon Pappadopoulo under the title *Théâtre tragique*, Paris, 1801.

A short epic poem celebrating the Russian victory over the Turks, by Michael Kheraskov (1733-1807), a well-known writer at that time but now completely forgotten, was translated by Le Clerc under the title *Le Combat de Tzesme*. Le Clerc included this very mediocre, pseudo-classic poem in his *Histoire physique, morale . . . de Russie ancienne*. It was published separately by an anonymous author in 1772, in octavo, and was given a complimentary notice in Grimm's *Correspondance littéraire*.[109]

The works of the Russian scientist, poet, and historian, Michael Lomonosov (1711-1765) were known through various articles containing excerpts from his works which appeared in the periodicals of the time.[110] Some of Lomono-

---

[108] *Journal étranger*, April, 1755; *Mercure de France*, April, 1755; *L'Année littéraire*, 1760, V, 194.

[109] Grimm, *Correspondance littéraire*, XVI, 10-21.

[110] *Mémoires de Trévoux*, December, 1769; *Nouvelle bibliothèque germanique de Formey*, II, 211; *Journal encyclopédique*, April, 1765.

sov's odes were translated by Levesque and Le Clerc and were included in their histories of Russia. Only the least important and incidental work of Lomonosov's, his *History of Ancient Russia,* had a French translation in its entirety. Translated in 1769 by Eidous, this work earned, as we have seen, considerable success.

It is to be noted that neither the works of Gabriel Derzhavin (1743-1816) an important poet and satirist, nor those of Denis Fonvizin (1744-1792), humorist and playwright, had French translations in the eighteenth century. Some of the best-known plays of Fonvizin appeared in French for the first time in a collection entitled *Chefs d'œuvre du théâtre russe,* Paris, 1823.

Empress Catherine's moral tales and plays enjoyed a certain degree of popularity, due chiefly to the propaganda of Voltaire, Diderot, and Grimm. Her *Czarewitz Chlore, conte moral,* translated by Formey and published in 1782, ran through several editions and was praised by Meister in the *Correspondance littéraire.* Her other tale, *Le Czarewitz Feveh,* received an enthusiastic review with a résumé of the story in *Correspondance littéraire* for 1790.[111] Among Catherine's dramatic efforts known to France, one can mention *O Tems! O Mœurs!* translated by Le Clerc and greatly admired by Voltaire and Diderot; also her short comedies for her private theater written in collaboration with several of her friends and published in Paris in 1799 under the title of *Théâtre de l'Hermitage de Catherine II.* In spite of Voltaire's, Diderot's, and Grimm's assertions to the contrary, none of the above-mentioned works possesses the least artistic value. Her correspondence with the French men of letters is perhaps of greater literary value. Some of Catherine's letters to Voltaire were published in Paris in 1785 as *Recueil des lettres de M. de Voltaire et de l'Impératrice de Russie.* Her correspondence with

111 Grimm, *Correspondance littéraire,* XVI, 85-98.

Grimm and Diderot, however, was not published in France until the second half of the nineteenth century.

In 1797 appeared the first translation from the famous historian and novelist, Nicholas Karamzin (1766-1826). His *Julie, nouvelle traduite de russe de M. Karamzine par M. de Bouilliers*, Moscow, 1797, received a long and very flattering review in the *Spectateur du Nord* for February, 1797.[112] The extreme difficulty of translating *Julie* into French and the fear of having failed in the task, led the translator to address to the author an apologetic poem which appeared in the Preface to the translation.[113] *Julie*, like the two subsequent novels of Karamzin translated into French, *Marpha; ou, La prise de Novgorod* (1804) and *La Pauvre Liza* (1808) was inspired by Rousseau, Richardson, and Sterne. In these novels Karamzin drew up a complete code of sentimentalism. We find in them a lively feeling for nature and rustic life, scorn for wealth, melancholy, tenderness, and the romanticizing of the past history of the nation. Like his novels, Karamzin's historical works, which began to be translated into French in the twenties of the nineteenth century, fulfilled the demand of contemporary fashion and ran through many editions.

Interest in Russian mythology and in popular poetry began to manifest itself in the last decade of the century. Already in the *Essai sur la littérature russe* by Dmitrievskiï, published in Leighorn in 1771 (republished in 1774) there

[112] *Spectateur du Nord*, I, 183-203.
[113] It runs in part as follows:

> Auteur charmant, je vous offre l'ouvrage
> Qui vous valut les plus flatteurs succès;
> Votre Julie a changé de langue
> Et dans ce jour elle parle français.
>
> .   .   .   .   .   .
>
> Puisse sur-tout l'écrivain séduisant,
> Qui la forma si douce et si jolie,
> A son aspect prendre un caressant,
> Et s'écrier: "c'est toujours ma Julie."

was some mention of the ancient Russian heroic tales, the *byliny*. In 1792 there appeared an essay by Michael Popov, *Description abrégée de la mythologie slavone*, which had a brief but enthusiastic review in the *Esprit des journaux* for October, 1792.[114] A long article by a Russian, written in the form of a letter signed "N. N.," containing selections from the *byliny* and the old folksongs, was published in the *Spectateur du Nord* for October, 1797.[115] Finally, many selections from ancient and contemporary Russian writers appeared in the first anthology of Russian literature published by Pappadopoulo and Gallais in 1800 and in a collection published in 1802 by François Pagès.[116]

These few examples of translations from Russian imaginative works are symptomatic of a growing interest in the cultural state of Russia. Voltaire, Diderot, Grimm, Levesque, and Thomas were, as we have seen in the preceding chapters of this work, the first to call the attention of their countrymen to the fact that Russia was beginning to produce men of outstanding literary talent. Frequently, the praise which they gave to the works of Kantemir, Lomonosov, or Sumarokov was scarcely deserved. Educated France, partly as a result of this propaganda of the philosophers, partly because of a general vogue for Russia in the second part of the century, was already beginning to manifest a certain curiosity in the literary and artistic developments in Russia.

The Russian material furnished to the eighteenth-century drama, poetry, and prose seems hardly sufficient to justify the use of the term "influence." This material, slight as it was, especially if one compares it with that of England

---

[114] *Esprit des journaux*, X, 409-410.

[115] *Spectateur du Nord*, IV, 53-72.

[116] François-Xavier Pagès (1745-1802) was a novelist and compiler of popular information; he was known chiefly for his works on the French Revolution and his compilations of the various accounts of travelers. None of his works survived him.

or even Germany, represents, nevertheless, a definite and well-sustained interest felt by the principal men of letters of the time in Russia and Russian history, from which they were wont to borrow on occasion, a plot, a character, or a theme. The creative genuis and the perplexities of Peter the Great's nature, the "liberalism" and the brilliance of Catherine the Great's reign, the picturesqueness of Menshikov's career, and the romantic *epopée* of the traitor and tragic lover, Mazepa, were some of the themes which left a strong impression on the French mind. Between 1760 and 1805 there were published at least sixteen plays (fourteen of which were produced) entirely on Russian subjects. Nine of these plays were serious melodramas; four, comedies and comic operas; and three, vaudevilles. Because of obvious dramatic and artistic weakness most of these plays failed to hold the stage. Nevertheless, Bouilly's *Pierre le Grand,* Desforges's *Feodor et Lizinka,* and Duval's *Le Menuisier de Livonie* achieved a certain popular success. Since 1805 plays on Russian subjects, for the most part dealing with Peter the Great and Menshikov's exile, continued to appear in increased number, some of them earning conspicuous popular approval.

Instances of Russian topics in the imaginative prose of the century are fewer than in the drama, though these too are indicative of a persistent interest in certain figures and themes of Russian history. Two historical novels, for example, can be mentioned, one on the Pseudo-Dimitrii by De la Rochelle (1715), the other centering about the Cossack chief, Mazepa, by Contant d'Orville (1769). A number of semifictitious tales and anecdotal accounts, dealing for the most part with Peter the Great, Menshikov, and Catherine the Great, appeared throughout the century. One might also include in this group prose *éloges* of Russian sovereigns by Fontenelle, Grimm, Sénac de Meilhan, and other lesser figures of the century. Just as in the drama, Russia continued to furnish material for fiction during the Empire and the Restoration.

The admiration of the eighteenth-century philosophers and men of letters for the creative genius of Peter the Great and Catherine the Great found its best expression in the poetry of the period. At least four epic poems on Peter the Great were attempted and numerous were the occasional eulogistic poems addressed to Russian sovereigns and courtiers, all of which reiterated the same themes: the personal virtues of the subjects of the author's inspiration and the incredibly swift progress of Russia.

In estimating the cosmopolitan tendencies in French literature during the second half of the eighteenth century, all these traces of Russian contributions which we have examined would seem to be sufficiently important to be taken into account.

The literary material surveyed in this chapter offers, as one would suspect, few instances where the local color and the psychology of the Russian people were depicted in anything but a rudimentary and superficial manner. The Russian locality and characters in the early eighteenth-century plays were apparently intended to produce merely an effect of *exotisme* of an oriental kind. In these early plays and tales the Russian people are depicted as primitive, barbaric, but also possessing a certain generosity of an oriental flavor. Later in the century, however, it is possible to discover a somewhat more precise characterization of the national type. Russians began to be portrayed as complex and contradictory natures. They were often depicted as cruel and generous, noble and mean, violent and gentle, primitive yet civilized. It is possible that the many contradictions of Peter the Great's nature, on which much was written during the century, contributed to the contemporary notion of the Russian national type. Furthermore, it is not only the Russian character that is described as contradictory; the mode of life and the very scenery of Russia abounds in sharp contrasts. Efforts to express these contrasts become toward the end of the century more and more apparent in the plays, poems, and tales dealing with Russia. The above tendency would lead one to conclude that Russian *exotisme* came to be considered in the latter part of the eighteenth century as something apart and not entirely identical with the *exotisme* of the Orient, for example, or that of other countries of the North. It had a certain characteristic or quality of its own.

One might say that none of the imaginative productions of the eighteenth century, Russian in subject, possessed sufficient artistic merit to survive its own time. To the student of the Franco-Russian relations they are of interest as symptoms of a growing intellectual and artistic rapprochement between the two nations. They represent a beginning, however humble, of the rich artistic inheritance which France received from Russia in the second half of the following century, in return for her own earlier contribution to the cultural development of Russia.

VIII

CONCLUSION

THE first part of this study shows that the points of contact between French and Russian society in the eighteenth century were widely distributed and varied in type. Two Russian monarchs and a large section of the aristocracy visited France, some of the latter to live there permanently; Russian students of art and naval science studied in France at various times; most of the outstanding representatives of philosophical, artistic, and literary France either visited Russia or corresponded with the Russian Court. The most frequent and intimate contacts between the two countries took place between 1756 (the establishment of a large Russian colony in Paris) and 1789. During this period the vogue for Russia appears to have been so strong in France that it threatened to overshadow even that of England. The revolution, naturally, put an end to this intimate relationship between the two countries. Under the Directorate and the Consulate, however, French society resumed its contacts with Russia and with a renewed interest. A vaudeville entitled *Allons en Russie,* produced in 1802, satirized this revived vogue or, as one of the characters called it, "fury," of going to Russia.

One can well ask, then, what was it that attracted so large a number of French aristocrats and intellectuals to a nation that was just beginning to emerge from a state of complete barbarism. In the light of this study several reasons suggest themselves. To begin with, Russia offered a vast field for the civilizing influences of France, which was flattering to the national pride of the French. In the second place, there was the growing admiration for the outstanding rulers of Russia and the spectacular transformation of a backward state into one of the foremost European powers. This admiration of Russia's successful assimilation of Western civilization was reflected in the correspondence, memoirs and belles lettres of the time. Another reason for France's attraction to Russia was, no doubt, the Frenchman's hope of gain and favors from the Russian Court. And many were those, among the literary men of France, who in one way or another benefited by their Russian connections. But aside from these rather obvious reasons, there were other more subtle, psychological elements which contributed to the Frenchman's curiosity and interest in Russia. Already in the second half of the eighteenth century we begin to find Frenchmen who notice certain temperamental affinities between themselves and the Russians. They begin to admire the gaiety, sociability, and graciousness of the Russian aristocracy (in addition to their knowledge of the French language and culture).

Il est très sûr [wrote the playwright Duval] qu'un Parisien qui se rencontrerait avec certaines Russes pour la première fois, pourrait très bien se croire avec des compatriotes.[1]

Mme Le Brun made similar observations.[2] And among later French visitors to Russia, Mme de Staël and De Maîstre and Marmier, such observations are frequent. But an even stronger element in this attraction of the French to the Russians was the dissimilarity in the national characteristics of the two countries. It was the attraction of the rational and logical-minded Frenchman to a people that were fundamentally irrational, complex, and contradictory. Throughout this study we have found many instances of the Frenchman's awareness of the contradictory and sharply contrasting qualities in the

---

[1] Alexandre Duval, Œuvres complètes, V, 397.
[2] Mme Vigée Le Brun, Souvenirs, chs. vii and xi.

Russian character, manners, and mode of life. This awareness did not originate in the eighteenth century but is to be found already in the early sixteenth-century German and English memoirs of travelers in Russia. As we have seen, these travelers, in describing the Russian life and people, emphasized the strange mixture of immorality and piety, luxury and poverty, hospitality and cruelty. These characteristics were later corroborated by the eighteenth-century Frenchmen—those who observed Russians in France [3] and those who visited Russia.[4]

On ne saurait trop le répéter [wrote Mme de Staël at the beginning of the nineteenth century], cette nation est composée de contrastes les plus frappants. Peut-être le mélange de la civilisation européenne et du caractère asiatique en est-il la cause.[5]

We have found the same emphasis upon sharp contrasts in Russian life and character in the dramas and tales on Russian subjects in the second half of the century.

At the beginning of the eighteenth century, as we have seen in the periodicals and memoirs of the time, France's attitude toward Russia was that of indifference and even contempt; it became that of interested curiosity after Peter the Great's visit to France in 1717 and reached a most flattering and friendly state toward the end of the century. In spite, however, of this rather remarkable change of attitude and the extensive Franco-Russian contacts, the average eighteenth-century Frenchman's knowledge of Russia was superficial and, in some respects, quite erroneous. This was certainly due, in part at least, to the best-known popular French accounts of Russia, such as Chappe d'Auteroche's, Voltaire's, Chantreau's, and Rulhière's (as well as some of the foreign ac-

---

[3] See conclusion to ch. ii. of this study.

[4] For example, Bernardin de Saint Pierre, Masson, Corberon, Abbé Chappe d'Auteroche, and De Ligne.

[5] Mme de Staël, De l'Allemagne, Paris, 1820, p. 273.

counts such as that of Captain Perry and others) which were superficial and biased. Besides conveying much erroneous information as to Russian history, geography, and ethnography, these works showed little grasp of national psychology and no understanding of Russia's old institutions and cultural background. The same is true of the French political writers of the century who, on various occasions, chanced to prophesy the destiny of the Russian Empire. Some, misled by the temporary and ephemeral manifestations of liberalism in the Russian government, tended to exaggerate vastly the Western influences upon the country. Others overemphasized the evils resulting from the absence of political and religious liberty. In either case, the most vitally important elements in the national development of Russia—the institutions connected with land and peasantry and the Greek-Orthodox religion—were misunderstood or willfully ignored. Many of these errors of judgment were corrected only by the early nineteenth-century visitors to Russia, notably by Mme de Staël and Joseph de Maîstre.

The material we have examined in the second part of this work, consisting of travelers' memoirs, popular histories, reviews in the literary journals, and, finally, traces of Russia in the political and imaginative literature of the century, is indicative of a well-sustained contemporary interest in Russia. The vogue for Russia was chiefly "literary," though quite tangible, and provided a certain amount of atmosphere for belles lettres in the second half of the century. The plays on Russian subjects produced between 1760 and 1805 and the large number of editions which some of the popular works dealing with Russia ran through would also seem to attest a vogue that was not entirely "literary" but, to some extent, popular, and that the Russian exoticism was not without interest to the average Frenchman.

In conclusion we might say that, in spite of many misunderstandings and errors of observation and judgment, a great deal was accomplished in the course of the century in mutual sympathy and understanding between the two nations. Throughout the century a constantly increasing and widening interest in Russia is clearly discernible. At first it limited itself to the geography, history, and ethnography of the country; later it centered around certain personages of Russian history; finally it embraced the cultural development of the country and the psychology of the common people. It is interesting and significant that as early as the latter part of the eighteenth century some of the enthusiastic russophiles recognized the beauty of the Russian language and the imaginative qualities of the Russian mind.

Les Russes ont un esprit facile et souple [wrote the academician Thomas in 1773], leur langue est, après l'italien, la langue la plus douce de l'Europe . . . les arts même de l'imagination, transportés dans ces climats pourront peut-être y prende racine et être un jour cultivés avec succès.[6]

These observations upon which Thomas based his prophecy might have been made by a Mérimée or a De Vogüé in the middle of the following century.[7] It was the eighteenth-century men of letters, like Thomas, Levesque, and others who were the first to bring to their countrymen's attention the creative potentialities of Russia. When Mérimée and De Vogüé "discovered" Russian literature, the educated French public was prepared to receive this cultural inheritance, thanks, in part at least, to the eighteenth-century precursors in Russian studies.

---

[6] Antoine Thomas, Œuvres, "Essai sur les éloges," (1773) II, 376.

[7] Mérimée, for example, wrote to Albert Stapfer in 1869 as follows: La langue russe est la plus belle langue de l'Europe, sans en excepter le grec. Elle est bien plus belle que l'allemand et d'une clarté merveilleuse. . . ."—A. Filon, Mérimée et ses amis, p. 294.

BIBLIOGRAPHY

Contemporary Works: Memoirs and Letters

Alembert, Jean d'. Œuvres et correspondances inédites de d'Alembert, publiés par M. Charles Henry . . . Paris, 1887. 23 cm.

Algarotti, Francesco, conte. Saggio di lettere sopra la Russia, Paris, Briasson, 1763. 20½ cm.

Allainval, Léonor Jean d'. Œuvres de l'abbé d'Allainval, Paris, La Petite bibliothèque des théâtres, 1785. 13½ cm.

Allonville, Armand, comte d'. Mémoires tirés des papiers d'un homme d'état . . . Paris, Michaud, 1831-1838. 13 vols. 21 cm.

Anthoine de Saint-Joseph, Antoine, baron. Essai historique sur le commerce de la Mer-Noire, Paris, H. Agasse, 1805. 22½ cm.

Argenson, René, marquis d'. Considérations sur le gouvernement ancien et présent de la France, comparé avec celui des autres états . . . second edition, Amsterdam, 1784. 22 cm.

———— Journal et mémoires . . . publiés par E. J. B. Rathery, Paris, Jules Renouard, 1859-1867. 9 vols. 26 cm.

Arnaud, François Baculard d'. Œuvres, Paris, Montard, 1781. 10 vols. 17½ cm.

Avity, Pierre d'. The Estates, Empires, and Principalities of the World . . . Translated out of French by Edward Grimstone . . . London, A. Islip, 1615. 33½ cm.

Bachaumont, Louis de. Mémoires secrets pour servir à l'histoire de la république des lettres en France . . . London, John Adamson, 1777-1789. 36 vols. 19 cm.

Barclay, John. The Mirror of Mindes; or, Icon Animorum . . . London, John Norton, 1631. 13 cm.

Barthélemy, Comte de. Gazette de la Régence (janvier 1715—juin 1719). Paris, Charpentier, 1887. 20 cm.

Belloy, Pierre Laurent de. Œuvres choisies . . . Paris, Masson et Yonet [181—?]. 14 cm.

Boissy, Louis de. Œuvres . . . Amsterdam and Berlin, 1758. 8 vols. 19 cm.

Bonchamps, Marie, marquise de. Mémoires de madame la marquise de Bonchamps, rédigés par madame la comtesse de Genlis . . . Paris, Baudouin frères, 1823. 20 cm.

Bouilly, Jean. Pierre le Grand, comédie, Tours and Paris, 1790. 19½ cm.

Bruce, Peter. Memoirs of Peter Henry Bruce . . . Dublin, Byrn, 1783. 21½ cm.

Bruin, Cornelis de. Voyages de Corneille Le Brun par la Moscovie en Perse et aux Indes Orientales . . . Amsterdam, Frères Wetstein, 1718. 2 vols. 34½ cm.

Buffon, Georges, comte de. Correspondance inédite de Buffon, recueillie et annotée par M. Henry Nadault de Buffon, Paris, Hachette, 1860. 2 vols. 22½ cm.

Buvat, Jean. Journal de la Régence, 1715-1723 ... Paris, 1865. 2 vols. 20 cm.

Carlisle, Charles Howard, first earl of [Miege, Guy]. La Relation de trois ambassades de M. le comte de Carlisle, Paris, Jaunet, 1857. 20 cm.

Carmontelle, Louis. Théâtre du prince Clenerzow ... Paris, 1771. 2 vols. in 1. 20½ cm.

Castéra, Jean. Vie de Catherine II ... Paris, F. Buisson, 1797. 2 vols. 20 cm.

Catherine II, Empress of Russia. Documents of Catherine the Great, The Correspondence with Voltaire and the Instructions of 1767, edited by W. F. Reddaway, Cambridge University Press, 1931. 22½ cm.

———— Les Lettres de Catherine II au prince de Ligne (1780-1796), publiées par la princesse Charles de Ligne ... Brussels and Paris, G. van Oest, 1924. 22½ cm.

———— Théâtre de l'Hermitage de Catherine II ... edited by J. Castéra, Paris, Gide, 1797. 2 vols. 20½ cm.

Chamfort, Sébastien. Caractères et anecdotes de Chamfort par von Bever, Paris, G. Cres, 1924. 19 cm.

Chancellor, Richard. "The Booke of the Great and Mighty Emperor of Russia ..." in R. Hakluyt's Collection, London, 1809. 31 cm.

Chantreau, Pierre. Voyage philosophique, politique, et littéraire fait en Russie pendant les années 1788-1789 ... Paris, Briand, 1794. 2 vols. 21½ cm.

Chappe d'Auteroche, Jean. Voyage en Sibérie ... Amsterdam, Marc Rey, 1769. 2 vols. 16 cm.

Cheverny, Dufort, comte de. Mémoires ... L'Ancien Régime (1731-1787) ... Paris, Plon-Nourrit, 1909. 20½ cm.

Condillac, Etienne de. Œuvres, Paris, Houel, 1798. 23 vols. 20½ cm.

Contant d'Orville, André. Mémoires d'Azéma, Paris, 1764. 20½ cm.

Corberon, Marie-Daniel Bourrée, baron de. Journal intime du Chevalier de Corberon ... introduction et notes par L. H. Lebonde, Paris, Plon-Nourrit, 1901. 2 vols. 21 cm.

Coxe, William. Travels in Poland, Russia, Sweden and Denmark, London, 1802. 5 vols. 21½ cm.

———— Account of Russian Discoveries between Asia and America, London, 1804. 19 cm.

Craven, Elizabeth, baroness. A Journey through the Crimea to Constantinople ... London, J. Robinson, 1789. 17½ cm.

Damas, Ange, baron de. Mémoires du baron de Damas (1785-1862), publiés par son petit-fils, le comte de Damas ... Paris, Plon-Nourrit, 1922. 23 cm.

Damas d'Antigny, Roger de. Mémoires du comte Roger de Damas, publiés par Jacques Rambaud ... Paris, Plon, 1912-1914. 2 vols. 23 cm.

Dangeau, Philippe, marquis de. Mémoires (1682-1720) ... Paris, Treuttel et Würtz, 1817. 3 vols. 19½ cm.

Dashkova, Ekaterina, princesse. Mémoires de la princesse Dashkoff, publiés par W. Bradford ... Paris, Franck, 1859. 20 cm.

Desforges, Pierre. Le Poète; ou, Mémoires d'un homme de lettres écrites par lui-même ... Hamburg, 1798. 4 vols. 17 cm.

Diderot, Denis. Œuvres complètes de Diderot, éd. Assézat, Paris, Garnier frères, 1875-1877. 20 vols. 23 cm.

———— Correspondance inédite, publiée par André Babelon, Paris, Gallimard, 1931. 2 vols. 22 cm.

Diderot, Denis. Letters to Catherine II, ed. by J. Grot, *Sbornik*, 1880, Vol. XXXIII.

—— Lettres à Sophie Volland, publiés par André Babelon, Paris, Gallimard, 1930. 3 vols. 22½ cm.

—— Three letters to Gesner, *Revue d'histoire littéraire de France*, 1908.

—— Lettres inédites de Diderot à Falconet, *Revue moderne*, 1866-1867.

Dorat, Claude. Amilka; ou, Pierre-le-Grand, Paris, Jorry, 1767. 23 cm.

Ducis, Jean. Œuvres posthumes . . . Paris, A. Nepveu, 1826. 3 vols. 21½ cm.

Du Deffand, M. A., marquise. Correspondance complète . . . publiée par le marquis de Saint-Aulaire . . . New ed., Paris, Levy, 1866. 3 vols. 21½ cm.

—— Lettres de la marquise du Deffand à Horace Walpole (1766-1780), London, Methuen and Co., 1912. 3 vols. 23 cm.

Duval, Alexandre. Œuvres complètes, Paris, J. N. Barba, 1822. 9 vols. 20½ cm.

Eon de Beaumont, Charles d'. Lettres, mémoires, négociations . . . London, Jacques Dixwell, 1764. 2 vols. 20 cm.

—— Mémoires . . . publiés par F. Gaillardet, Paris, E. Dentu, 1866. 20 cm.

Epinay, Louise, marquise d'. Mémoires et correspondance . . . Paris, Volland, 1818. 3 vols. 21 cm.

—— La Signora d'Epinay e l'abate Galiani, lettre inedite (1769-1772) . . . int., and notes by F. Nicolini, Bari, Laterza, 1929. 20½ cm.

Esterházy, Valentin, comte. Mémoires . . . publiés par E. Daudet, Paris, Plon-Nourrit, 1907. 2 vols. 23 cm.

Falconet, Etienne. Correspondance de Falconet avec Catherine II . . . publiée par Louis Réau . . . Paris, Champion, 1921. 25½ cm.

Favart, Charles. Mémoires et correspondance . . . publiés par A. P. C. Favart, Paris, Collin, 1808. 3 vols. 20½ cm.

Fletcher, Giles. "Of the Russian Commonwealth," in Russia at the Close of the Sixteenth Century, edited by Sir Edward Bond, London, Hakluyt Society, 1856. 22 cm.

Fontenelle, Bernard de. Œuvres . . . Paris, Salmon, 1825. 5 vols. 21½ cm.

Fonvizin, Denis. Sochinenïïa, pis'ma . . . (Works), St. Petersburg, Efremov, 1866. 22 cm.

Fornerod. L'Antidote; ou, Les Russes tels qu'ils sont . . . Lausanne, 1799. 21½ cm.

Fortia de Piles, Alphonse, comte de. Voyage de deux Français en Allemagne, Danemarck, Suède, Russie, et Pologne en 1790-1792 . . . Paris, Desenne, 1796. 5 vols. 20 cm.

Genlis, Stéphanie, comtesse de. Mémoires inédites de Madame la comtesse de Genlis sur le XVIII⁰ siècle . . . Paris, Ladvocat, 1825. 8 vols. 20 cm.

—— Théâtre d'éducation . . . Paris, Lecointe et Durey, 1825. 5 vols. 17½ cm.

Geoffroy, Julien Louis. Cours de littérature dramatique, Paris, Blanchard, 1819-1820. 5 vols. 21 cm.

Georgel, Jean François, abbé de. Mémoires pour servir à l'histoire des évènements de la fin du dix-huitième siècle . . . Paris, Alexis Eymery, 1818. 6 vols. 20½ cm.

Georgi, J. G. Russland; Beschreibung aller Nationen des russischen Reiches . . . Leipzig, Verlage der Dykischen Buchhandlung, 1783. 2 vols. in 1. 28½ cm.

Golovina, Varvara, Countess. Memoirs of Countess Golovine . . . London, David Nutt, 1910. 22½ cm.

Grimm, Friedrich Melchior, Correspondance littéraire, philosophique, et critique, par Grimm, Diderot, Raynal, etc . . . publié par Maurice Tourneux, Paris, Garnier frères, 1877-1882. 16 vols. 24½ cm.

——— Correspondence with Catherine II of Russia, Russian Antiquity (*Russkaîa starina*), 1893, and Russian Archives (*Russkiî arkhiv*), 1878.

——— Gazette littéraire (1753-1790), "Etudes sur Grimm par Saint-Beuve et Paulin Limayrac . . ." Paris, Didier, 1854. 17 cm.

Hakluyt, Richard. Collection of early Voyages, Travels, and Discoveries of the English Nation, London, R. H. Evans, 1809-1812. 5 vols. 31 cm.

Herberstein, Sigmund, Freiherr von. Notes upon Russia, translated by R. H. Major . . . London, Hakluyt Society, 1851-1852. 2 vols. 22 cm.

Jaucourt, Chevalier de. Article on Russia in the Encyclopédie; ou, Dictionnaire raisonné des sciences, des arts, et des métiers, par une société de gens de lettres . . . Neufchâtel, Samuel Faulche, 1751-1765. 17 vols. 39½ cm.

Jenkinson, Anthony. "Voyage d'Antoine Jenkinson pour découvrir le chemin du Cathay . . ." in J. Bernard's Recueil de voyages au Nord, Amsterdam, 1725-1738. 17 cm.

Kantemir, Antïokh, Prince. Sochineniîa (Works) . . . St. Petersburg, Efremov, 1867. 2 vols. 22½ cm.

Korb, Johann. Diary of an Austrian Secretary of Legation at the Court of Czar Peter the Great, London, Bradbury and Evans, 1863. 2 vols. 19 cm.

La Combe, Jacques. Abrégé chronologique de l'histoire du Nord . . . Amsterdam, Chatelain, 1763. 2 vols. 17 cm.

——— Histoire des révolutions de l'Empire de Russie, Paris, 1760. 17½ cm.

La Harpe, Jean François de. Abrégé de l'histoire générale des voyages . . . Paris, 1780-1801. 32 vols. 21 cm.

——— Œuvres . . . Paris, 1820-1821. 16 vols. 21 cm.

La Martinière, Pierre de. A New Voyage into the Northern Countries . . . London, 1674. 14½ cm.

La Messelière, comte de. Voyage à Pétersbourg; ou, Nouveaux mémoires sur la Russie . . . Paris, Panckoucke, 1803. 20½ cm.

La Rivière, Pierre Mercier de. L'ordre naturel et essentiel des sociétés politiques . . . London, Nourse; Paris, Desaint, 1767. 2 vols. 17 cm.

Lauzun, Armand, duc de. Mémoires du duc de Lauzun (1747-1783) . . . publiés par Louis Lacour . . . Paris, Poulet-Malassis, 1858. 19 cm.

Le Brun, Marie Vigée de. Souvenirs . . . New York, Worthington, 1879. 21½ cm.

Le Clerc, Nicolas Gabriel. Histoire physique, morale, et politique de la Russie ancienne et moderne . . . Versailles and Paris, 1783-1794. 6 vols. 19 cm.

Lenglet Dufresnoy, Nicolas. De l'usage des romans . . . Amsterdam, 1734. 2 vols. 17½ cm.

Le Sage, Alain René. Le Théâtre de la foire . . . Paris, Pierre Gandouin, 1723-1734. 9 vols. 17½ cm.

Lescallier, Daniel. Voyage en Angleterre, en Russie, et en Suède . . . Paris, Firman Didot, 1800. 22 cm.

Levesque, Pierre. Histoire de Russie . . . Nouv. éd., Hamburg and Brunswick, P. F. Fauche, 1800. 8 vols. 19½ cm.

Ligne, Charles-Joseph, prince de. Mémoires et mélanges historiques et littéraires . . . Paris, Dupon et Cie., 1827. 5 vols. 21 cm.

Ligne, Charles-Joseph, prince de. Lettres de prince de Ligne à la marquise de
Coigny ... publiés par Henri Lebasteur ... Paris, Champion, 1914. 19½ cm.

Louis XV. Correspondance secrète inédite sur la politique étrangère ... publié
par M. E. Boutaric, Paris, Henri Plon, 1866. 2 vols. 24 cm.

Mably, Gabriel Bonnot, abbé de. Œuvres ... Paris, Charles Desbrière, 1794-1795.
15 vols. 21 cm.

Maistre, Joseph Marie, comte de. Lettres et opuscules inédites ... Paris, Vatan,
1851. 2 vols. 19 cm.

———— Mémoires politiques et correspondance diplomatique de J. de Maître ...
publiés par Albert Blanc ... Paris, Librairie Nouvelle, 1853. 19½ cm.

Manstein, Christof Hermann von. Mémoires historiques politiques et militaires
sur la Russie ... Nouv. éd., Paris, Saillant, 1772. 18½ cm.

Marais, M. Journal et mémoires (1664-1737) sur la Régence et le règne de
Louis XV ... Paris, Didot frères, 1863-1868. 4 vols. 23 cm.

Marbault. Essai sur le commerce de Russie avec l'histoire de ses découvertes ...
Amsterdam, 1771. 19½ cm.

Margeret, Jacques. Etat présent de l'Empire de Russie, Paris, Poitier, 1855. 22
cm.

Marmontel, Jean. Œuvres complètes ... Nouv. éd., Paris, Verdière, 1819. 19 vols.
21½ cm.

———— Mémoires d'un père pour servir à l'instruction de ses enfants ... Paris,
M. Peltier, 1805. 4 vols. 19 cm.

Masson, Charles François. Mémoires secrets sur la Russie pendant les règnes de
Catherine II et de Paul I ... Avant-propos et notes par M. F. Barrière ...
Paris, Firman Didot, 1863. 18½ cm.

Mayerberg, Augustin, Freiherr von. Relation d'un voyage en Moscovie, Paris,
Franck, 1858. 2 vols. 16 cm.

Mercier, Louis Sébastien. Tableau de Paris ... Paris, Pagnerre, 1853. 19 cm.

Métra, François. Correspondance secrète, politique et littéraire (1774-1785) ...
London, John Adamson, 1787-1790. 18 vols. 16 cm.

Milton, John. "A Brief History of Moscovia," in his Works, New York, Columbia University Press, 1932.

Mirabeau, Honoré, comte de. Doutes sur la liberté de l'Escaut ... London, G.
Faden, 1784. 22 cm.

Montesquieu, Charles de Secondat, baron de. Correspondance ... publiée par F.
Gebelin et A. Morize ... Paris, Champion, 1914. 2 vols. 24½ cm.

———— Œuvres complètes, Paris, Garnier frères, 1875-1879. 7 vols. 24 cm.

Moreau, C. F. Allons-en Russie, Paris, Fages, 1802. A pamphlet. 22 pp. 21 cm.

———— Mincétoff, parodie de Menzikoff, Paris, Barba, 1808. 20 cm. [Bibliothèque
dramatique—2ᵉ série.]

Münster, Sebastian. Cosmographiae universalis, Basil, 1550. 31 cm.

Neuilly, Ange, comte de. Dix années d'émigrations ... souvenirs et correspondances ... publié par Marice de Barberey ... Paris, Charles Douniol, 1865.
22½ cm.

Oberkirch, Henriette Louise, baronne d'. Mémoires ... publiés par le comte
Léonce de Montbrison ... Paris, Charpentier, 1869. 2 vols. in 1. 17 cm.

Olearius, Adam. Voyages du Sieur Adam Olearius, Leyden. P. Vander Aa, 1719.
22½ cm.

Perry, John. The State of Russia under the Present Czar, London, B. Tooke. 1716. 20 cm.

Pius II, Pope. Asiae Europaeque elegantissima descriptio, Paris, 1534. 15 cm.

Pixerécourt, René Charles Guilbert de. Théâtre choisi ... Paris, 1841-1843. 4 vols. 22½ cm.

Pontecoulant, Adolphe, comte de. Souvenirs historiques et parlementaires ... (1764-1848), Paris, Levy, 1861-1865. 4 vols. 23 cm.

Prévost, Antoine François, Œuvres ... Paris, Boulland-Tardieu, 1823. 39 vols. 20 cm.

Raynal, Guillaume Thomas. Philosophical and Political History of the Settlements and Trade of the Europeans in the East and West Indies ... translated from the French by J. O. Justamond ... revised edition, London, Strahon and Cadell, 1798. 6 vols. 19 cm.

Richardson, William. Anecdotes of the Russian Empire ... London, Strahon and Cadell, 1784. 21½ cm.

Richelieu, Armand Emmanuel, duc de. "Papers and Documents relating to the Life and Activity of the Duke Richelieu (1766-1822)," edited by A. Polovtsev, Sbornik, St. Petersburg, 1866, Vol. LIV. [In Russian.]

Rousseau, Jean-Jacques. Œuvres complètes ... Paris, P. Dupont, 1823-1826. 25 vols. 21 cm.

———— Œuvres et correspondance inédites de J. J. Rousseau ... publiés par M. G. Streckeisen-Moultou ... Paris, Michel Levy frères, 1861. 23 cm.

Rousset de Missy, Jean. Mémoires du règne de Pierre le Grand ... Amsterdam, 1726-1728. 4 vols. 20 cm.

Rulhière, Claude Carloman de. Œuvres, Paris, Menard et Desenne, 1819. 4 vols. 20 cm.

Saint-Pierre, Bernardin de. Œuvres complètes ... mises en ordre et précédées de la vie de l'auteur par Aimé-Martin ... Paris, Méguigon-Marvis, 1818. 12 vols. 21 cm.

———— Empsail et Zoraïde ... drame publié pour la première fois par Mauris Sourieau, Caen, L. Jouan, 1905. 20½ cm.

Saint-Simon, Louis, duc de. Mémoires de Saint-Simon ... Nouv. éd., Paris, Hachette, 1879-1928. 41 vols. 23 cm.

Sauvage, Jehan. Mémoire du voyage en Russie, publié par L. Lacour [Le Trésor des pièces rares ou inédites], Paris, 1855. 18½ cm.

Scherer, Jean Benoit. Histoire raisonnée du commerce de la Russie ... Paris, Cuchat, 1788. 2 vols. 20 cm.

Ségur, Louis-Phillipe, comte de. Œuvres complètes ... Paris, A. Eymery, 1824-1830. 33 vols. 20½ cm.

Sénac de Meilhan, Gabriel. "Letters of Catherine the Great to Sénac de Meilhan ..." Sbornik, St. Petersburg, 1885, Vol. XLII. [In Russian.]

———— Lettres inédites de la marquise de Crequi à Sénac de Meilhan ... Paris, Potier, 1856. 18½ cm.

Staël-Holstein, Anne Louise, baronne de. Œuvres complètes ... publiés par Mme Necker de Saussure ... Paris, Treuttel et Würtz, 1820. 17 vols. 20 cm.

Stählin, Jacob von. Original anecdotes of Peter the Great, Dublin, Byrne and Jones, 1789. 19 cm.

Struys, Jean. Les Voyages de Jean Struys en Moscovie, en Tartarie, en Perse ... publiés par M. Glanius ... Amsterdam, Jacob van Meurs, 1681. 25½ cm.

BIBLIOGRAPHY 307

Swinton, Andrew. Voyage en Norwège, en Danemarck et en Russie... Paris, 1798. 2 vols. in 1. 22 cm.

Tarente, Princesse de. Souvenirs... (1789-1792), publiés par Louis de la Trémoïlle, Paris, Champion, 1901. 20½ cm.

Thomas, Antoine Léonard. "Correspondance inédite entre Thomas et Barthe (1759-1785)," éd. par M. Henriet, *Revue d'histoire littéraire*, 1917-1929.

——— Œuvres..., Nouv. éd., Amsterdam and Paris, Montard, 1773. 4 vols. 17½ cm.

Tooke, William. View of the Russian Empire during the Reign of Catherine the Second... London, Longman and Rees, 1799. 3 vols. 21½ cm.

Tudela, Benjamin. The Itinerary of Benjamin of Tudela, critical text... by Marcus Adler, London, H. Frowde, 1907. 22 cm.

Valfons, Charles, marquis de. Souvenirs... (1710-1786)... notice par M. Georges Maurin, Paris, Emile-Paul, 1906. 21 cm.

Voltaire, François Arouet de. Œuvres complètes de Voltaire... Nouv. éd., par Louis Moland, Paris, Garnier frères, 1877-1885. 52 vols. 23½ cm.

Weber, Friedrich Christian. The Present state of Russia, London, 1723. 20 cm.

Whitworth, Charles. "An Account of Russia as it Was in 1710," in R. Dodsley's Fugitive Pieces, Vol. II, Strawberry Hill, 1758. 19½ cm.

Wille, Johann Georg. Mémoires et journal... publiés par G. Duplessis... Paris, Jules Renouard, 1857. 2 vols. 20 cm.

Williams, John. Histoire des gouvernements du Nord... Amsterdam, 1780. 4 vols. 17 cm.

MODERN WORKS

Aleksinskiï, Grigoriï. Russia and Europe, London, T. Fisher, 1917. 23 cm.

Armaillé, Marie, comtesse d'. La Comtesse d'Egmont d'après ses lettres inédites à Gustave III... Paris, Perrin, 1890. 18 cm.

Babeau, Albert. Les Voyageurs en France depuis la Renaissance jusqu'à la Révolution, Paris, Firman-Didot, 1885. 19 cm.

Baldensperger, Fernand. Le Mouvement des idées dans l'émigration française (1789-1815)... Paris, Plon-Nourrit, 1924. 2 vols. 20 cm.

Bayet, Albert. Les Ecrivains politiques du XVIIIᵉ siècle... Paris, Armand Colin, 1917. 21 cm.

Bellier-Dumaine, Charles. Alexandre Duval et son œuvre dramatique, Paris, Hachette, 1905. 21 cm.

Bonnefon, Paul. La Société française du XVIIIᵉ siècle... Paris, Armand Colin, 1905. 19 cm.

——— Mémoires de Marguerite de Valois... Paris, 1920. 19 cm.

Caro, Elme. La Fin du dix-huitième siècle... Paris, Hachette, 1880. 2 vols. 18½ cm.

Cart, Théophile. "Le Voyage en Laponie de Regnard," *Revue des cours et conférences*, 1900.

Catalogue de la section des Russica; ou, Ecrits sur la Russie en langues étrangères... St. Petersburg, Imprimerie de l'Académie Impériale des Sciences, 1873. 2 vols. 25½ cm.

Daudet, Ernest. Histoire de l'émigration pendant la Révolution française... Paris, Hachette, 1905-1907. 3 vols. 20½ cm.

Desnoiresterres, Gustave. Le Chevalier Dorat et les poètes légers au XVIII°
siècle, Paris, Perrin, 1887. 19 cm.

Dodds, Muriel. Les Récits de voyages, sources de L'esprit des lois de Montesquieu,
Paris, Champion, 1929. 21 cm.

Douhaire, P. "Les Relations de la Russie et de la France au XVIII° siècle,"
Le Correspondant, 1882.

Ducros, Louis. Diderot, Paris, Perrin, 1894. 21 cm.

Florovskiĭ, A. Two Political Doctrines ... the "Nakaz" and Diderot, Belgrade,
Russian Scientific Institute of Belgrade, 1929. [In Russian.] Pamphlet, 18
pages. 20 cm.

———— Un Légiste français au service de la Tsarine Catherine II (Charles de
Villiers), Paris, Revue historique de droit français et étranger, 1924. Pamphlet,
18 pages. 19 cm.

Foucaux, Marie (Mary Summer). Quelques salons de Paris au XVIII° siècle ...
Paris, L. Henry May, 1898. 23 cm.

Fould, Paul. Un Diplomate au XVIII° siècle—Louis-Augustin Blondel ... Paris,
Plon-Nourrit, 1914. 22½ cm.

Gaiffe, Félix. Etude sur le drame en France au XVIII° siècle, Paris, Armand
Colin, 1910. 23½ cm.

Gauthier-Villars, Henri. Le Mariage de Louis XV ... Paris, Plon-Nourrit, 1900.
22½ cm.

Godefroy, Frédéric. Histoire de la littérature française, Paris, Gaume et Cie.,
1879. 2 vols. 23 cm.

Hall, Evelyn (Tallentyre, S. G.). The Friends of Voltaire, New York, Putnam's
Sons; London, Smith, Elder and Company, 1907. 21½ cm.

Hartog, Willie G. Guilbert de Pixerécourt, sa vie, son mélodrame ... Paris, Champion, 1913. 25½ cm.

Haumant, Emile. La Culture française en Russie (1700-1900), Paris, Hachette,
1910. 25½ cm.

Herpin, Clara (Perey, Lucien). Histoire d'une grande dame au XVIII° siècle, la
princesse Hélène de Ligne, Paris, Calmann Lévy, 1887. 22½ cm.

———— Une Femme du monde au XVIII° siècle ... Dernières années de Mme
d'Epinay, son salon et ses amis d'après des lettres et des documents inédits,
par L. Perey et Gaston Maugras, Paris, Calmann Lévy, 1883. 22 cm.

Hillbrand, K. "Katharina II und Grimm," Deutsche Rundschau, 1880.

IAkobson, Liubov'. Russland und Frankreich in den ersten Regierungsjahren
der Kaiserin Katharina II ... Berlin, Ost-Europa Verlag, 1929. 23½ cm.

Inklaar, Derk. François-Thomas de Baculard d'Arnaud, ses imitateurs en Hollande et dans d'autres pays ... Paris, 1925. 24½ cm.

Johansson, Johan Viktor. Etudes sur Denis Diderot, Paris, Champion, 1927.
19½ cm.

Kurz, Harry. European Characters in French Drama of the Eighteenth Century
... New York, Columbia University Press, 1916. 21 cm.

Larivière, Charles de. La France et la Russie au XVIII° siècle, Paris, Soudier,
1909. 20½ cm.

La Roncière, Charles de. Histoire de la marine française ... Paris, Plon-Nourrit,
1899-1932. 6 vols. 22 cm.

BIBLIOGRAPHY 309

Leger, Louis Paul Marie. La Russie intellectuelle, études et portraits ... Paris, Jean Maisonneuve et fils, 1914. 25½ cm.

Lenient, Charles. La Comédie en France au XVIII° siècle ... Paris, Hachette, 1888. 2 vols. 18 cm.

Leroy, O. Etudes morales et littéraires sur la personne et les écrits de J. F. Ducis ... Paris, Dufey et Vézard, 1832. 21½ cm.

Liubimenko, Inna, "Les Etrangers en Russie avant Pierre le Grand," Revue des études slaves, 1923 and 1924.

———— "Le Rôle comparatif des différents peuples dans la découverte et la description de la Russie," Revue de synthèse historique, December, 1929.

Loménie, Louis de. Beaumarchais and His Times ... London, Addey and Company, 1856. 4 vols. 18 cm.

Lozinski, G. "Le Prince Antioche Cantemir, poète français," Revue des études slaves, 1925.

———— "La Russie dans la littérature française du Moyen Age," Revue des études slaves, 1929.

Mansuy, Abel. Le Monde slave et les classiques français au XVIe-XVIIe siècles, Paris, Champion, 1912. 25½ cm.

Martino, Pierre. L'Orient dans la littérature française au XVII° et au XVIII° siècles, Paris, Hachette, 1906. 25 cm.

Mathorez, Jules. Les Etrangers en France sous l'ancien régime, Paris, Champion, 1919-1921. 2 vols. 25½ cm.

Maugras, Gaston. Duc de Lauzun and the Court of Marie Antoinette, London, Osgood, McIlvaine and Company, 1896. 23 cm.

Maury, Fernand, Etude sur la vie et les œuvres de Bernardin de Saint-Pierre, Paris, Hachette, 1892. 22½ cm.

Micard, Etienne. Un Ecrivain académique au XVIII° siècle: Antoine-Léonard Thomas (1732-1785), Paris, Champion, 1924. 25½ cm.

Michaud, Joseph François. Biographie universelle ancienne et moderne, Paris, Michaud frères, 1811-1862, 85 vols. 20½ cm.

Miller, K. French émigrés and Russia in the reign of Catherine II, Paris, "Rodnik," 1931. [In Russian.] 25½ cm.

Molloy, Joseph. The Russian Court in the Eighteenth Century, New York, Charles Scribners, 1905. 2 vols. 24½ cm.

Mornet, Daniel. French Thought in the Eighteenth Century, New York, Prentice Hall, 1929. 19½ cm.

———— Les origines intellectuelles de la Révolution française, Paris, Colin, 1933. 25½ cm.

Notovich, Nicolas. La Russie et l'alliance anglaise, Paris, Plon-Nourrit, 1906. 23½ cm.

Oulié, Marthe. Le Cosmopolitanisme du Prince de Ligne (1735-1814), Paris, Hachette, 1926. 23 cm.

Oursel, Paul. La Diplomatie de la France sous Louis XVI, Paris, Plon-Nourrit, 1921. 22½ cm.

Patouillet, Jules. "Les Relations intellectuelles entre la France et la Russie," La Revue de Paris, March and April, 1920,

Peignot, Gabriel. Recherches historiques littéraires et bibliographiques sur la vie et les ouvrages de M. de la Harpe ... Dijon, Frantin, 1820. 19 cm.

Pellisson, Maurice. Les Hommes de lettres au XVIIIᵉ siècle ... Paris, Armand Colin, 1911. 18½ cm.

Peloux, Charles, Vicomte du. Répertoire général des ouvrages modernes relatifs au dix-huitième siècle français (1715-1789), Paris, Ernest-Grund, 1926. 25 cm.

Petit de Julleville, Louis. Histoire de la langue et de la littérature française, Paris, Colin, 1910-1924. 8 vols. 25½ cm.

Petitot, Claude Bernard. Répertoire du Théâtre François ... Nouv. éd., Paris, Faucault, 1817-1818. 25 vols. 20 cm.

Pierling, Paul. La Russie et le Saint-Siège ... Paris, Plon-Nourrit, 1896-1901. 3 vols. 23 cm.

―――― La Sorbonne et la Russie (1717-1747), Paris, Ernest Leroux, 1882. 22½ cm.

Pingaud, Léonce. Les Français en Russie et les Russes en France ... Paris, Perrin, 1886. 22 cm.

―――― "Le Duc de Richelieu en Russie," Le Correspondant, May and June, 1882.

Praal, Louis, "Les Prédictions de Diderot, J. J. Rousseau, et Condillac sur la Russie," Mercure de France, August, 1918.

Rambaud, Alfred. "Catherine II et ses correspondants français," Revue des deux mondes, January and February, 1877.

―――― Recueil des instructions données aux ambassadeurs et ministres de France ... Russie ... Paris, Félix Alcan, 1890. 2 vols. 28 cm.

―――― "Paris et Saint-Pétersbourg à la veille de la Révolution," La Revue politique et littéraire, June, 1878.

Réau, Louis. "Les Artistes russes à Paris au XVIII° siècle," Revue des études slaves, 1923.

―――― Les Relations artistiques entre la France et la Russie, Paris, Champion, 1925. 25½ cm.

Russkiĭ arkhiv (Russian Archives), Moscow, 1863-1892. [A monthly historical publication.]

Russkaia starina (Russian Antiquity). St. Petersburg, 1870-1896. [A monthly historical publication.]

Sayous, Pierre. Le Dix-huitième siècle à l'étranger, Paris, Amyot, 1861. 2 vols. 21½ cm.

Sbornik, St. Petersburg, 1867-1912. [The magazine of the Imperial Russian Historical Society.]

Scherer, Edmund. Melchior Grimm, l'homme de lettres ... Paris, Calmann-Lévy, 1887. 22½ cm.

Ségur, Pierre, marquis de. Le Royaume de la rue Saint-Honoré, Paris, Calmann-Lévy, 1897. 20 cm.

Shmurlo, Evgeniĭ. Voltaire et son œuvre "Histoire de l'Empire de Russie sous Pierre le Grand," Prague, editions 'Orbis,' 1929. 22 cm.

Sipovskiĭ, Vasiliĭ. Karamzin ... St. Petersburg, Demakov, 1899. [In Russian.] 23½ cm.

Sommervogel, Carlos. Table méthodique des "Mémoires de Trévoux" (1701-1775), Paris, Auguste Durand, 1864-1865. 2 vols. 19½ cm.

Sorel, Albert. The Eastern Question in the Eighteenth Century, London, Methuen and Company, 1898. 20 cm.

Stenger, Gilbert. La Société française pendant le Consulat ... Paris, Perrin, 1903. 21 cm.

Tastevin, Félix. Histoire de la colonie française de Moscou, depuis les origines jusqu'à 1812, Paris, Champion, 1908. 20½ cm.

Telfer, John Buchan. The Strange Career of the Chevalier d'Eon de Beaumont ... London, Longmans, Green and Company, 1885. 25 cm.

Texte, Joseph. Jean-Jacques Rousseau et les origines du cosmopolitisme littéraire ... Paris, Hachette, 1895. 18 cm.

Tieghen, P. von. L'Année littéraire (1754-1790), Paris, F. Rieder et Cie., 1917. 20½ cm.

Tourneux, Maurice. Diderot et Catherine II ... Paris, Calmann-Lévy, 1899. 23 cm.

Tronchon, Henri. "Un Préromantique français en mission chez les Russes: Diderot," Revue des cours et conférences, December, 1929.

Vandal, Albert. Louis XV et Elisabeth de Russie, Paris. Plon-Nourrit, 1882. 24 cm.

Vorontsov family. Arkhiv Kniazia Vorontsova ... (Archives of Princess Vorontsov), published by Bartenev, Moscow, 1870-1895. 40 vols. [In Russian.] 24 cm.

Waliszewski, Kazimir. A History of Russian Literature, New York, D. Appleton and Company, 1900. 19½ cm.

——— Peter the Great, London, Heinemann, 1897. 2 vols. 20½ cm.

——— "Relation du voyage de Pierre le Grand," Revue de Paris, 1896.

Zimmermann, Erich. Pierre-Laurent Buirette de Belloy, sein Leben und seine Tragödien ... Leipzig, 1911. 24 cm.

ARTICLES ON RUSSIA IN THE EIGHTEENTH-CENTURY PERIODICALS

Journal des savants (1680-1750): VI, June 27, 1678, Review of Scheffer's *Histoire de Laponie*. XV, August 2, 1688, review of an anonymous *Voyage historique en Moscovie*. XVII, April 25, 1689, article on the Russo-Turkish wars. XXVI, May 19, 1698, review of an anonymous *Voyage historique en Moscovie*. XXVI, June 16, 1698, review of an anonymous *Relation curieuse et nouvelle de Moscovie* ... XXXIII, May 4, 1705, review of an anonymous work on Russo-Swedish wars, *Les Campagnes de Charles XII* ... XXXIV, May 10, 1707, *ibid*. XXXIX, January 23, 1708, *ibid*. XLI, August, 1708, review of *Nouveau voyage vers le Septentrion* ... XLV, August, 1709, literary news from Russia; short reviews of books published in Russia (chiefly on religious and scientific topics). XLVII, August, 1710, a long article on Russian religion and a review of N. Borgio's *Exercitatio historico-theologica de statu ecclesiae et religionis Moscoviticae* ... XLIX, June, 1711, review of *Les Campagnes de Charles XII* ... (Vol. IV). Considerable space devoted to Tsar Peter's character and reforms. LVIII, August, 1715, an article on Peter the Great's reforms. LXI, April, 1717, a review of a book on universal geography;

includes descriptions of Russia. LXIV, September, 1718, a lengthy review of a *Recueil de voyages au Nord* . . . ; this collection includes an account of Jenkinson's trip to Russia and of Ferrand's descriptions of *Tartares*. Three volumes of this collection appeared in 1715. LXV, March, 1719, review of Corneille le Bruin's trip to Russia. LXVII, March, 1720, review of a *Traité du génie, des mœurs, et des occupations des principales nations de l'Europe* . . .; includes comments on Russia. LXX, November, 1721, article on the geography of Russia, correcting many errors in contemporary maps of the country; includes descriptions of St. Petersburg. LXXV, October, 1724, review of *Histoire de l'Académie royale des sciences* . . . ; includes letters exchanged between Peter the Great and the Academy on the occasion of the Tsar's election to this learned body. LXXVII, September, 1725, a long review of *Nouveaux mémoires sur l'état présent de la Grande Russie ou Moscovie* . . . (by Weber). This review is the most detailed account of Russia published to date in the *Journal des savants*. LXXIX, July, 1726, review of Rousset de Missy's (Nestesuranoi's) *Mémoires du règne de Pierre le Grand* . . . LXXX, December, 1726, l'Abbé Girard's translation and review of the funeral oration on Peter the Great, delivered by Feofan, Archbishop of Pskov and Narva. LXXXI, April, 1727, a long review of the third and fourth volumes of de Missy's (Nestesuranoi's) *Mémoires du règne de Pierre le Grand* . . . LXXXVI, December, 1728, review of an anonymous *Mémoires du règne de Catherine I* . . . LXXXIX, December, 1729, review of the first volume of the *Memoirs of the St. Petersburg Academy of Sciences*. XC, January, 1730, an account of Tsar Peter's visit to the French Academy of Sciences. XCII, December, 1730, literary news from Russia, including a list of scientific books published in Russia. CII, April, 1734, Fontenelle's *Eloge des académiciens* . . . including his *Eloge du Czar Pierre I*. CIX, May, 1736, review of *Le Militaire en solitude; ou, Le Philosophe Chrétien* . . . ; contains a character sketch of Peter the Great.

Mémoires de Trévoux (1701-1775): May, 1717, review of Tournemine's *Histoire des Russiens que nous appelons Moscovites, tirée des monuments et des auteurs les plus croyables;* review of an anonymous *Histoire abrégée du Czar régnant Pierre Alexievicz* . . . ; review of *Diarium itineris in Moscoviam anno 1698 perillustris et magnifici domini Ignatii de Guarient et Rall*, Vienna, 1717, in folio; review of *Exercitatio historico-theologica de statu Ecclesiae et Religionis Moscoviticae, Praeside Nicolas Borgio*, Lubeck, 1709, in 8º; review of Perry's *Etat présent de la Grande Russie* . . . December, 1717, review of the *Recueil de voyages au Nord par J. Bernard*, Amsterdam, 1715-1738, 10 vols. in 12º. February, 1719, review of *Apologia pro Joanne Basilide II, magno duce Moscoviae* . . . Vienna, 1711, in 4º. November, 1722, discourse on the new map of the Caspian Sea. August and September, 1725, review of Weber's *Nouveau mémoire sur l'état présent de la Grande Russie ou Moscovie* . . . September, 1725, review of Rousset de Missy's (Nestesuranoy's) *Mémoires de Pierre le Grand* . . . July, 1737, discourse on Kamtchatka by P. Castel. February, 1750, review of D'Allainval's *Anecdotes du règne de Pierre I*. January, 1751, review of Outhier's *Journal d'un voyage au Nord en 1736 et 1737* . . . December, 1758, review of Strahlenberg's *Description historique de l'Empire Russien*. August, 1760, review of La Combe's *Histoire des révolutions de l'Empire de Russie*. February, 1768, review of Kéralio's translation of Müller's *Voyage en Sibérie* . . . January, 1769, review of Chappe d'Auteroche's *Voyage en Sibérie* ... June, 1769, review of Algarotti's letters on Russia. December, 1769, review of Lomonosov's history of Russia. February, 1770, translation of a treaty between Catherine II and Stanislaus Augustus. June, 1774, review of *Versuch einere neuen Einleitung in die russische Geschichte* ... Riga, 1773. November, 1775, review of Betskii's *Les Plans et les status des différents établissements ordonnés par sa Majesté Impériale Catherine II.*

Choix des Journaux: VIII, 187, and IX, 169, articles on the Moscovite envoys. XII, 47, an article on Peter the Great. XXIV, 157, review of Struys' account of his trip to Russia. XXV, 5, and XXXVI, 5, articles on Tsar Peter's visit to France. XLIII, 25, review of a translation of Tsar Peter's manifesto. LXXVI, 51, review of *Mémoire sur la fortune du Comte de B* ... (Marot de Brasset).

Bibliothèque raisonnée des ouvrages des savants de l'Europe (1728-1753): VI, 447, a short discourse on the etymology of "Moscovie." II, 86, a short list of histories of Russia. II, 66-70 and 72-85, a short review of memoirs of Peter the Great and a sketch of his character by Abbé de St. Pierre. XVII, 260, review of Rousset de Missy's memoirs of Peter the Great. XL, 376, a short article, "L'Idée de la puissance de Moscovie sur mer."

Le Journal littéraire de la Haye (1713-1735): IV, 92, on the origin of the word "Moscovite." VII, 443, a short review of de la Rochelle's historical novel, *Le Czar Démétrius*, La Haye, Von Dole, 1716. XV, 189-190, a short article on Peter the Great and the Academy of Inscriptions. XIX, 427, review of Voltaire's history of Peter the Great's reign. XXII, 391, a short article, "Pierre le Grand; fautes qu'on lui reproche."

Jean Le Clerc's Bibliothèque universelle 1686-1693): VII, 64, an article, "Russiens: leur conversion miraculeuse." XXIV, 216, an article on the conquests of the Tatars.

Jean Le Clerc's Bibliothèque ancienne et moderne (1714-1727): X, 435, an article on the area of the Russian Empire. V, 461, an article on Peter the Great. VIII, 178, on Russia and Roman Catholicism.

Nouvelle bibliothèque germanique, by S. Formey (1746-1760) [1]: XI, 448, an account of Peter the Great's visit to Mme de Maintenon. VI, 321, and XXV, 364, articles on Gmelin's trip to Siberia. II, 211, article on Lomonosov. IV, 16-21, comments on the etymology of "Russia."

L'Année littéraire (1754-1790): 1760, V, 194, *Lettres d'un jeune seigneur russe à M. de* ... on the state of Russian literature, particularly on Lomonosov and Sumarokov with translations of extracts from their works. 1771, VII, 217, a letter to the editor on the collection of plays published under the title: *Théâtre Clénerzow*, purporting to be a translation from the Russian.

Journal étranger (1754-1762): April, 1755, an article on Sumarokov's tragedy, *Sinave et Trouvore*; contains long excerpts translated from Russian. February, 1760, a short article on the fireworks display in honor of the Empress Elizabeth, and a description of the Russian court life.

---

[1] This publication has many articles of a scientific nature, pertaining to Russia: especially accounts by the members of the Academy of Sciences. Cf. table of *N.B.G.*, Amsterdam, Schreuder, 1760.

Journal encyclopédique (1756-1780): I, January, 1756, short review of *La Vie de Pierre-le-Grand, par Alexandre Gordon d'Achintoul* ... London, 1755. VII, April, 1757, résumé of Strube de Piermont's discourse on the origin and development of the Russian law, delivered in the Imperial Russian Academy of Sciences. XXXV, May, and XXXVI, June, 1760, long review with excerpts from La Combe's *Histoire des révolutions de l'Empire de Russie* ... XXXVII, September and October, 1760, long review with excerpts from the first part of Voltaire's *History of Peter the Great.* XLI, January 1 and 15, 1761, reviews of Algarotti's *Saggio di lettere sopra la Russia* ... XLVI and XLVII, September, October, and November, 1761, reviews of the reports of the Imperial Academy of St. Petersburg. LV, November, 1762, letter to the editor from St. Petersburg regarding the last revolution and Catherine's offer to D'Alembert. LVI, December, 1762, a long critique of Voltaire's *History of Peter the Great* (by Müller), and extracts from a letter addressed to the Hamburg journal *Allgemeinnuetziges.* LVII, February, 1763, reprint of Catherine II's letter to D'Alembert inviting him to come to Russia. LIX and LX, May 1 and 15, 1763, reviews of the second part of Voltaire's *History of Peter the Great.* LXIII, November, 1763, Voltaire's short panegyric poem to Catherine II. LXV, February, 1764, review of Contant d'Orville's *Mémoires d'Azéma* ... LXXV, April, 1765, a long review of a work in German, *Gelehrte Abhandlungen* ... by A. Bushing, Leipzig, 1764, on the state of literature in Russia—a good source of information on the state of poetry and eloquence in Russia, including abstracts from many Russian books. LXXIX, October, 1765, exchange of epistles in verse between Voltaire and Count Shuvalov. LXXV, July, 1766, anecdotes concerning Peter the Great. XCIV, August, 1767, a long review of Dorat's tragedy *Pierre-le-Grand.* XCVII, January, 1768, an article on the Russian clergy. CXII, December, 1769, review of Lomonosov's *History of Russia.* CXVIII, September, and CXIX, October, 1770, review of Chappe d'Auteroche's *Voyage en Sibérie.* CXXIV, May, 1771, review of Coxe's account of Russia. CXXVIII, December, 1771, *Antidote ou examen d'un mauvais livre* ... a critique of Abbé Chappe d'Auteroche's *Voyage en Sibérie.* CXXXVIII, March, 1773, review of D'Anville's *L'Empire de Russie considéré dans son origine et ses accroissements.* CXLII, September, 1773, a letter to the editor on the subject of the article on the "Knout" [i.e., *Knut*] in the *Dictionnaire philosophique.* CXLIII, October, 1773, review of the journal of Peter the Great. CLXXIX, April, 1778, review of a German ethnological work on Russia: *Description de toutes les nations soumises à l'Empire de Russie.* CXCIV, March, 1780, review of Meyer's *Briefe über Russland.* CXCV, April, 1780, article on the production of Dorat's tragedy, *Pierre le Grand.* CXCVII, July, 1780, review of an English historical and ethnographical work on Russia.

Esprit des journaux (1791-1793): 1791, XII, 348-351, review of a short play translated from Russian (*Qui veut tromper se trompe*) and produced successfully in Stockholm. 1792, VI, 137-149, La Harpe's article on Rulhière's posthumous works, 1792, VIII, 83-88, review of a Russian book on a scientific trip to the Crimea, 1792, X, 30-56, and XI, 65-84, a long review of *Anecdotes intéressantes et secrètes de la cour de Russie* ... Bruxelles, La Haye, and Paris, 1792. 6 vols., in 8º. This review gives long extracts, chiefly on

Peter the Great, Menshikov, and Catherine II. 1792, X, 86-96, review of Georgi's description of St. Petersburg—*Versuch einer Beschreibung* ... St. Petersburg, Müller, 1792, 2 vols. in 8⁰. 1792, X, 409-410, Mikhail Popov's *Description abrégée de la mythologie slavonne* ... 1793, II, 109-115, review of Abbé Becconti's *History of Turkey, Germany, and Russia*, 1793, X, 33-39, review of Chantreau's *Voyages philosophiques* ... 1793, XI, 5-44, and XII, 31-41, review of Pallas's *Voyages*.

Le Spectateur du nord (1797-1800): January, 1797, I, 155, short notice on *L'Ombre de Catherine II aux Champs Elysées*, an imaginary dialogue. February, 1797, I, 183-203, review of and extracts from De Bouilliers's translation of Karamzin's novel: *Julie*. March, 1797, I, 435-436, review of Rulhière's *Histoire ou anecdotes sur la révolution de Russie en l'année 1762*. October, 1797, IV, 53-72, a letter on Russian literature signed N. N.

INDEX